SETON HALL UNIVERSITY
HG8039 .D38 1987   MAIN
Lloyd's :

073 00150192 1

D1190765

DATE DUE

AUG 1 3 1995	

GAYLORD   PRINTED IN U.S.A.

A VIEW
OF THE ROOM
Lloyd's
Change and Disclosure

A VIEW
OF THE ROOM
Lloyd's

Change and Disclosure

Ian Hay Davison

SETON HALL UNIVERSITY
McLAUGHLIN LIBRARY
SO. ORANGE, N. J.

ST. MARTIN'S PRESS
NEW YORK

HG
8039
D 38
1987

Copyright © Ian Hay Davison, 1987

All rights reserved. For information, write: Scholarly & Reference Division,
St. Martin's Press, Inc., 175 Fifth Avenue, New York, NY 10010

Printed in the United States of America in 1987

ISBN 0-312-01333-7

Library of Congress Cataloging-in-Publication Data

—CIP applied for—

To the external members of Lloyd's
on whose behalf the mission was carried out.

Contents

Contents

Acknowledgements

Even before I left Lloyd's in early 1986 a number of my friends in the market, on the Corporation staff and outside Lloyd's encouraged me to record my experiences and the history of the reform of that institution from 1982 to date. They felt, as I feel, that these matters should be written down for the guidance of posterity. In preparing my book I had to wait until Sir Patrick Neill's report was completed lest my public views should undermine the authority of his conclusions. Sir Patrick's report on regulatory arrangements at Lloyd's was published on 22 January 1987. Thereafter I was free to set forth my own opinions on the reform of one of Britain's greatest, and most unusual, financial markets.

These views are founded on three year's intensive study of the Lloyd's market from the privileged position of an independent insider – privy to the currents of opinion in the market and yet independent as a non-member of the society – followed by a year's reading and reflection. In writing this book I have been greatly assisted by the support of my firm Arthur Andersen & Co who, while affording me the facilities to prepare it, take no responsibility for the contents. Many of my friends at Lloyd's have offered guidance and advice. It would be invidious to identify them – they know how grateful I am.

Specific thanks are due to Professor Dean Berry of the London Business School who first suggested the idea of the book; to my former adviser on self-regulation, David Stebbings, who was reading and commenting on the manuscript up to his sad death in March 1987; to John Newton who helped me on press and public relations matters during my time at Lloyd's and whose continuing steady advice, for which I remain immensely grateful, has kept me out of trouble with the press ever since; to my secretary, Majorie Smith, who typed many drafts of the book carefully, patiently, and accurately – and never complained once; and finally and especially to my wife, Morny, who read all the drafts and translated them, painstakingly and lovingly, into decent English. The stylistic and punctuational felicities are entirely hers, the errors are entirely mine.

Ian Hay Davison
London WC2
21 April 1987

I

A Necessary Rupture

The monthly meeting of the Council of Lloyd's on 5 February 1987 was
held as normal round the enormous table in the reproduction Adam
ballroom from Bowood House which serves as the council chamber for
the society: three massive crystal chandeliers cast a sparkling reflection
across polished mahogany. The council's most important piece of business
that Wednesday morning was to receive the resignations of four of its
number: four of the sixteen who work day to day in the business of
insurance at Lloyd's. These resignations presaged the end of the 200-year
hegemony over the affairs of the society by its working members;[1] they
ushered in a further set of reforms that will place control in the hands of
those members of the society who do not work at Lloyd's, now four-fifths
of the membership,[2] and eight outside councillors appointed with the
approval of the Governor of the Bank of England. These constitutional
changes in the regulation of Lloyd's were the kernel of the proposals for
reform produced by a government inquiry under Sir Patrick Neill that
had reported two weeks earlier.[3] Lloyd's prompt reaction to Sir Patrick's
proposals reflected a climate of political and public opinion which, due to
the recent Guinness affair,[4] was running strongly against the City. Lloyd's
had no choice but to concede Sir Patrick's demands at once: the Conservative Government, faced with a general election within the next 12
months, was not prepared to countenance insurrection in its own backyard.

Fifteen months earlier I had submitted my resignation from the post of
Deputy Chairman and Chief Executive of Lloyd's. My resignation produced
two effects: first, Lloyd's was forced, in the critical climate that followed,
to appoint a successor to myself vested with virtually identical powers
and independence, although when I resigned such a reappointment was
at first resisted; and, second, the Government took action about the defects
in the constitution of Lloyd's.

I

Parliament's concern had begun in April 1985 when large losses by Lloyd's members served by the unfortunate PCW agency had produced a spate of letters from indignant members of Lloyd's to their MPs, mostly Conservatives. These concerns were aggravated in August and September by revelations about the extent to which parallel underwriting syndicates continued to be used by insiders at Lloyd's to benefit themselves at the expense of the innocent outside members. My resignation confirmed, as it was meant to, that despite a major three-year programme of reform, the constitutional structure of the Society of Lloyd's remained defective for its principal task: the regulation of the market. The council took the resignation, with some justification, as an affront. But it was a necessary rupture. They did not appear to share my view that further major changes were needed: changes which would not have occurred without the outside pressures caused by my resignation and the resulting Neill Inquiry.

In autumn 1985 a Bill to reform the regulation of City investment markets was due to be debated in the House of Commons. The Lloyd's market had been left out of the Bill on largely technical grounds. To many Tory MPs this seemed illogical and wrong. Following my resignation, the reasons for which were explained in a public letter,[5] there was pressure to amend the Bill and include Lloyd's. This pressure was met by an announcement in January 1986 that Sir Patrick Neill would chair a government inquiry into the regulation of the Lloyd's market and the extent to which it matched the needs of those who invest there.[6]

The defects in the constitution to which Sir Patrick's report drew attention arose from changes at Lloyd's over twenty years. Outsiders had been admitted to the membership which had thereby ceased to be an exclusive club. With traditional arrogance some insiders had treated these outsiders with disdain. Such an attitude was tolerated given the continued profitability of Lloyd's membership and the absolute probity of the insiders who were running the society.

From the middle of 1982 it became increasingly apparent that there was something seriously wrong. A handful of powerful insiders involved in the Howden, PCW and Brooks & Dooley affairs had taken advantage of the Lloyd's climate of arrogant secrecy to milk their backers of millions. Fraud occurs in the City from time to time. Rarely are those who suffer the private investors, even less frequently is it true that the perpetrators of the fraud are the trustees for the investors. These were not frauds *on* Lloyd's, they were frauds by insiders at Lloyd's on their own members. The probity of the insiders could no longer be taken for granted.

The cases of outright plunder were few: less than twenty Lloyd's men were ultimately to be disciplined in respect of abuse of their fiduciary duties towards the members they served. When I joined Lloyd's I had announced my determination to pick out the rotten apples. I then thought that to exclude the wrongdoers would solve the problem. But it was not as simple as that. Many of the apples were to some extent tacky, and the barrel itself appeared to many observers to be infected. The problem was that misunderstandings about the fiduciary duties of Lloyd's agents towards the members were universal. Impartial observers were shocked by the ignorance and indifference of the Lloyd's community to its most basic legal and moral obligations. As Neill says, 'Many members of the Lloyd's community in senior positions were not even vaguely aware of the legal obligations on agents to act at all times in the best interests of their principals, not to make secret profits at their principals' expense and to disclose fully all matters affecting their relationship with their principals.'[7] Save in rare cases, these misunderstandings had not led to fraud. But a number of the most prominent agents had made improper tax arrangements which could not have been carried out had they performed their duties as agents.

A second difficulty was the close relations which appeared in the public mind to exist between the wrongdoers and the ruling circles at Lloyd's. The latter stoutly defended their innocence, yet three of the committee of 1982 were subsequently to face disciplinary charges by Lloyd's and the involvement of some members of the committee with parallel syndicates was generally known. The majority of the committee members had done no wrong by the standards of the time, a minority had done no wrong at all, but their authority was fatally damaged by these associations.

The events at Lloyd's between the late summer of 1982, when the major scandals emerged, and the publication of the Neill Report in January 1987, which brought to an end the control of Lloyd's by the market professionals, are the subject of this book. We shall trace the factors that led to the need for reform at Lloyd's and review the steps taken to bring about the revolution that took place over five years. Two issues of wide public and political significance emerge.

The first concerns changing attitudes towards government regulation of financial markets. Britain has always espoused self-regulation, by which the rules are made, and in extreme cases applied, by those whose affairs are to be regulated. This contrasts with other countries – the United States and France – where government agencies handle the task of regulating investor markets. In this context it is significant that the current reforms at Lloyd's were initiated by disclosures about improprieties at Howden's, a large Lloyd's broker. The disclosures came about because Howden's had been bought by an American company, Alexander & Alexander, which is quoted on the New York Stock Exchange and subject to the rules of the United States Securities and Exchange Commission (SEC). US practice requires that, in the event of a takeover bid when the acquiring company is unable to audit the books of the target company before committing itself, an audit must be carried out afterwards. It was thanks to the application of this American practice rule that the public, and Lloyd's, first became aware of the activities of the 'Gang of Four' who dominated the Howden board. Similarly information given to the SEC by the New York arbitrageur Ivan Boesky first revealed the existence of alleged improper arrangements for share price support in connection with the Guinness bid for Distillers in 1986.

Both these instances raised questions about the efficacy of self-regulation for controlling markets. A government agency, as in the USA, appears to go further than analogous agencies here in probing wrongdoing and exposing financial malefactors. The British Government's reaction has been to shift the emphasis in its pronouncements from the value of self-regulation as a flexible, speedy, efficient and cheap tool of market regulation, to the importance of properly supervising self-regulatory markets and including an appropriate level of outsider involvement. The Neill Report closes a chapter in the history of City self-regulation because it propounds the new maxim that investment markets should henceforth allow for a substantial degree of independent scrutiny of market practitioners.[8]

The Neill Report is the most up-to-date study of self-regulation available now: its clear conclusion about the importance of providing adequate supervision of self-regulatory markets will be fundamental to the future reform of investment markets in general.

The second significant element in the Lloyd's story is the light it throws upon the role of professional accountants in British commercial life. Accountants prepare accounts. They audit accounts and assist in settling tax liabilities. In advising on tax they may propose arrangements to ameliorate a company's tax burden: for example to claim allowances provided for in the taxing statutes. They may go further in suggesting a corporate reorganization that has the overall effect of reducing tax. Such a reorganization will be legitimate if the Revenue are able to see what has been done and challenge it if they wish. The line between legitimate tax avoidance and illegitimate tax evasion is broken when the arrangements are not transparent and essential details are concealed from the Revenue. Auditors, in checking and approving the accounts, should give the Revenue comfort that nothing has been concealed.

Accountants were at the heart of the major misconduct at Lloyd's. Underwriters and brokers may have taken money, and ultimately paid the price for doing so, but in each case an accountant planned the arrangements and failed to warn his principal of the dangers of what they were doing. More generally, the dubious tax arrangements that were such a widespread feature of the Lloyd's of the 1970s were planned by accountants and audited, or to be strictly factual, *not* audited, by accountants.

It was therefore not inappropriate to ask an accountant to supervise the reform of the situation. In November 1982 I was paying one of my routine visits to New York. After work I played squash with one of my American partners in the extremely comfortable surroundings of the University Club on Fifth Avenue. The game over, I was enjoying the old-fashioned marble-lined showers which produce a veritable Niagara of warm water when I was interrupted. In America even shower rooms have telephones. Dripping and wrapped in a towel I received a phone call from the Chairman of Lloyd's. Sir Peter Green asked me to undertake the chairmanship of a Lloyd's working party to inquire into the Lloyd's audit requirements and make recommendations on implementing the accounting proposals of the Fisher Report.[9] I was to be assisted by two outsiders – an accountant and a lawyer – and four leading members of the Lloyd's market. The *Financial Times*, announcing this on 6 November 1982, said that I would be asked to make recommendations by the end of December and that the inquiry had the support of the Department of Trade and Industry (DTI) and the Bank.

At that time my own knowledge of Lloyd's was an observer's. I had helped to advise C. E. Heath Ltd, a Lloyd's broker founded by Cuthbert Heath, over a takeover in 1970, and my firm, Arthur Andersen & Co., had subsequently been appointed auditors. As Managing Partner of Arthur Andersen's London office since 1966 and of its UK practice since 1973, I had been involved in building up the business in the UK from a total staff of 180 in 1966 to about 2,000 by 1982. But I had had time for other matters, investigating fraud in particular. As joint DTI inspector, with Michael Sherrard QC, I had investigated the disappearance of Mr John Stonehouse MP in November 1974 and the complex web of fraudulent arrangements surrounding the British Bangladesh Trust, a secondary bank later to be called the London Capital Group. In March 1978 I was asked by the Treasury to investigate a fraud at the Grays Building Society in which £8 million, half the balance sheet, had been extracted by the secretary over a period of forty years, and apparently spent on women and racing. As a member of the Price Commission from 1977 to 1979 I

5

had been involved in reviews of the banking, unit trust and estate agency businesses. I had been a long-standing member of the Council of the Institute of Chartered Accountants, and I had recently been appointed Chairman of the Accounting Standards Committee (ASC), a body sponsored by the six accounting institutes and charged with the task of developing accounting standards for the use of British industry, commerce and the public sector. As the new chairman I sought extra members for the committee whose status needed raising by an influx of fresh blood drawn from a wider circle than members of the accountancy bodies. I called upon the Governor of the Bank of England and discussed the matter with him in the spring of 1982. Gordon Richardson, whom I had not met before, is a keen supporter of self-regulation. He wanted to see it succeed in the accountancy field, and backed me in my efforts to recruit important figures from the City and industry to serve on the ASC. As a result I owed him an obligation that was to be repaid somewhat sooner than I expected.

The new Lloyd's working party had barely started its meetings when on 22 December 1982 I was asked to call on the Governor of the Bank. He knew that I was on my way to Lloyd's and inquired mildly if I had considered taking on the job of Chief Executive of Lloyd's. The answer was no, such a thought had never entered my head. Although I protested that I knew little about Lloyd's and was not a member, he persisted, regarding both these reservations on my part as additional qualifications for the job. 'I am not asking for a life sentence, three to five years will do,' he said. With that comment and observing the gleam in his eye I knew I would be hard pressed to find convincing reasons to refuse him.

I spent the Christmas holiday thinking hard. I had resigned the post of Managing Partner at Arthur Andersen in the preceding May after sixteen years, and I was ready for a fresh challenge. Lloyd's was, and is, an institution of vital national importance. The job to be done was daunting, but it would involve things I knew about: the unravelling of fraud and the development of accounting rules. Gordon Richardson had pointed out that there was a critical responsibility for communication with the press and this was something I was used to doing. It was clear that if I were to do my job properly I would be unpopular at Lloyd's – no agent of change imposed from outside attracts much praise – but I thought I could put up with that for three years. But above all I admired Gordon Richardson and he had asked me: I would not have accepted for anyone else.

All through my time at Lloyd's echoes of my accounting career recurred. The most important, irreversible thing that I did was to establish disclosure: once the accounts of syndicates were properly prepared, audited and published to the world the external members of Lloyd's could be their own police force.

I undertook my task at Lloyd's as an assignment, not as a career move. I agreed to do the job for a limited term, three to five years, and as an agent of change: to clean up the market, launch the new rule book and, as far as I was able, to alter the structure of the society so that power could be shifted and a recurrence of the iniquities of the late 1970s avoided. This book is my report on that assignment. It explains why Lloyd's had to change and how those changes were brought about. It goes further, impelled by the extensive reforms suggested by Neill, to comment on those suggestions and point the way to further change. An ex-cabinet minister member of Lloyd's said to me at lunch one day: 'Never underestimate the conservatism of a British institution.' His warning was right, but even at Lloyd's change has proved to be possible.

PART I

A PECULIAR INSTITUTION

II

Lloyd's in the World Insurance Market

By any standard Lloyd's of London is a remarkable place. It is a large and flourishing survivor of Britain's mercantile and imperial past, in many ways a strange relic, but none the less a valuable one. Lloyd's is particularly remarkable in the Britain of the 1980s, for its size and for its peculiar structure. These two factors provide the background for this book.

Note that I describe Lloyd's as a place. That is what it is: a Room where the business of insurance is carried on. Until the Fundamental Rules of Lloyd's were repealed by the Lloyd's Act 1982 they included the regulation: 'All underwriting business transacted in Lloyd's shall be conducted in the underwriting rooms and not elsewhere'.[1] Although, because of the expansion of Lloyd's into the motor insurance market, the rule is an anachronism, it still describes the way in which the preponderance of business is carried on.

Lloyd's business is founded on ships. The marine market is, by 200 years, the senior of the four principal insurance markets at Lloyd's. Marine insurance, which at Lloyd's includes the insurance of cargoes, is powerfully influenced by the society.[2] Even today, despite the paucity of Britain's merchant fleet, the insurance of over 40 per cent of the world's merchant ships passes through the hands of the underwriters in the Room and, although Lloyd's takes a rather smaller share of the total risk, the London market, which covers Lloyd's and the insurance companies grouped into the Institute of London Underwriters, sets the rates and the terms of insurance for the world's merchant fleets. Although aircraft have largely replaced ships as transporters of people Lloyd's still dominates. Insurance slips covering virtually all of the world's commercial aircraft are 'shown in the Room at Lloyd's'.[3] The Lloyd's market is very influential in setting the rates which the world's airlines and their passengers must pay for insurance cover.

But neither the marine nor the aviation market is the largest sector at Lloyd's. The business of non-marine underwriters accounts for about 42 per cent of Lloyd's volume.[4] It includes property and casualty risks, windstorm, earthquake, fire, burglary, product liability and jeweller's block insurance.[5] The last class of business initiated the non-marine market when Cuthbert Heath wrote a policy 100 years ago to cover, in one 'block', all the risks to a jeweller's stock. Before Heath's time such non-marine business as there was was written as a side line by marine syndicates, and this tradition has carried on under the rule that a marine underwriter may take incidental non-marine risks up to 10 per cent of his capacity.[6]

Although Lloyd's holds a pre-eminent position in the world's marine and aviation insurance markets, this is not the case with non-marine business where Lloyd's share of the world's markets is under 1 per cent.[7] None the less Lloyd's is influential because of its ability to accept large and complex risks which no insurance company elsewhere in the world would be willing to lead or even to share. For example, the professional indemnity insurance of the world's eight largest accounting firms, each of whose practices is dominated by their American business, is underwritten at Lloyd's although other markets share the risks.

None of these markets is static. Lloyd's market share changes from year to year, and so does the nature of the risks underwritten. Increasingly in recent years Lloyd's has tended to specialize in reinsurance: in insuring the insurers. Every insurance underwriter must balance the risks on his book by laying off some element of it, as a bookmaker lays off his bets. He may do this by accepting only a portion of the risk, by co-insuring; or he may accept a larger share, and reduce his exposure by reinsurance. Either this will be done by facultative reinsurance related to a specific risk; or, more commonly, he will arrange a contract or treaty with another insurer by which the latter accepts a share, or quota, of risks of a certain class. Alternatively he may arrange a treaty to reinsure his entire account for the year against loss. Reinsurance is a large and growing business in which Lloyd's is the most specialized market.

As the insurance habit has spread to an ever-growing proportion of the world's population the administrative problems of servicing multiple risks have grown. Third World countries, eager to assert their independence, have established their own insurance companies and closed their markets to direct insurers from overseas. Increasingly, Lloyd's has come to provide the reinsurance capacity for such new and often undercapitalized insurance companies, and for the world's insurance retail giants. Today more than 50 per cent of Lloyd's business is reinsurance, and the proportion is even larger in the non-marine and aviation markets.

The last of the four major markets at Lloyd's, motor insurance, is quite different. It now accounts for 11 per cent of Lloyd's volume of business and, with about 16 per cent of the UK domestic motor market, Lloyd's is the largest domestic insurer of cars. Motor insurance is essentially a retail business: the underwriter's customer is the individual driver or fleet owner. Claims are small, and frequent. Individual premiums are small by Lloyd's standards. Business is thus essentially a tariff business, and the Lloyd's syndicates are organized like small tariff companies. They have moved out of the Room to suburban or provincial locations from where they deal directly with high-street brokers who retail motor insurance to the public. The motor underwriters write insurance business that is quite alien to Lloyd's: standard policies with standard conditions and premiums charged according to a predetermined tariff; the typical underwriter in the Room at Lloyd's writes 'bespoke insurance' with the premium and policy wordings determined by his and his fellow underwriters' assessment of the particular risk and of the circumstances of the case.

The three main classes of business in the Room at Lloyd's – marine, non-marine and aviation – compete energetically and successfully in the world insurance market. The City of London once dominated the world financially. Its elaborate and powerful network of financial institutions was originally established to invest in and support Britain's overseas trade and its related imperial expansion. It ignored the investment needs of domestic industry in the nineteenth century in favour of rubber plantations in Malaya, gold mines in South Africa, railways in the Argentine, cotton in the United States, indigo plantations in Bengal and the needs of foreign governments everywhere.

With Britain's decline the City has lost its world lead in finance. Although it is, by any standards, a major financial centre, the City's banks are not the world's largest; nor are its stockbrokers, money brokers, commodity dealers or shipping lines.[8] But there is one business in which the City of London still leads the world and that is insurance: probably the only field of endeavour in which Britain is still the world's leader measured by size as well as by skill, enterprise and inventiveness, and Lloyd's is in the forefront. In 1985 73 per cent of Lloyd's business was export.[9] Sixty-eight per cent[10] is transacted in dollars and about 55 per cent relates to risks in the United States, easily Lloyd's largest market, followed by the UK and Japan. The earnings of Lloyd's in foreign markets contributed, in 1985, over £1.9 billion to the British balance of payments – a figure approaching the £2.1 billion earned by the entire British banking system.[11]

In 1939 the possibility of a German invasion presented a major threat to Lloyd's American business, even then an important share of the market. In a period of a few days on the eve of the declaration of war Lloyd's American Trust Fund was established in New York. All Lloyd's dollar premiums are held in trust in this fund, whether they originate in the USA or not, and dollar claims are met from it. The fund is managed for Lloyd's underwriters by Citibank and its size makes Lloyd's one of the largest customers of one of the world's largest banks. Most of the fund is invested in US Treasury Bonds, a safe haven for short-term money. Lloyd's holdings of US Treasury Bonds makes Lloyd's the largest private investor in the US Government – it provides about nine days' worth of America's annual public-sector borrowing requirement.[12] It should be said in explanation that US Treasury Bonds are particularly attractive to Lloyd's underwriters for tax reasons: domestic US insurers prefer tax-exempt bonds like those issued by many US local government entities.

Lloyd's is big in the US by other standards. It is the largest operator in the reinsurance market, its premium income being three times that of the largest American-owned reinsurance company. Lloyd's contribution to the US Treasury puts it next to the top of the list of taxpayers in the property and casualty insurance industry. While I was at Lloyd's I paid regular visits to the USA and was surprised at first by the courtesy and attentiveness with which I was received by Lloyd's American bankers. When I learnt of the scale of our US operations I realized that the natural courtesy of my hosts was supported by an appreciation of the importance of the Lloyd's account.

Why is it that Lloyd's can still lead the market in insurance when, in other fields, Britain's position reflects its relative financial weakness? It would be nice to say that it is due to the flexibility and inventiveness of the underwriters and brokers, and the skill with which Lloyd's assets are invested, but that would not be true. The two largest economies in the free world are Japan and the United States. In the former the desire for a high degree of economic self-sufficiency has made it extremely difficult for foreign insurance companies to obtain licences to operate: no other nation has such a small proportion of its domestic insurance needs served by foreigners. But insurance is a worldwide business, especially in the field of large risks and reinsurance. Lacking a domestic market in which foreigners regularly operate, it is difficult for the Japanese to do insurance business in other countries: they lack the skills (although they don't lack the financial resources), and they find it difficult to get licences to operate in foreign countries whose own insurance companies cannot enter Japan. So the Japanese rely on foreigners for the reinsurance of risks too large to cover in their own markets and much of this business continues to come to Lloyd's.

With the growing skills which the Japanese are exhibiting in world financial markets the situation may change, and Lloyd's will certainly suffer if it does.

The large American market is, however, more secure for a totally different reason. Alone among the major fields of commercial endeavour in the United States, insurance is regulated by the individual states, and not by the Federal Government in Washington. As a result there is no 'common market' for insurance in the USA. Fifty states regulated by fifty different insurance commissioners have laid out a regulatory maze through which American insurance companies find their way with difficulty and at considerable expense. In this world Lloyd's participates as an outsider, except for the two states – Illinois and Kentucky – where Lloyd's is directly licensed. Elsewhere in the USA it does not have to meet the complex regulations laid down for domestic insurers. Lloyd's is, however, limited to writing reinsurance and surplus lines business – insurance risks that the local companies do not wish to take because they are too large or complex – the very stuff that Lloyd's thrives on. Lloyd's US business is split 2:1 between reinsurance and surplus lines. How secure is this market? In my opinion, it is quite secure, because a real risk of losing the American market would arise only if Washington were to legislate for insurance to become a federal matter. That would be a political move which would hardly find favour with the individual states and their politically appointed insurance commissioners; a move that can, I think, be discounted for the present. Meanwhile Lloyd's takes great care to be a good citizen of the USA by paying its taxes, keeping its dollar premiums in New York, and encouraging American citizens to become members.

Lloyd's relative absence from the European market is a more troubling matter. Since 1945, as the empire has declined, Britain's economy has become increasingly bound up with that of Europe: 44 per cent of our exports now go to the Common Market. But only 9 per cent of Lloyd's overseas business is with Europe. The reason lies in the fact that in virtually every country that came under the rule of Napoleon insurance is regulated by government as if it were a public monopoly. Rates and covers[13] are fixed by governments and in some countries it is illegal to insure with a foreign insurance company or through a foreign insurance intermediary. The reason for this tight regulation is protection for the consumer against the possible default of the insurer; the effect is higher prices for less cover than would be available in a freer market such as London. Opening up the Common Market to Lloyd's insurers remains a major task.

Lloyd's is also important as a place to work; its buildings in Lime Street in the City are the centre of the London insurance market. About four thousand work under the spacious atrium of the new Lloyd's building which houses the largest single working market in the City. Another two thousand work for the Corporation of Lloyd's at its offices in Lime Street, Fenchurch Street, Chatham and Colchester. With an annual budget of £100 million they provide necessary back-up services for the Lloyd's market. But over forty-five thousand people work for the organizations that operate in the Lloyd's market: some work for the brokers and the underwriting agents, others are employed by the host of specialist companies supporting those who work in the Room: the investment fund managers, loss adjusters, data-processing bureaux, lawyers and accountants.

This is a book about the structure of Lloyd's and the changes being made to that structure. It is not a treatise on insurance. Nevertheless it will be helpful to an understanding of recent changes there to see how Lloyd's fits into the world insurance scene and to note certain changes in that scene.

The worldwide market for insurance is growing. Premiums grew tenfold between 1960 and 1980. In 1982 North America accounted for 51 per cent of world insurance business, Europe for 28 per cent (the UK represents 6 per cent) and Japan for 13 per cent. Over the twenty-year period the North American share of world insurance business had declined from 72 per cent, the European share had grown from 21 per cent and the Japanese share from 2 per cent.[14]

Within this booming trend a regular economic cycle emerges. Insurance seems to be the same as pig-farming when it comes to the laws of economics because the costs of entering the industry are low. Insurers make profits. More insurers enter the market. They reduce their prices to attract more business. Insurance becomes unprofitable. The weakest go out of business. The market tightens and insurance rates rise. Insurers make profits again and the cycle is repeated. It appears that the cycle has a typical interval of eleven years and that 1983 represented the trough of the most recent insurance cycle. The current worldwide pattern of high interest rates has made this cycle more violent. Insurance as a business offers the operator a positive cash flow. He receives his premiums before claims are made. If premium rates are set correctly the insurer should always be in funds, and these funds can be invested to show a profit, given high interest rates and falling inflation as has recently been the case. In the last decade the profits from investing insurance funds have been so attractive that insurers have been willing to cut their underwriting rates and make losses on their underwriting account in order to invest the cash flow.

This is fine, as long as the business continues to grow, and the settlement of claims can be deferred. But in the end an underwriting loss must produce an overall loss and as a consequence of the recent business downturn many insurers, especially in the US, have been forced to raise their rates and cut back the volume of business they handle. Some have gone out of business.

Lloyd's is uniquely fortunate in this cycle because of the peculiar structure of the market: underwriters are sole traders and not corporations. Unlike an insurance company there are no shareholders expecting to receive a dividend every year. A Lloyd's underwriter can afford to wait and turn away unprofitable business until rates rise. Rates have risen in the last three years and as a result Lloyd's is enjoying better profitability in 1985, 1986, and 1987.

Four special factors, all emanating from the United States, have affected the Lloyd's market in recent years.

The first, and in economic terms the most serious, is the problem of court settlements in the US. The system of jury trial for civil cases, with jurors awarding the damages, and contingent fee arrangements by which the plaintiff's counsel is paid only if he wins, out of what he wins, makes litigation cheap and rewarding for an American with a claim for damages. A jury is likely to be generous in its support of an apparently impoverished plaintiff in a case against a faceless insurance company. Recent US court settlements, met by underwriters at Lloyd's, have produced dramatic and absurd judgments. In one case a suit was brought over environmental pollution, which was traced to creosote in railroad sleepers. The judge placed the liability on the Lloyd's insurers who had covered the railroad company in 1896 when the sleepers were laid. In another case a young couple broke into an apartment complex. They had been drinking; the girl dived into the swimming pool, and as the pool was half empty, she broke her neck. The pool manufacturer, insured at Lloyd's, was found to be liable. A third case involved a truck driven along a California highway. There was an accident for which the truck driver was responsible. He was not insured, neither was the trucking company, but the freight container carried on the back of the truck was covered, at Lloyd's. Underwriters were held to be liable for damages to the injured third party.

Not only are attributions of liability distant and capricious, the damages concerned can often be very large, driven up by trial lawyers with a financial interest in the size of the settlement and emboldened by the fact that it is not the practice in the American courts to award costs against an unsuccessful suitor: each side normally bears its own costs regardless of the outcome.

This legal climate has produced some bad losses for the non-marine market dealing in long-tailed North American business – risks where the settlement of claims will take a long time. But the overall effect of these on the fortunes of Lloyd's should not be exaggerated: such business accounted for 12 per cent of Lloyd's volume in 1982, and produced most of the losses in that year.[15]

The other three factors are the development of captive insurance companies, the influx of American insurance brokers into London, and the introduction of the insurance exchanges in the USA and Canada.

Captive insurance companies grew up in the 1970s. Some very large American industrial companies, concerned at the apparent high cost of insurance, looked at building up self-insurance reserves as an alternative. From an actuarial point of view it is attractive. But there is a snag. American tax legislation does not allow a tax deduction for a payment made by a company into its own reserves. A deduction would, however, be available if the payment were made to an insurance company owned by the principal: in other words a captive insurance company. But there is another snag: the captive insurance company must be able to show the US Internal Revenue Service (IRS) that it is a genuine insurance company, that is, that it has more than one customer.[16]

During the 1970s a host of such companies were established, often in offshore tax havens like Bermuda, the Bahamas and the Cayman Islands, in order to take advantage of the fact that in such places any interest accruing on invested funds would be tax free. Many of the companies were operated for their owners by insurance brokers who understood the business. Some of them made losses, especially on the proportion of outside business which the IRS rules required them to handle. They were sitting targets for a broker with a problematical risk.

Lloyd's was affected in a number of ways. The growth of the captives increased world insurance capacity and in general must have driven rates down. The subsequent decline of captives helped Lloyd's to recover some of this business at much more profitable rates. All captives needed reinsurance and some of this must have come to Lloyd's, partly compensating for the direct business lost. The captives provided capacity for placing some of Lloyd's underwriters' own reinsurance. But the most serious effect was that certain Lloyd's underwriters were to mimic the US companies and start their own captive insurance companies offshore for the same reason, to obtain a tax deduction for making a reserve.

The commercial insurance broking market in the US is dominated by a limited number of firms led by Marsh McLennan, Alexander & Alexander and Johnson & Higgins. These firms, with others nearly as large, are collectively known as the 'alphabet brokers' because they are usually referred to by their initials. Much of their very large commercial business comes to London, by direct placing or in the form of reinsurance for their American insurance company clients. In the last ten years the alphabet brokers have been buying Lloyd's brokers to gain access to the London market without having to use a British-owned intermediary. The largest, Marsh McLennan, acquired Bowring's, one of the four largest Lloyd's brokers, in 1979. It was the inquiries following the acquisition by Alexander & Alexander of Howden's, another Lloyd's broker, at the end of 1982 which brought to light the extent of the wrongdoing at the heart of the Lloyd's market.[17]

If the pattern of US acquisitions of London brokers represents the application of the maxim 'if you can't beat 'em, join 'em', the establishment of insurance exchanges in the United States represents the reverse. Three exchanges have now been established in the United States to provide a service to insurance brokers similar to that provided by Lloyd's. A fourth has just opened in Toronto. The New York exchange is much the largest: its total volume in 1985 was $310 million, down from $346 million the year before.[18] This was less than one-tenth of Lloyd's premium income at the time, and Lloyd's income is growing. The two exchanges in Chicago and Miami are smaller. Although the American exchanges provide a convenient meeting place for the exchange of insurance and reinsurance risks, they do not provide the additional capital that Lloyd's makes available through its unique structure of individual membership with unlimited liability. The syndicates which operate on the American exchanges all trade with limited liability and their capital is, for the most part, contributed by US insurance companies who thereby reduce their own ability to write direct business.

When the US exchanges were proposed at the end of the 1970s there was considerable apprehension at Lloyd's that American business would be lost. This has not happened.

Lloyd's remains a large and powerful force in the world insurance market. Despite the scandals that have surrounded it in the last five years, there is no evidence that the volume or profitability of the insurance written at Lloyd's has suffered. In the three years I was at Lloyd's, from 1983 to 1986, the overall volume of premium income doubled.[19] That premium income made a contribution to the balance of payments and to the nation's financial strength which makes the success of Lloyd's important to the success of Britain and its reform vital to that success. To understand these reforms and why they were needed it is necessary to understand the second remarkable feature of Lloyd's, its structure.

III

The Structure of the Market

The seventeenth century was a period of expansion and prosperity for the nation states of Europe. In France the Sun King Louis XIV reigned over a nation larger, in the territorial sense, than it had ever been. Holland traded across the world and its merchants brought home riches to the counting houses of Amsterdam. For Germany and England however it was a period of strife: the Thirty Years' War and the Civil War, in which religion played a large part. The Restoration of 1660 and the accession of William and Mary to the throne of England in 1689 cemented the foundations for a new century in which Britain would build up its trade to compete with and then eclipse the Dutch and ultimately to challenge and defeat the mighty French.

Dutch commercial practices were much in vogue in Restoration London. The foundation of the Bank of England in 1694 by City merchants was based on the obvious success of the Dutch banking houses in supporting that nation's trade. In this prosperous commercial climate Edward Lloyd opened his coffee house some time before 1689. We know it was before that date because the first published reference to Lloyd's is an advertisement in the *London Gazette* in March of that year offering a reward at Edward Lloyd's coffee house for a lost gold watch.

There is no evidence that business transacted in the early coffee house had much to do with insurance. But it is known that Edward Lloyd made his premises a centre for marine intelligence by providing facilities for sea captains, a Captains' Room, to encourage those returning from voyages to call in and give the latest reports of ships sighted. In 1734, fifty years after the first edition of *Lloyd's News*, published by Edward Lloyd himself, a committee of Lloyd's subscribers launched a daily report of shipping intelligence. This was *Lloyd's List*, still published daily and beating by fifty years the claim of the London *Times* to be the world's oldest daily newspaper. Having seen some of the early bound volumes of *Lloyd's List* in the Guildhall Library, I must admit that the dull recital of lists of ships, dates and destinations on octavo paper would hardly qualify as a daily newspaper today.

Early insurance was much like gambling. A merchant tended not to insure his ship until it was already overdue and the risk of loss was real. Then he would, in the eighteenth century that is, seek out and insure it with someone who didn't know it was overdue.[1] Intelligence was vital, and Lloyd's provided an ideal location to do marine insurance since that was where the latest marine intelligence was to be had.

Strangely, the practice of insuring overdue ships continues and overdue risks can still be broked in the Room. Here the broker acts for an underwriter with a policy on an overdue ship to see if he can reinsure the risk, at a pretty hefty premium of course, with other marine syndicates. The difference today is that both parties, the insurer and the reinsurer, know the latest intelligence.

Much of the efforts of the Committee of Lloyd's and of the staff of the Corporation of Lloyd's over the years has been directed at improving the flow of shipping information into the Room where the Loss Book records all marine casualties. In the last century, before the days of wireless, emphasis was placed upon a worldwide network of signal stations to receive and transmit, by semaphore, news of ship sightings from sea to land. Sir James Hozier, who was Secretary of Lloyd's from 1874 to 1906 (and Sir Winston Churchill's father-in-law) devoted his career to expanding and strengthening the network of signal stations. The advent of wireless telegraphy brought the stations to an end and only one now remains, at Gibraltar.

But the collection of intelligence continues, much of it reported in by the Lloyd's Agents. There are 403 of these,[2] one in every major port around the world, including several behind the Iron Curtain. The Lloyd's Agents, not to be confused with the underwriting agents who form the main subject of this book, bid for the right to put up the Lloyd's crest in their harbour-side offices. They report all merchant shipping movements in and out of their ports by telex to Lloyd's of London Press at Colchester. This provides the input to the daily edition of *Lloyd's List*, the weekly *Shipping Index and Voyage Record* and the daily computer tapes which are made available to the maritime authorities in London and Washington. The same network, leading into Lloyd's at Colchester, brings news of wrecks and other maritime calamities and it is from Colchester that seagoing tugs and rescue vessels are called out. The business of collecting and publishing marine intelligence makes a profit of three-quarters of a million pounds a year towards the corporation's expenses.

Until the Napoleonic Wars Lloyd's was small and obscure. The members of the society, which became self-governing about 1770, finally settled into premises in the Royal Exchange opposite the Bank of England in 1773. Here the Room was located and it was in this building that Lloyd's flourished during the Napoleonic Wars. Risks at sea were high then and, as always in times of calamity, underwriters prospered. John Julius Angerstein, for many years Chairman of Lloyd's, was able to amass a private display of such splendid pictures that they formed on his death the foundation of the National Gallery collection.

Lloyd's set up a Patriotic Fund to reward brave naval officers who had, by their efforts, saved British merchant shipping. The fund ran into political difficulties when the government of the day found that Lloyd's was publicly, and generously, rewarding admirals whom Whitehall had not chosen for public notice: Lloyd's private enterprise form of battle honours was not felt to be helpful to the national interest. Since Napoleonic times the fund has been more discreet, and today it gives assistance to needy ex-servicemen. The Committee of Lloyd's has taken on the function of awarding medals both for long service and for meritorious acts.

The nineteenth century was a period of great maritime prosperity for Britain. Free trade flourished under the White Ensign of the Royal Navy and the British merchant fleet was the world's largest. Lloyd's prospered too and moved into the second floor of the new Royal Exchange, which was built in 1844 to replace the building destroyed by fire in 1838. Towards the end of the century non-marine business was introduced at the initiative of Cuthbert Heath, as historic a figure at Lloyd's as Angerstein had been a century earlier. It was he who telegraphed instructions to his San Francisco agent after the fire and earthquake of 1906 to pay all policy holders in full, regardless of the detailed wordings of the policies. This shrewd action brought great credit to Lloyd's at a time when many American companies were restricting their claims. Many attribute Lloyd's standing in the States today to its reputation, dating from that time, for paying legitimate claims promptly and in full.

After the First World War the business of Lloyd's had outgrown the Royal Exchange and the society moved down the road to Leadenhall Street, where in 1928 Lloyd's occupied, for the first time, its own building. The Room here again became too small, and in 1958 a new building was erected on the other side of Lime Street. Subsequently the 1928 building was demolished and Richard Rogers' brilliant exercise in stainless steel and glass was opened on that site in 1986. Owning the two sites on either side of Lime Street, Lloyd's is one of the City's largest freeholders and its property assets are worth in excess of £250 million.

In order to understand the structure of the organization that owns and operates the Room at Lloyd's one must grasp the fact that Lloyd's is a market place where people do business. The Corporation of Lloyd's, created by Act of Parliament in 1871, owns the market place which is the Room, and provides facilities for the transaction of insurance business. It, and its servants, do not engage in the business of insurance. That business is carried on by the members of the Society of Lloyd's who collectively form, and own, the corporation. There are in practice four principal types of member at Lloyd's, although some, brokers in particular, do not have to be members of the society to do insurance business in the Room. Lloyd's is a market place with strict rules about the functions of each type of participant. As the Stock Exchange was until recently, it is a single-capacity market in which each participant is confined to one principal role. The structure is based on the concept of the intermediary, or broker, who deals with the customer and allows the underwriter, who is at the heart of the business, to concentrate on the pricing and evaluation of risks.

To make clear how Lloyd's works I shall deal with the principal participants in the Room in turn.

First, the brokers: there are just over two hundred and fifty Lloyd's brokers, among whom are the largest organizations at Lloyd's; about twenty are quoted companies or are owned by quoted companies. The largest of the Lloyd's brokers dominate the market: nearly 40 per cent of the business in the Room is placed by the top three firms[3] and 65 per cent by the top twelve. These brokers are international in scale and have offices, branches, affiliates or, in the case of the American-owned brokers, parents overseas. Their departments specialize in different types of risk, and in the case of smaller broking firms, the company may limit itself to one type of business (for example reinsurance). But the function is always the same, to define the assured's insurance problem, to seek out the best underwriters in terms of price and financial security, to persuade underwriters to underwrite the risk at an acceptable premium and with suitable conditions, to prepare the policy for the underwriter to sign, and to deal on behalf of the insured with any claims that may arise. A broker will also act for the underwriter in placing his outward reinsurance business.

Initially brokers, who under the title 'subscribers' are one of the oldest categories of Lloyd's members, also engaged in the business of under-writing. When limited companies were first admitted as underwriting agencies in the 1930s most of the new companies also operated a brokerage account. From 1936 onwards the 'broker-agents', as they were known, accounted for a sufficiently large percentage of the market to cause the Committee of Lloyd's considerable concern. The committee was concerned at the thought that, if the brokerage business passed into the hands of outsiders (which the committee thought it would be wrong to try to prevent), the agency business would also pass out of the hands of individuals connected with Lloyd's. The matter was extensively discussed but it was not until 1954 that the Chairman of Lloyd's approached the chairmen of the various companies involved and asked that their agency activities should be transferred into separate companies.[4] In the 1960s, when the committee finally outlawed them, there were still twenty-five companies acting in two capacities as broker-agents. The story did not end there. In 1982 when Parliament legislated against brokers having interests in agency companies, no less than 70 per cent of the Lloyd's underwriting agents were broker owned or controlled.

The larger brokers place a minority of their customers' risks at Lloyd's, the balance going to the insurance companies in the UK and overseas. This is either because the risk lies outside Lloyd's field, for example life insurance, or because Lloyd's will not write the business, or because its terms are too onerous or its rates too high. Lloyd's brokers have now outgrown the Lloyd's market and operate on a scale in which Lloyd's plays a minor but significant role. Yet the large brokers are still proud to use the Lloyd's name, describing themselves as 'Lloyd's Brokers'. However, their size and standing no longer make them easily amenable to the direct discipline and regulation of Lloyd's.

But the brokers are still the marketing arm of Lloyd's: they bring in the business to the underwriters who, with certain exceptions (chiefly the motor market) may only deal with a customer through a Lloyd's broker. There is however a developing tendency for underwriters to meet customers in order to obtain better information about risks.

The second participant is the underwriter. There are just over three hundred underwriters divided into the four principal markets: marine, non-marine, aviation and motor. Each operates from a box in the Room, a tiny cubicle looking much like the coffee-house booth from which its design originates. The underwriter will have a deputy and a number of clerks or entry boys, who note the risks accepted and the claims settled. A typical underwriter will manage no more than ten people, so his overhead costs will be small. This is because the broker undertakes the tasks of defining the risk, on a slip, preparing the policy and processing the claims. The duties of checking and signing policies, settling claims and clearing accounts between brokers and underwriters are all handled

on behalf of underwriters by staff of the Corporation of Lloyd's. This
sharing of overhead expenses gives the Lloyd's underwriter a tremendous
cost advantage over his company competitors who must support the cost
of a marketing and office staff out of their underwriting income, although
a company underwriter does not have to pay as much commission as a
Lloyd's underwriter normally allows to the broker.[5]

Lloyd's underwriters specialize. They do so not only within the four
markets, but in more specialized classes of risk within the market: war
risks, London market excess of loss reinsurance, product liability or satel-
lites. The list is endless. For each class of risk there are a few leading
underwriters who, because of their specialized knowledge, will be expected
by their colleagues to take the lead and set the rate and the wordings.
The broker presents a slip giving details of the risk to a leading underwriter.
Until a leader has put down his 5 per cent or 10 per cent line on the slip
the followers will not sign. Having secured his leading signature the
broker then completes the slip in the Room or he may complete it outside
the Room in the company market. In signing the slip an underwriter,
usually on his sole authority, commits himself and the members of the
syndicate for whom he writes to pay all claims that may arise on the
policy that will ultimately be prepared from the completed slip. It is
a serious responsibility. Lloyd's has produced a breed of idiosyncratic
individualists to carry that responsibility. Underwriters rarely have any
formal training but learn their trade from their seniors on the box. It is a
trade in which failure can be easily measured: by a loss ratio regularly
exceeding 100 per cent of premiums. The selection process is, therefore,
rigorous and expensive. The system of single capacity by which an underwriter deals with the outside world only through a broker makes him
isolated. Few underwriters have any management experience, given the
small size of their staffs, and many do not have a university education.
These reasons explain the weakness of the Committee of Lloyd's underwriters in the face of the political difficulties they faced over the last
decade.

The role of the underwriter is threefold: to accept risks, at a stated
premium and at appropriate wordings; to settle claims; and to reinsure
his book of risks. The fourth function of underwriting, the management
of the fund of premiums held to meet claims, is commonly handled for
the underwriter by the underwriting agent.

The development of the underwriting agency system at Lloyd's matches
the growth and increasing complexity of Lloyd's itself. Originally underwriters dealt on their own account as sole traders in the business of
insurance. With the need to insure larger risks the underwriter would

agree to act for a syndicate of underwriters; although each would be liable only for his share of the risk. In legal terms the liability was several not joint. The insurance policy would list, on the reverse, the names of the underwriters on each syndicate headed by that of the active underwriter. It is from this practice that underwriting members of Lloyd's came to be called 'Names'.[6]

Before 1914 syndicates were very small and the active underwriter handled his own insurance affairs and those of his Names personally. In 1904 the Committee of Lloyd's recognized the concept of the underwriting agency when it introduced a rule that an underwriter could have only one agent for marine business. Later the same rule was applied to the other markets. By 1930 the main functions of the underwriting agent, as an intermediary between the active underwriter and the Names, were established.

They are twofold: to manage syndicates and to handle the Lloyd's affairs of the members. It is the duty of the managing agent to perform four functions in managing a syndicate: to underwrite risks, to reinsure risks as may be appropriate, to settle claims, and to manage the premiums trust funds in which premiums are held pending the settlement of claims. The first three of these functions are discharged through an individual, the active underwriter, who is an employee of the agent.

The second role is that of handling the Lloyd's affairs of the members. The members' agent must find potential members of Lloyd's, guide them through Lloyd's complex admission procedures, advise them as to which syndicates to join, manage the personal reserves which each agent will require his members to leave with him against the possibility of under-writing loss, and resolve the tax liabilities that will arise in respect of the Names' membership of Lloyd's.

Not all agents perform both these functions, about one-third of the two hundred and fifty or so agents perform the member service functions only, one-quarter confine themselves to managing syndicates, and the balance, just over 40 per cent of the total number, combine managing and member duties.[7]

In the last twenty years there has been a growing trend for Names to spread their business across a number of syndicates and thus to spread the overall risks. In 1968 the average underwriting member of Lloyd's was on three and a half syndicates. By 1985 the average had grown to ten.[8]

Because of the 'one agent/one class' rule a member can only have access to the syndicates managed by another agent operating in the same market through the medium of a sub-agency agreement between his own agent and the agent whose syndicate he wishes to join.

He can, however, go direct to the second agent if he has no other agent for business in that market. As a result of the one agent/one class rule there has grown up a plethora of sub-agency agreements between members' agents, anxious to have access to the best syndicates for their Names, and managing agents anxious to obtain Names to add to the capacity of their syndicates. In 1968 three of the largest agencies had fourteen, nine and six sub-agency agreements respectively. By 1982 the same three had sixty, forty-eight and thirty sub-agency agreements. Two other managing agents among the largest had over one hundred, and ninety, in 1982.[9]

Agents are remunerated by their Names through a fixed fee or 'salary' and a profit commission payable on the underwriting profits and on the earnings performance of the syndicate funds. In the case of a syndicate membership obtained through a sub-agency agreement, the fee and commission will be split between the managing agent and the members' agent, with the managing agent taking the lion's share; the relative size of this share varies from time to time depending on the balance in the market between the underwriter's need for Names to increase his capacity and the Names' eagerness to get on to a profitable syndicate.

As already referred to, Lloyd's brokers played an active part in the development of the agency system. Having access to capital and extensive contacts among their customers, they were well placed to provide the capital needs of underwriting agencies, especially at times when heavy taxation and death duties made it likely that some agents would have to give up without the introduction of outside capital, and to provide the system with a continual flow of Names to support the growth of the market; Names who looked to the good name of their broker for comfort and assurance that the underwriting arrangements made on their behalf were as sensible and sound as they could be.

The specialist members' agents, of whom there are about eighty, are a phenomenon of the last twenty years when the need for increased membership at Lloyd's gave scope to those with access to potential Names but no skills in underwriting management. An agent who confines himself to the members' support function has the advantage that he can single-mindedly pursue his Names' interests because he has no obligation to keep a syndicate going. His disadvantage is that he has no right of access to any syndicate but must negotiate with the managing agent and will invariably find that his Names are given lower priority than the managing agent's direct Names. The Name who goes direct to a managing agent will be sure of getting on to the syndicates managed by that agent, but is likely to be the last to hear when it is time to come off those syndicates.

He will have the advantage that the desire of other agents for places on his own agent's syndicates will give him reciprocal access to a wider range of syndicates. There is no simple answer: some Names prefer to talk to the organ grinder; others prefer to deal through the monkey.

When Parliament imposed divestment upon Lloyd's in 1982 it allowed an exception. Brokers could continue to own members' agencies as long as they did not engage in underwriting. The Parliamentary Committee debated the desirability of going further and requiring that the functions of managing and members' agents be divorced but this did not find favour. The new Act imposed divestment but not divorce. Statutory divestment has required that the ownership of agents who controlled 70 per cent of the market be transferred into other hands. This has been a source of major disturbance during a period, 1982 to 1987, when Lloyd's has been occupied with more important reforms.

The fourth category of participant at Lloyd's is the Name, or underwriting member. There are, in 1987, just under thirty-two thousand underwriting members of Lloyd's, each venturing his or her entire personal fortune on the world insurance market. Each must show Lloyd's that he has means of at least £100,000, and will be expected to deposit with the corporation cash or liquid investments to the value of £50,000. He or (since 1970) she,[10] is then free to join one or more syndicates and to write a premium income up to five times his deposit. If the Name wishes to join a certain syndicate his agent will contract for him to take a certain line on that syndicate. Lines are usually expressed in multiples of £10,000 and the active underwriter for that syndicate is then empowered to accept premiums on behalf of that Name up to the total of his line. The Name is then liable for any claims that may arise. But that liability is not limited to the Lloyd's deposit, the certified means, or even the premium limit; it is unlimited. Names are liable down, as the traditional phrase goes, to their last waistcoat button. The ratios between deposits, means and premium limits are laid down by Lloyd's so that it can satisfy the Department of Trade each year that each member is solvent and that all are able to meet the claims expected to be made upon them.[11]

Originally Names at Lloyd's were all workers in the market themselves, but since 1945, with the rapid growth of the membership of Lloyd's, an increasing proportion are outsiders. At the latest count 82 per cent of the Names were external members who were, in fact, nothing other than passive investors in the syndicates in which they participated. While the numbers of brokers, active underwriters, syndicates and agents has not increased greatly since 1945 the number of members has. Since 1970 the number of members of Lloyd's has grown dramatically, so that the

6,000 in 1970 rose to 8,600 in 1976, 18,600 in 1980 and almost 32,000 by 1987. The character of the membership has changed in other respects: 17 per cent are now foreigners (8 per cent are from the USA) and 22 per cent are women. More than any other factor this dramatic change in the size and character of the membership led to the downfall of the old regulatory regime at Lloyd's.

The principal participants in the Lloyd's insurance market are the brokers who bring in the business, the active underwriters who price it and write it, the underwriting agents who manage the underwriters and get together the Names to back the syndicates, and finally, the Names themselves who, pledging their assets without limit, provide the capacity for Lloyd's to compete as successfully as it does in the world insurance market.

The staff of the corporation, none of whom or their wives or husbands may be a member of Lloyd's, provide the support services to the underwriters: the marine intelligence, the policy signing office,[12] the claims offices and the agency network in overseas ports; and they regulate the market: admitting members, approving and monitoring brokers and underwriting agents, investigating breaches of the rules of Lloyd's, holding and investing the deposits and the other reserve funds of a very wealthy institution. Headed by the deputy chairman and chief executive they number about two thousand, including the red-and-black-liveried waiters who are the real descendants of Edward Lloyd and his staff of kitchen maids and waiters.

The staff is under the overall governance of the Council of Lloyd's elected from the membership and charged by Parliament with 'the management and superintendence of the affairs of society' and empowered 'to regulate and direct the business of insurance at Lloyd's'.[13]

IV

The Legal and Financial Structure of Lloyd's

The Insurance Companies Act 1982 governs the business of insurance in the UK. Under its provisions it is unlawful to operate an insurance company unless the regulations of the Act are followed. There are rules about minimum capital, solvency ratios and annual returns to be made to the Department of Trade and Industry (DTI). The DTI must also be satisfied that the controllers of insurance companies are 'fit and proper persons'. All these provisions are designed to protect the public from the possibility that a claim under an insurance policy will not be met because the company is insolvent, or fraudulent. Insurance inevitably involves an element of trust: the insurer takes the insured's money in exchange for a promise, evidenced by an insurance policy, to pay a claim if it arises. The business of insurance is governed by the legal doctrine of *uberrimae fidei* – the utmost good faith: both parties, insurer and insured, must deal entirely openly and fairly with each other if the trust on which the contract is based is to survive.

Having stated that 'no person shall carry on any insurance business in the United Kingdom' unless authorized by the DTI the Act promptly makes three exceptions: for trade union strike funds, registered friendly societies, and Lloyd's. Lloyd's therefore occupies a unique position of immunity from direct legislation which gives it a measure of self-government and of self-regulation. Underwriters at Lloyd's are not, however, entirely exempt from the Act. The policy holder must still be protected and the Act lays three requirements on Lloyd's underwriters: all premiums must be held under a trust deed from which claims may be settled; the underwriter's accounts must be audited each year and a certificate produced that the underwriter is solvent; and the Council of Lloyd's must file an annual return summarizing the extent and character of the insurance business done by the members of Lloyd's. The first two provisions relate to each member individually so that there must, by law, be 32,000 trust funds and 32,000 solvency certificates – one for each underwriting member of Lloyd's.

Because of Lloyd's exemption from the Insurance Companies Act the internal government of the society is covered by separate legal provisions. In 1769 a committee of Lloyd's subscribers, dismayed at the amount of gambling that was then rife at Lloyd's, opened a New Lloyd's Coffee House, run by a 'master' on behalf of the two hundred or so subscribers.[1] In 1811 in response to complaints from Parliament about the insolvency of certain underwriters the subscribers signed a trust deed to put their constitutional house in order. This deed governed the Society of Lloyd's until 1871, much as the Stock Exchange is governed by a trust deed today. In 1871, after the Committee of Lloyd's had found itself unable to expel a member who had, so they alleged, defaulted on a claim,[2] Lloyd's secured a private Act of Parliament. This Act laid down the 'Fundamental Rules of Lloyd's': the membership was to be divided between underwriting and non-underwriting members, and only the former could underwrite at Lloyd's; all business had to be conducted in the Room on behalf of individuals and not partnerships or companies; and underwriters in the Room could only deal with other members or subscribers, so that only Lloyd's brokers could place business at Lloyd's. Under this Act the committee became increasingly concerned about the solvency of underwriters. At first guarantees were called for, but by the 1880s the present system of deposits was in widespread use. In 1882 the committee fixed the minimum deposit at £5,000: this is £200,000 at today's prices compared to the minimum deposit today of £50,000. The 1871 Act established an elected committee of twelve and gave the society the power to make bye-laws subject to the approval of the Recorder of the City of London. Further Acts, in 1888, 1911, 1925 and 1952 updated the founding statute. The most important change was in 1911 when the committee was given power to suspend a member for up to two years if he had been guilty of any act or default discreditable to him as an underwriter, or otherwise, in connection with the business of insurance.

By the 1970s it had become apparent that the 1871 Act, designed for governing a small society all of whose members were active in the Room, was no longer adequate. The sanction of expulsion could only be applied by a four-fifths majority at a general meeting, after a finding of guilt by two arbitrators, one appointed by the committee and one by the defendant. These provisions were used once, in 1982, when Christopher Moran was expelled. Clearly they were too cumbersome for a society which in 1982 had almost 20,000 members, 16,000 of whom were not active at Lloyd's.

The new Lloyd's Act, passed by Parliament on 23 July 1982, established a totally new regime for Lloyd's. It had four provisions.

1 A Council of Lloyd's was established to supersede the old committee. The council was to have a tripartite membership of twenty-eight: sixteen 'working' members elected from the six thousand members active in the market at Lloyd's; eight elected from the external inactive membership of the society; and three nominated members appointed by the council subject to the approval of the Governor of the Bank of England. The nominated members cannot be members of Lloyd's. Their number was subsequently increased to four when, as Deputy Chairman and Chief Executive of Lloyd's, I was made a nominated member of the council on 14 February 1983. The old Committee of Lloyd's, made up of the sixteen working members of the council, still exists.[3]

2 The new council has the power to pass bye-laws which under the 1871 Act could only be enacted by a general meeting of members.

3 A Disciplinary Committee was established which may include lay members and need not be composed of members of the council: this committee can expel, suspend, fine, reprimand or censure a member and its reports may be published. There are rights of appeal and the council may exercise a right of clemency to modify the punishment.

4 Finally, the Act requires divestment – associations between Lloyd's brokers and underwriters to be ended by 23 July 1987.

Lloyd's brokers are covered by the Act. They are members of the Lloyd's community in their capacity as subscribers and most are also individual members. But they are also subject to the Insurance Brokers Registration Council (IBRC) established by the Insurance Brokers (Registration) Act 1977. This Act attempted to regulate the activities of insurance brokers by limiting the use of the title 'Insurance Broker' to registered organizations, and applying regulations and a code of practice to those so registered. Lloyd's brokers are the largest group within the British Insurance Brokers Association (BIBA), the body of brokers registered under the Act. They form a powerful constituency which strongly influences BIBA whose members are mostly small provincial brokers handling retail, rather than commercial, business. The Act lays down minimum standards of size and financial strength: many BIBA members complain that their competitors have escaped the burden of these standards by dropping the word 'broker' from their trading name in favour of insurance 'consultant'. Lloyd's brokers are currently exempted from some of the detailed rules of the IBRC on the footing that, being subject to the rules of Lloyd's, they must already meet higher standards.

The business of insurance has been supervised for many years by the Board of Trade, now the Department of Trade and Industry. The DTI is therefore Lloyd's sponsoring department, and is particularly concerned with the annual solvency test, laid down under the Insurance Companies Act 1982. The Bank of England, whose primary contact in Whitehall is the Treasury, has a general role in the supervision of City markets of which Lloyd's is one. The Lloyd's market is involved with two sets of external relationships: with policy holders, in which the DTI is directly and statutorily concerned; and with the external members, who, although not strictly speaking investors, have a relationship with their agents like that of a shareholder with his stockbroker. Relations between members and their agents are not governed by Whitehall but by the Council of Lloyd's under the provisions of the 1982 Act. In this area Lloyd's is self-regulatory. Both the DTI and the Bank of England are interested to see that the self-regulatory powers are properly exercised.[4]

Self-regulation is a peculiarly British method of supervising financial markets and Lloyd's is a first-class example of the advantages and disadvantages of the method. For self-regulation to work effectively there are a number of preconditions. In the first place there must be a closed circle of members to whom the rules are to be applied, and it must be profitable to be a member of the closed circle and financially disadvantageous to be excluded. Second, there must be statutory backing for the self-regulatory regime so that a member with a grievance cannot defeat the system by recourse to the courts. Third, the members of the self-regulatory society must be willing to accept that proper rules are more helpful to the conduct of business than a complete free-for-all. Fourth, the self-regulatory process will not work unless there are adequate procedures for consultation. If Parliament vests legislative powers in a private body it follows that any proposed subordinate legislation by that body should be subject to public review in the same way as bills in Parliament. The consultative process must extend outside the circle of members so that laymen can also express a view. But consultation does not mean consensus: it is not appropriate to allow a veto power to any member of the society, as was once the case with Lloyd's rule-making arrangements. Provided that views on proposed legislation have been properly canvassed and considered by the self-regulatory body it is entirely right that the body should be free to decide what should be done.

The fifth prerequisite for effective self-regulation is the active participation, on a voluntary basis, of those to whom the rules are to be applied. Self-regulation has many attractions for Whitehall. Self-regulatory legislation is much cheaper: the drafting is done by practitioners and not civil servants. It has more important advantages. Practitioners are better able to define the questions being addressed and to prepare rules to prevent malpractices because they are more familiar with the market. A repentant poacher makes the best gamekeeper. But underwriters and brokers are not usually expert legislators, and skilled staff are needed to turn the practitioners' propositions into effective legal language.

Finally, it is vital that the public interest be properly observed. As Adam Smith said, 'People of the same trade seldom meet together, even for merriment or diversion, but the conversation ends in a conspiracy against the public.'[5] The public interest means the interests of *all* parties other than the insiders themselves: in the case of Lloyd's, the interests of external members and policy holders as opposed to working members. In a modern self-regulatory organization great care must be taken to protect the public interest.

Such a self-regulatory regime covering a well-defined market, with appropriate statutory backing, acceptance by the market of the need for rules, adequate procedures for consultation before legislation, and active involvement in legislation by practitioners can, provided that the self-interest of the regulators does not damage the superior interests of those outside the circle of practitioners, produce a more efficient regulatory framework than Whitehall can. It is efficient because the rules are likely to be more closely adapted to the needs of an efficient market: they can be made more quickly and if necessary changed more quickly. Self-regulators do not have to wait for a gap in government business to fit legislation into a parliamentary timetable. Further, rules made by a society are more likely to be accepted and followed by those to whom they are to be applied than rules made by outsiders. This offers a further advantage. Offences against statutes are crimes and are punished in the courts according to criminal standards of evidence and proof. Parliamentary legislation is a clumsy instrument for raising standards because rules must be drafted in such a way that only really grievous offences are criminal. Statutes must establish a minimum standard of behaviour, breach of which is a crime. A self-regulatory regime, because it is based more upon consent than compulsion, is able to control through codes of practice rather than statutes. Such codes can establish higher standards: they are based on the premise that compliance with the spirit of the rules is the essence of the rules themselves. Parliament cannot expect the public to obey anything more than the letter of the law. Members of Lloyd's, and other self-regulatory organizations, can be expected to do more: to obey the spirit of the law.

But there are disadvantages to a self-regulatory regime. It may be lackadaisical, lacking the will or the authority to do its task effectively. Alternatively, it can be officious and overzealous with too many rules inadequately enforced. But the greatest disadvantage is unquestionably the freedom it gives to vested interests. Unless the market professionals show considerable self-restraint there will always be a danger of Adam Smith's maxim coming into play: rules will be inadequately enforced against chums or exercised overzealously against hated competitors; there will be an unwillingness to legislate until offences have become too widespread; there will be a tendency not to see the improprieties of current attitudes because 'things have always been done that way'; and judgments will too frequently veer towards supporting current market practice rather than protecting the public interest.

The key to effective self-regulation must, therefore, be adequate arrangements to control and obstruct vested interests.

The discussion so far makes no distinction between legislation and execution: writing the laws and applying them. Self-regulation may be defined as a system under which the rules are made by those to whom they are to be applied. But such a definition begs a question which was to be central at Lloyd's in the 1980s: who is to apply the rules? It is self-evident that there is a much greater danger of vested interest coming into play in the enforcement of rules than in their promulgation. Enforcement proceeds case by case. It is carried out in private. Personal relationships are at issue, as are considerations of competition between enforcer and enforced. It is therefore essential if the public interest is to be properly secured by a self-regulatory regime, to be punctilious in excluding anyone with a vested interest from applying the rules in the market place. This was to prove extraordinarily difficult at Lloyd's with its small number of market professionals from which the amateur market regulators were to be drawn, and with the extensive cross-memberships of syndicates. Furthermore there was an unwillingness to concede that there was a point at issue. To many at Lloyd's self-regulation meant, and means today, self-government, in which the legislative, executive and judicial branches are all in the control of the market professionals.

A curious feature of the business of insurance is that you don't actually need capital, save for a trivial investment in a desk and a pen, since premiums are collected first and claims paid later: the business enjoys a positive cash flow, unless something goes wrong and claims exceed premiums, when capital must be called upon. In insurance, capital serves principally to provide reserves for the protection of the policy holders in case of loss.

Lloyd's has put this fact to good use by employing the concept of uncalled capital. Underwriters do not call upon their Names to contribute until there is a loss on a particular year of account and capital is needed: then they have the right to call for as much as the circumstances may require. Names at Lloyd's have unlimited liability, but only in respect of their own share of the syndicate's loss; in the words of the standard Lloyd's marine policy, 'each for his own, not one for another'. In legal terms Names have several, not joint and several, liability. The security of a Lloyd's policy depends on the ability of each Name who has subscribed to that policy to meet his obligations under the policy as and when they fall due. A Lloyd's policy is signed by the corporation on behalf of underwriters. The Society of Lloyd's itself warrants that legitimate claims under the policy will be met and has rules to ensure that this will be the case. There are four lines of defence.

First, in accordance with the Insurance Companies Act, all premiums must be placed into a premiums trust fund, on behalf of policy holders.[6] This fund must only be used for the payment of claims and must, by the rules of Lloyd's, be invested in secure short-dated investments. After three years the active underwriter will take a view of the possible future claims that may be expected to fall on the fund and will calculate a closing reserve. Most of the balance of the fund will be used to buy a reinsurance policy, called a reinsurance to close, the terms of which will indeminify the fund against all future claims. Any balance then left in the trust fund is profit and can be withdrawn for the benefit of the Name. If the trust fund is in respect of certain very complex classes of business, or the syndicate's affairs are in an uncertain state, the account may be left open for a fourth year or longer until the closing reserve can be calculated with sufficient accuracy. It is wrong to assume that this three-year accounting system at Lloyd's exists because of any inability on the part of Lloyd's underwriters to keep their books up to date. The system is designed principally to defer the distribution of profit until the pattern of claims settlement can be seen with reasonable clarity.

In practice the other party with whom the reinsurance to close policy is usually taken out is the same syndicate, but for the next year of account. In fact, a Name participating on the syndicate for a given year contracts with the same syndicate for the next year of account and is thus, in a sense, contracting with himself. This may smack of Alice in Wonderland but it becomes important when, as frequently happens, the constitution of a syndicate changes from year to year and hence a continuing Name's fractional interest in the outgoing reinsurance to close differs from his fractional interest in the incoming reinsurance to close. The whole thing is rather like a game of pass-the-parcel with each player representing the syndicate for a different year of account.

If the premiums trust fund proves inadequate and the calculation of the reinsurance to close reveals a loss the second line of defence is called on – the deposits and personal reserves. Each Name at Lloyd's is required to place a deposit with the corporation pro rata to his premium income limit. For external members the current figure is 20 per cent for UK residents and 28 per cent for foreigners.[7] The agent will also normally require a Name to leave personal reserves with him, accumulated out of past profits. In addition the Revenue-approved Special Reserve Fund Scheme allows a Name to set aside a small tax-deductible amount of his underwriting income. These reserves and deposits are there to meet losses in case of need. If the Lloyd's deposit is used for this purpose the Name will be required to reduce or cease underwriting until the deposit is made good.

If the deposits and reserves prove inadequate Lloyd's can then turn to the Name's certified means. Before becoming a member of Lloyd's an individual must show by producing an accountant's certificate to that effect that he has independent means, excluding his home, of at least £100,000. He must renew that certificate if he later increases his under-writing limits and must undertake not to allow his means voluntarily to drop below the certified level. The Lloyd's deposit and reserves form part of the means. The level of certified means determines the level of premium income the Name is permitted to write by a ratio of 1 : 2.5; a Name may accept premium income, and the related risks, up to two and a half times his or her certified means. Although there is no maximum level of means, the maximum premium income which an individual Name may write is £1.3 million, which requires him to show means of £520,000.

The Name's underwriting obligations are unlimited. If his means are not enough to meet claims then Lloyd's must turn to the fourth and last line of defence: the Central Fund. Lloyd's Central Reserve Fund was established by a trust deed in 1927 out of a small levy paid by every Name in proportion to his premium income. It has always existed for the protection of policy holders, so that claims can be met when Names lack means. For the Central Fund to be used a Name must be declared in default; Lloyd's then has a right of suit on behalf of the fund against any Name on whose behalf disbursements are made. Since the 1982 Act, the assets of the Central Fund have been legally merged with those of the Society of Lloyd's, and the total available to meet the claims of defaulting Names is now about five hundred million pounds.[8] This may not seem much in relation to a market capacity of £10 billion, but it should properly be viewed as a fund to cover the possible default of individual underwriters, each undertaking an average volume of business of £220,000.

In the last five years, and most dramatically in 1986, there have been attempts to 'borrow' the Central Fund to provide security for the liabilities of Names whose solvency position is not clear because of allegations of fraud or accounting deficiencies. I shall comment further on this in relation to the PCW case.[9]

These four lines of defence: Premiums Trust Fund, deposits and reserves, certified means, and Central Fund, provide backing for a Lloyd's policy that compares very favourably with that behind a company policy – Lloyd's ratio of premium income to assets is 1.2 : 1. This compares with a norm of 4 : 1 in the US and 2 : 1 among the top companies in the UK.

These lines of defence are subject to two systems of check. First, the level of premium income accepted by each underwriter on behalf of his Names is continuously reviewed. Insurance regulators everywhere use premium income as a surrogate for exposure to risk when laying down rules about levels of solvency and assets. By definition, risk exposure cannot be measured, but risk will vary proportionately to premium. Taking one year with another, an insurance company's premium income will cover the risks it undertakes or it won't make a profit. Since the insurance industry as a whole makes a profit, it follows that although risk cannot be measured, premium income will do as a substitute. By ensuring that Names do not exceed their limits of premium income Lloyd's ensures that their assets should cover the risks they undertake.

The second check is the annual solvency test, formerly called the Lloyd's audit. This originated in 1908 when, in response to a scandal in which an underwriter bankrupted several Names,[10] a manifesto was signed by the leading underwriters of the day led by Cuthbert Heath. It said: 'We the undersigned underwriters would agree to hand into the Committee of Lloyd's annually a statement signed by an approved accountant that we were in the possession of assets reasonably sufficient to wind up our underwriting accounts.' Rules for an annual audit of solvency were duly introduced and in the next year, when new insurance companies legislation was introduced requiring deposits and returns from insurance companies, Lloyd's was exempted. This was the genesis of Lloyd's self-regulatory status.

Each year Lloyd's lays down minimum reserves for each class of business in its first, second, third and subsequent years of development. Under-writers are required to calculate their reserves by reference to these minima, but they must provide more reserves if the record of claims requires it. The solvency returns for each syndicate are amalgamated so that the total exposure of each Name at Lloyd's is calculated. A certificate must be signed by an approved auditor in respect of each Name certifying that he has assets, whether in his premiums trust fund, deposits or personal reserves, to cover his liabilities. Any deficiency must be made good before the certificate is signed. Names who cannot produce certificates of solvency are declared to be in default and Central Fund assets are earmarked to cover the deficiency. When every Name has been accounted for in this way, that fact is signified to the Department of Trade and to those overseas regulators who also require Lloyd's to provide an annual proof of solvency.

The work of checking solvency certificates has by statute to be carried out by an accountant approved by the Committee of Lloyd's. This work has traditionally been in the hands of a limited panel of relatively small firms of chartered accountants who specialized in Lloyd's work. Four firms account for 76 per cent of the syndicates.[11] There were a number of defects in these arrangements.[12]

Each Name at Lloyd's has unlimited liability and must expect to pay out cheques in some years, although he may expect to receive cheques in most. Names who are nervous of the risks they run are able to take out a personal policy of reinsurance to back up the arrangements that each of their underwriters will have made to reinsure his syndicates. Such a personal stop-loss policy will cover the Name each year against the risk of an overall loss in the year. That is, against the risk that all his syndicate underwriting results plus all the investment returns on his premiums trust fund, will show a negative result because of underwriting losses on one or more of his syndicates. Because a Lloyd's Name must have unlimited liability, such a personal stop-loss policy cannot be without limit: there must be a maximum loss covered, but the upper figure can be, and usually is, fixed at an improbably high level.

Should he be unlucky the Name has a second option. He can consider whether his agent is perhaps to blame, and if he has a case he can sue his agent. By the rules of Lloyd's, each agent must carry errors and omissions insurance so that if he is sued he will have the means to settle a claim for damages.

There are structural snags to these arrangements: because both personal stop-loss and agents' errors and omissions insurance are usually placed within the Lloyd's market. This results in a security weakness, because stop-loss reinsurances are using the asset-backing behind a Lloyd's policy twice. The Lloyd's security chain has been pledged once to back the claims of direct external policy holders. It is then pledged a second time to cover the risks of stop-loss policies. Although there are rules which prevent a Name participating in a syndicate which writes his

39

own stop-loss policy there is a clear element of double counting. There are also regulatory weaknesses because underwriters of agents' errors and omissions insurance are not excluded from the regulatory activities of the committee and council where deliberations as to an agent's behaviour can affect a claim against him by his Names. A complete solution would be provided by a rule that personal stop-loss policies, and agents' errors and omissions insurance, must be placed outside the Lloyd's market.[13]

PART II

THE DEVELOPING CRISIS

V

The Advent of Speculation

In 1965 a severe American wind-storm led to historic changes in Lloyd's; Hurricane Betsey produced losses on a scale that Lloyd's had not seen since the end of the Second World War. The average Name lost £6,000 in 1965 and over £3,000 in 1966. The whole market showed a loss of 8 per cent on premium income in 1965. The effect of the three loss-making years of 1965, 1966 and 1967 on those who work at Lloyd's was serious and is not forgotten today: workers in the market are allowed privileged access to membership; these privileges mean that they don't have to have the financial resources of ordinary external members and the economic risks they run are consequently greater. However, in the long run the effect on the external membership was of greater importance.

In the twenty years following 1946 Lloyd's membership grew slowly and steadily: from 2,000 to over 6,000. Then, as a result of the Hurricane Betsey disaster, the number coming forward for election each year halved and resignations doubled. For the first time in recent history the membership of Lloyd's began to fall: it fell for four years, and only began to recover in 1971. This happened against the background of an upturn in the insurance cycle. Rates were hardening and there was good business to be written, but underwriters lacked the capacity to respond. Lord Cromer, a former Governor of the Bank of England, was invited in November 1968 to chair a committee to examine the required growth of Lloyd's capacity, the likely growth of underwriting membership, the existing capital structure, and alternative methods of providing capital backing for underwriting.[1]

Cromer concluded that Lloyd's must stay in the business of insuring large risks and that it must therefore increase its capacity. He proposed a number of changes to make membership more accessible: a lower means requirement; simplified deposits; higher premium income limits and a

43

larger allowance for reinsurance which has the effect of increasing capacity for a given level of security. The Committee of Lloyd's quickly accepted these proposals and at the same time opened the membership to foreigners and women.

These changes, together with a return to profitability in world insurance markets, produced dramatic increases in membership. By the end of the decade – 1980 – the number of members had trebled to 18,600; it reached 31,500 in 1987. Not only did the number of members grow but the nature of the society began to change. Cromer had noted that whereas in 1958 two-fifths of the applicants for external membership had been landowners or farmers, that proportion had dropped to one-fifth by 1968.[2] The ratio of external to working members changed too: one-third of the membership worked in the market in 1968, whereas today that proportion is one-fifth. Lord Cromer's Committee showed considerable foresight when it said: 'nor is it surprising that the recent run of losses should lead to a more critical attitude by some Names towards agents. We think it would be a mistake to assume that this more critical attitude is a passing phase. Many Names are waiting to see what comes out of the present review of the organisation of Lloyd's. Many have also made substantial losses which only a long series of profitable years will wipe out. In present conditions Names are likely to look for something akin to the relationship which would exist if they were shareholders in a company and expect at least the same degree of accountability and consideration as is generally extended today to the shareholder.'[3] Pursuing this theme, the Cromer Committee called for Lloyd's to require agents to publish audited syndicate accounts to their Names, to give a report on prospects for the two open years, and not to increase a Name's share in a syndicate or transfer him to another syndicate without his approval. Annual meetings of Names on syndicates were also proposed.

Pointing out that a small number of agents treated their Names in a thoroughly cavalier fashion, the Cromer Committee thought that, thanks to the practice at Lloyd's whereby the agent receives a commission on the profits of the syndicates but makes no contribution to the losses, agents' charges were higher than could be justified. It proposed that agents should be required to inform the Committee of Lloyd's, in confidence, of the financial arrangements in the conduct of each syndicate, the results of this survey to be published in a generalized form.[4]

Although the Committee of Lloyd's adopted the Cromer proposals to ease the conditions of membership there was, at best, only a partial follow-up of the proposals concerning agents, and none at all for the proposals for the management of Lloyd's which included the appointment of a chief executive.[5] The Committee of Lloyd's decided that the Cromer Report should not be published. It is a wide-ranging survey of the affairs of Lloyd's, of interest to the Names, the authorities and the public. It is, however, somewhat critical of agents and it is difficult to resist the conclusion that the decision not to publish was prompted by the fact that the Committee of Lloyd's consisted then (it was eventually published in 1986) of an overwhelming majority of agents. Had it been published at the time it is possible that pressure from Names for the reforms called for would have brought about changes in the agency system that should have avoided some of the disasters that followed. In the event the changes were made, fifteen years too late.

The Cromer Report introduced a decade in which the behaviour of Names changed radically. During the booming 1970s when for five years out of six profits averaged over 8 per cent, the agency business grew as the membership of Lloyd's grew. Members' agencies, virtually unheard of in the 1960s, sprang up as entrepreneurs with access to blocks of potential Names sought to serve the needs of the market – and make some money doing so. As the membership grew the nature of Lloyd's changed inexorably and permanently. It ceased to be a small tight-knit association in which working members predominated – a members' club – and increasingly became an investment market in which members did not hesitate to enforce their rights at law. Two critical cases signalled this change.

The first, the *Savonita* case, concerned a claim against Lloyd's in respect of a damaged cargo of Fiat cars carried on board the *Savonita*. The original broker was doubtful of the bona fides of the claim and hesitated to present it for payment. The customer changed his broker to Willis Faber and in the end settlement was made. The difficulties between the two brokers, one of whom was not himself a member of Lloyd's while the other was at the heart of the Lloyd's establishment, led to an internal inquiry, but only after an adjournment debate in the House of Commons in which Jonathan Aitken MP criticized the Chairman and the Committee of Lloyd's.

The inquiry report was published at the end of 1978. In publishing it the committee chose a curiously inept way of handling the press. Newspapers were allowed to have copies of the report only if they agreed to sign a document beforehand acknowledging that 'having regard to the privileged nature of the report, neither the board of inquiry nor the Committee of Lloyd's will accept responsibility for the accuracy or otherwise of the report'. In addition, newspapers were required to indemnify the board and the committee in advance for any legal costs arising from publication. However sound this course of action may have been legally it was disastrous from a public relations point of view and from that time on the press have been suspicious of what they see as unpardonably pompous and arrogant tendencies on the part of Lloyd's.

The difficulties behind the *Savonita* case concerned a suspect claim at Lloyd's: rightly or wrongly, the original broker from his investigations suspected that the claim might be fraudulent, while Willis Faber, from their investigations, concluded, rightly or wrongly, that the claim was not fraudulent. Lloyd's has suffered from suspect claims from time to time; sadly there is nothing unusual about this in the world of insurance. The second case, the Sasse affair, was much more serious. Used to handling matters between underwriters and customers, Lloyd's now had to learn new skills on a second front: relations between Names and agents.

A binding authority is an arrangement under which a Lloyd's underwriter grants the authority to bind risks on his behalf and that of his Names to a third party or 'cover-holder'. The cover-holder is often a broker and is usually operating overseas. By this device the Lloyd's syndicate gains access to retail business overseas. A binding authority, or 'binder', should only be granted to a highly reputable cover-holder and the underwriter should monitor the development of the business closely. The Non-Marine Association at Lloyd's has for many years operated a system of checking the bona fides of cover-holders, but such a binder was granted by the Sasse syndicate in 1975 to an American cover-holder – Harrison – without the usual checks. The binder was used improperly to insure derelict properties in the South Bronx area of New York. Massive losses ensued and fraud was alleged. The Names on the syndicate were faced with calls for large sums in circumstances which they found difficult to follow and of which they had been told nothing. For the first time in Lloyd's history the Names refused to pay.

The problem was compounded by the actions of the Committee of Lloyd's in intervening in the management of the damaged syndicates. The Names alleged that the Corporation of Lloyd's itself shared responsibility for their plight. The litigation between Lloyd's and a group of its Names hit the headlines. The protesting Names formed themselves into associations out of which grew today's Association of Lloyd's Members. It was apparent to the Committee of Lloyd's that the constitutional arrangements that had served for a society of a few hundreds, all of whom were engaged in the business of insurance at Lloyd's, would no longer work in the new climate of investor Names. The Sasse affair was resolved by a compromise in which the whole society undertook to bear some of the Sasse losses. The general question that had arisen – the changing nature of relations between Names and agents – led to the appointment of the Fisher Committee.

Sir Henry Fisher has had an unusual career: a distinguished lawyer who became a high court judge, he resigned from the bench to become a merchant banker and has just finished a term as Master of Wolfson College, Oxford. In February 1979 he was asked by the Committee of Lloyd's to undertake an inquiry into self-regulation at Lloyd's and in particular to review the constitution and the powers of the committee. The committee included two distinguished outsiders – Mr Robin Broadley of Baring's, the merchant bankers, and Mr David Watt, then director of the Royal Institute of International Affairs. Four senior working members of Lloyd's completed the group.

The Fisher Committee reported in May 1980. Its terms of reference make clear that the question of whether self-regulation was appropriate to Lloyd's was not to be considered. The report said: 'We have no doubt that Lloyd's would be best served by a properly conducted system of self-regulation.'[6] But no arguments were advanced to support this thesis, which would remain unexplored until Sir Patrick Neill's Inquiry was appointed in January 1986.

The Fisher Report laid down a charter for reform at Lloyd's. It concerned itself principally with legal and structural matters. Much the most important conclusion was that there should be a new Lloyd's Act, whose contents have been described in an earlier chapter. The most radical element of the Act was to be the establishment of a Council of Lloyd's, in which the ultimate power of regulating the market would vest, and which would include representatives of the external members of the society and 'three nominated members ... appointed by the Council ... and confirmed by the Governor for the time being of the Bank of England: Provided that a person who is a member of the Society ... shall not be eligible for appointment as a nominated member.'[7] The majority would still be working members, brokers or underwriters, most of whom would be agents as well, and the chairman and elected deputy chairmen would continue to be market professionals. Having proposed that the council should have the power to pass bye-laws, Fisher's next proposal was that the contractual undertakings between participants in the market and the Corporation of Lloyd's, which largely governed the behaviour of market members, should be replaced by a comprehensive system of bye-laws. Agents and brokers would all be required to re-register with Lloyd's to new tighter standards. The Act should give the council wide investigatory and disciplinary powers. Recognizing the difficulties caused by the Sasse case, binding authorities were to be regulated; as suggested by Cromer, audited syndicate accounts were to be required.

But the most dramatic reform introduced by Fisher was divestment by the brokers of their agency interests. At the time of the Fisher Inquiry 70 per cent of the syndicates at Lloyd's were broker-controlled.[8]

The concern of the Committee of Lloyd's in 1954 that underwriting agency activities be conducted through separate companies from insurance broking activities has already been noted.[9] Cromer commented further on the matter in 1970: 'There is a conflict of interests which cannot be ignored.... There can be little question that the Lloyd's underwriting syndicate and the Lloyd's broker are essentially complementary to each other in forming the Lloyd's market as a whole. Although complementary, and this is a cardinal point, they are not interchangeable.... If a conflict were to arise between an insured and an underwriter who happened to be an employee (even indirectly) of the broker to the insured the problem is most difficult. But, short of a conflict of this kind, we find it difficult to accept that, in exercising judgment of what he is to accept and what to refuse, an underwriter who is an employee of a broker-owned agency can at all times be wholly impartial.'[10] The committee of the day did not take up the suggestion of negotiations to resolve the problem.

Sir Henry Fisher returned to the question of conflicts of interest in 1980. He saw three dangers: that the underwriter might be forced to accept risks contrary to his better judgment and the interest of his Names; that the broker might give the business to his own syndicates contrary to the interests of his assured; and that collusion between broker and controlled underwriter would limit the degree of competition between underwriters in the Lloyd's market. He concluded: 'The question is whether the undoubted difficulties, both of principle and of practice, of a compulsory divestment by Lloyd's brokers of shares in managing agencies should be allowed to override this logic. We have discussed this problem at length and the majority of us have reached the conclusion that divestment should be enforced and the formation of such links prohibited for the future.'[11] He went on to consider the further question of whether, when brokers were no longer allowed to control managing agencies, they should be allowed to control members' agencies and hence to influence an underwriter by threatening to take their Names off his syndicates. The Fisher working party concluded that, although divestment was necessary, the divorce of brokers from members' agents was not, provided that the Committee of Lloyd's introduced a rule that there should never be more than a certain percentage of one syndicate's Names coming from any one members' agent.

Fisher's arguments were accepted by Parliament: the 1982 Act decreed that associations between managing agents and Lloyd's brokers were to be terminated by July 1987. Lloyd's brokers were allowed to continue their members' agencies. In other words, Parliament favoured divestment by which brokers were to cease their connections with the underwriting activities of agencies but did not support divorce – the separation of brokers from the members' services activities of agencies. Nor did Parliament favour the divorce of underwriting activities from members' service activities; combined managing/members' agencies were allowed to continue and indeed now dominate the agency business.

The Lloyd's Bill started through Parliament as a private Bill in November 1980. Before then a general meeting of Lloyd's members had endorsed the Bill and accepted that divestment, as recommended by Fisher, should be recognized in it. What was not agreed at that stage was that the Act itself would impose divestment, and not leave it to be implemented at a later stage under the aegis of the new Council of Lloyd's. The Bill's passage through Parliament was controversial: some members objected to the clause that granted the Council of Lloyd's immunity against suit by members of the society in respect of actions committed in the discharge of its regulatory duties; others, led by individuals from Howden's and Minet's who were to figure in later disciplinary proceedings, argued against divestment by which some Lloyd's brokers stood to lose considerable sums in profits. The House of Commons Select Committee on the Bill took an active interest, favouring statutory divestment, and also divorce, from which they were dissuaded by the vote of a further general meeting of the members of Lloyd's. But statutory immunity from suit at the hands of the members, a very necessary provision for the effective regulation of the market, stayed in the Bill. On 23 July 1982 the Lloyd's Act became law. A leader in the influential New York daily, the *Journal of Commerce*, said at the beginning of August that Lloyd's, its troubles behind it, could now look forward to some years of calm prosperity while the changes required by the Act were carried out.

Before I discuss the dramatic developments of the latter half of 1982 that led to my appointment, it is necessary to explain a second undercurrent of change at Lloyd's: this concerned reinsurance.[12] The genesis of these developments lay in the late 1960s when premiums rose sharply in a world insurance market shocked by the serious losses caused by Hurricane Betsey. Although premiums and profits were high in the 1970s, the insurance market was tight. Underwriters were unable to find reinsurers for their active, profitable but risky, accounts. They therefore decided to make their own arrangements, and a handful of agents set up reinsurances with insurance companies in such a way that the companies bore no risk. Typically the terms of such a 'funding' or 'banking' policy were that the claims under the policy could not exceed the premiums, plus the interest earned by the insurance company on those premiums, less a commission to the reinsurers. The reinsured could determine when a claim was due: in other words, he could call down the money at any time. In many cases the terms of the policy were such that any unclaimed balance could be rolled forward as a reduction in the premium payable for the next year of account. Such a policy was called a 'roller'.

These arrangements were capable of increasing degrees of refinement in which, in some cases, the line between permissible tax avoidance and criminal tax evasion became somewhat blurred. First, the money could be placed with a reinsurance company offshore so that interest would accrue tax free. Second, the money could be placed with a reinsurance company owned by the agent himself so that the commission would not be lost. In such cases a higher rate of commission might be charged, benefiting the agent at the expense of his Names. Third, although the value of the reinsurance policy *could* be brought into account when reckoning up the assets of the syndicate to calculate the reinsurance to close, in many cases this was not done. As the books of the syndicate bore no trace of the assets held under the policy, but only recorded a reinsurance premium paid, concealment was easy. Fourth, as the reinsurance premiums were paid away from the syndicate and not accounted for or audited, they provided a fund from which dishonest agents could steal, and in a few notorious cases that is what they did.

Often the funding arrangements included supporting opinions from auditors and counsel and, in one or two cases, clearance from the audit department at Lloyd's and even from the Revenue itself. The fact that such care was taken from the start confirmed the doubts of their authors about the tax deductibility of such reinsurance arrangements, arrangements which, with varying degrees of refinement, became widespread among a small circle of the larger agents: perhaps thirty in all. It was a circle which included some of those who were later to be found guilty of misdemeanours and also a number of members of the committee. Thanks to the modern practice of Names spreading their interests, and their risks, among many syndicates, many managed by agents other than their own, such doubtful arrangements ultimately affected 92 per cent of the Names.

Lloyd's rules, since the 1950s, have confined themselves to requiring underwriters to arrange that their reinsurances 'conform to the basic concept of honourable trading' which requires that there be a genuine risk of loss on the part of the reinsurer. A letter from the Committee of Lloyd's to underwriters in December 1958 drew attention to the questionable tax deductibility of certain roller reinsurance premiums. Notwithstanding this advice, during the 1970s rollers flourished and in

October 1985 were alleged to have reached £100 million in value. The lack of adequate accounting rules at Lloyd's, coupled with the fact that there was no requirement for syndicate accounts to be audited, helped to conceal the true facts from the Names and the Revenue.

The distinction between genuine policies of reinsurance and funding policies is clearly illustrated in the report of the Hart disciplinary inquiry: 'Where there is a genuine risk reinsurance contract, the premium is received by the reinsurer on his own behalf. He is under no obligation to repay the premium (unless the policy is avoided). His liability (if any) is to pay in respect of claims falling within the terms of the reinsurance contract. Where there is a "funding policy", the purported reinsurer receives the "premium" on behalf of the Syndicate, and not on his own behalf, he invests it, not as part of his own funds, but as funds of the Syndicate, sometimes called "escrow funds"; and when called on by the active underwriter pursuant to the arrangements between them, he repays the "premium" (with or without interest and/or any gain derived from its investment) to the syndicate.'[13]

In summary, the practice was this: payments were described as reinsurances which were in fact general reserves, and tax deductions were obtained for these payments. The underwriter then had an additional secret fund under his hand which could be called upon to meet later losses and hence to smooth profits. The evidence is that, overall, funds flowed out in the 1970s and back in the loss-making 1980s although many syndicates drew down in the late 1970s and made further arrangements up to 1982. The Revenue was concerned by the fact that deductions were claimed in years when the top tax rate was 98 per cent and the funds recalled into tax when the top rate had dropped to 60 per cent.

Exchange controls, abolished in 1979, played an influential part in such arrangements. Funds could be moved abroad under the guise of reinsurance and then used for investment purposes. To have moved the funds ostensibly for investment would have been difficult and might have meant paying the dollar premium which existed in the 1970s, and which became payable if dollars were bought for investment. Reinsurance was thus an attractive route for moving funds for exchange control, as well as tax reasons. Islands such as Bermuda and Cayman were popular locations for offshore reinsurance funds because of local rules about secrecy, the fact that interest would be earned there tax free, and that they were in the sterling area. In 1973 Bermuda and the Caribbean islands were excluded from the British exchange control net. Such locations as Gibraltar, the Isle of Man and the Channel Islands, which remained inside the sterling area, then became more attractive because, while no exchange control permission was required for fund transfers, there was little or no local income tax.

It must be said that underwriters were no less affected than other businessmen by the climate of the late 1970s when tax avoidance became something of a crusade. While the top rate of tax on earned income was 75 per cent, and that on unearned income 98 per cent, Lloyd's underwriters were not alone in seeking ways of making what they saw as perfectly legitimate and proper provision against future disasters. The Treasury, under Sir Stafford Cripps in 1947, had instigated arrangements by which each member of Lloyd's could reserve up to £7,000 tax free against future losses. But the figure had not been adjusted since 1956 and gave little cushion against an increasingly risky business. The roller arrangements were products of the times, but that does not make less excusable the breach of the agents' duty implicit in the transactions. Under agency law every agent has a duty to account to his principal, who in the Lloyd's context is the Name, for the use he makes of the principal's funds. He must never make a profit for himself out of such funds without the express agreement of the principal given with full knowledge of all the facts. The roller arrangements breached those rules because of the secrecy involved and because, in some cases, agents charged fees or commissions on the fund without the express agreement of the Names. In a few notorious cases they went a step further and misappropriated the funds.

Each year since 1908 Lloyd's has carried out a solvency test assisted by a panel of approved auditors.[14] The collective behaviour of this group when faced with the arrangements I have just described, and the more serious breaches of agency duty which I shall come to, provide an object lesson for accountants.

Having the legal duty of preparing the Annual Certificate of Solvency, and acting as they did for the underwriting agents who are mainly small concerns with limited staff, many of the panel auditors had taken on the task of keeping the books for their clients and preparing the tax returns for agents and their Names. Twenty years ago the Institute of Chartered Accountants introduced rules restricting auditors from keeping the books of their clients because of the inevitable lack of independence involved: an auditor should not be called upon to check his own work. The reaction of the panel auditors at Lloyd's, with which the committee concurred, was to establish 'joint audits', by which one of the signatories to the auditor's certificate kept the books and the other audited them. It was frequently not clear how the duties were divided and what responsibility each of the joint auditors had for the work. Certainly one, the bookkeeper, could not also be the auditor if the strict rules of the profession were to be applied.

The number of firms on the Lloyd's audit panel remained very small. Until a recent spate of mergers with larger, non-Lloyd's, accounting firms, none of the leading members of the panel was a household name in accounting terms. The Committee of Lloyd's did not appreciate the perils in this situation, no doubt assuming that the requirements of the market were so peculiar that only a small number of auditors experienced in the work could be relied upon to do it. Until 1985, any newcomer to the panel was required to serve a period of probation as a joint auditor with an existing panel member.

Each of the small panel firms became increasingly bound up with Lloyd's, and in isolated cases had partners who were not only members of Lloyd's, but members of the syndicates they audited. Because of their significant involvement in Lloyd's work some of the panel firms drew a substantial proportion, and in a few cases the majority, of their total fee income from such work.

A further problem was the fact that the panel auditors, appointed to audit the syndicate by the agent, frequently acted both as auditor to the agent and auditor to the syndicate for whom the agent acted. The conflict of interest is obvious: it is always a matter of judgment how much of the overhead expenses of the underwriter should be borne by the agent out of his fee and profit commission and how much may properly be charged directly as an expense to the underwriting account of the individual Name. An auditor acting for both sides is in a difficult position when commenting on the fairness of this judgment. For a number of reasons, therefore, there was a continuing risk, not always avoided, that the panel auditors at Lloyd's lacked independence from their clients: some kept the books; some were too dependent upon Lloyd's for their fee income; the panel formed a small group specializing in an arcane area of accounting work; and the different interests of Names and their agents were not adequately reflected in the audit arrangements.

But there was a more serious problem. Despite their title, the panel auditors were not in fact charged with carrying out an audit at all. Their duty was described by Lord Cromer: 'The main function of the auditor is to provide a certificate to the Committee of Lloyd's that the Name has sufficient funds at Lloyd's to meet his obligations.'[15] Agents, underwriters, Names and the committee were all under the misapprehension that the work done by the panel auditors was an audit, in the commonly accepted sense of that word: an independent opinion on the veracity of a set of accounts. But it was not – a point which the panel auditors, to give them

53

their due, had occasionally drawn attention to. The accounts of an underwriting syndicate, and the determination of its profits, depend upon how much reserve is necessary to close the accounts. The figure for this closing reserve is provided by the underwriter in the form of the reinsurance to close. Some of the panel auditors were still living in the days, which I recall from my apprenticeship as an accountant thirty years ago, when auditors accepted a certificate of stock 'at director's valuation': they did not consider it part of their duty to *audit* the reinsurance to close, yet the result of the syndicate for the year of account was wholly dependent on this one figure.

Under these circumstances it is no surprise that some of the auditors missed the scandals and failed to point out the impropriety of what was going on. They were not charged with performing an audit to normal auditing standards, and although they clearly had knowledge of some of the matters that were going on, they may well not have fully appreciated their implications. In any case, regrettably, they did not see it as their duty to draw the Names' attention to what was happening. Had they been stronger firms, or wiser in the affairs of the world, or perhaps more willing to ask difficult questions, they might have exposed the frauds earlier. But the fact is they did not.

VI

The Autumn of 1982

United States business is vital to Lloyd's and, despite its apparent Englishness, Lloyd's business has been at least half American since the Second World War. As the volume of the world's insurance business grew so did the size and geographic scope of the great American broking houses based in the nation that provides almost half the world's insurance premium income. Much of their reinsurance business and of their more complex direct insurance business is placed in the London market of which Lloyd's is the centre. Lloyd's rules require that any business coming to an underwriter must be placed through a Lloyd's broker: the American brokers were therefore forced to go through intermediaries whose skills duplicated their own. It would make economic sense for each to merge with or acquire its own Lloyd's broker.

The Committee of Lloyd's has historically been dominated by underwriters, although brokers have always had an important voice. Chairmen of Lloyd's are usually underwriters although a distinguished minority have been brokers. The committee has always been ambivalent on the question of permitting Lloyd's brokers to be owned by foreigners – which usually means Americans. On the one hand, they fear their inability to control elements of the market having such enormous financial muscle – elements which are able to gobble up the business handled by the more traditional English brokers. On the other hand, the underwriters are keen to attract business to Lloyd's and don't wish to offend a vitally important source of that business.

The last thirty years have been marked by increasingly half-hearted attempts by the committee to prevent outsiders taking over Lloyd's brokers. The so-called '20 per cent rule', which is alleged to forbid any holding by a foreign interest above 20 per cent in a Lloyd's broker, has been broken so often that it is clearly a dead letter. The committee still attempts to stop insurance companies from owning Lloyd's brokers on the footing that they would have an impossible conflict of interest. But American brokers of standing are now clearly free to buy: the takeover of Bowring's by Marsh McLennan, the largest of the alphabet brokers, has already been referred to.[1]

In this climate it was obvious that the acquisition of Alexander Howden by Alexander & Alexander, the second-largest of the alphabet brokers, would be unlikely to be challenged by the regulatory authorities.[2] Howden's was, in 1982, a fast-growing broker with an extensive reinsurance book. It owned a number of reinsurance companies including the Sphere/ Drake. The management of Howden's was in the hands of four members of Lloyd's: Messrs Grob, Comery, Page and Carpenter, later known as the Gang of Four. The Lloyd's underwriting activities of Howden's made a significant contribution to the group's profits: their chief underwriter, Ian Posgate, was the largest marine underwriter in 1982. He wrote for about six thousand Names, over one-quarter of the then Lloyd's membership, and handled not far short of 10 per cent of the entire premium income of Lloyd's.[3] This represented a high degree of concentration, but it was not all that unusual: in an average year in each of the two large markets, marine and non-marine, ten underwriters write half the business. Ian Posgate was, however, an undoubtedly popular star with a large number of external members. He was also a reluctant fifth member of the Howden board, having come under the wing of Howden's in 1970 at the insistence of the Committee of Lloyd's which was concerned at his overwriting of premium income and wished him to be properly controlled. Posgate was a controversial figure in the Lloyd's market. His free-wheeling and aggressive underwriting methods had earned him the enmity of his competitors in the marine market on the floor of the Room. He was seen as being one who would break conventions and cut rates to get business – he was certainly not a team player. But his popularity at Lloyd's was great enough for him to be elected to the committee at the end of 1981.

The acquisition of Howden's would give Alexander & Alexander the direct access to the Lloyd's market they were seeking. In early 1982 the deal was done and the new owners began to move in. Under American securities practice it was necessary for the acquiring company to carry out a full audit of their new subsidiary. Such a check could not be carried out before as Howden's was a public company and the rules of the UK Stock Exchange would have forbidden such disclosures to a potential buyer. Deloitte's carried out a 'fair value' audit. This revealed that a large proportion of the assets of Howden's was missing, mostly from Sphere/Drake, the wholly owned reinsurance company subsidiary.

In a statement filed with the Securities Exchange Commission in Washington reporting this discovery, Alexander & Alexander said that they were suing the Gang of Four and Mr Posgate. The company alleged that: 'Beginning as early as 1975, funds totalling approximately $55 million, including payments purporting to be insurance and reinsurance premiums from Howden insurance companies and quota share premiums from Howden managed insurance underwriting syndicates, of which Mr Posgate was the underwriter' were paid improperly to certain entities.

On 1 September 1982 A&A gave Lloyd's the first news of Deloitte's discovery. On 16 September Lloyd's was told that Ian Posgate was implicated and he was suspended from the market and from his place on the committee. On 20 September following the filing of the statement with the SEC the DTI announced in London that inspectors would be appointed under Section 165 of the 1948 Companies Act, into the affairs of the Howden Group.

Lloyd's learned about a further development on 29 October. A&A reported that questionable reinsurances had been placed by Howden's on behalf of the PCW syndicates. Peter Cameron-Webb was another marine underwriter, but with a more conformist style than Mr Posgate. He had been trained by Janson Green, the agency later operated by Sir Peter Green, then Chairman of Lloyd's, but had left to start his own operation when Janson Green was still under the command of Sir Peter's father Toby Green. With his partner, accountant Peter Dixon, he had placed reinsurances of his syndicates with entities which he owned in Gibraltar, the Isle of Man and Guernsey. About forty million pounds was alleged to have been moved in this way. Cameron-Webb had retired from Lloyd's at the end of 1981 and taken up residence abroad. As soon as A&A reported their discoveries to Lloyd's, Dixon, who then ran the PCW agencies, agreed to suspend himself from the market.

The PCW agency had been acquired by the large publicly quoted Lloyd's broker, J. H. Minet & Co., in 1970. Following the policy of the committee at the time, which was anxious to avoid unnecessary conflicts of interest, Minet's were denied access to details of the PCW underwriting activities, the auditors at the agency were different from those of the parent broker, and Minet's was allowed only one nominee director on the board of the agency subsidiary. This was their Chairman, John Wallrock. It appeared that, without the knowledge of the board of Minet, Wallrock had shared in some of the personal benefits obtained by Cameron-Webb and Dixon at the expense of the Names on the syndicates they managed. He resigned and the DTI appointed Section 165 inspectors into the affairs of the Minet Group.

A third similar scandal broke just before Christmas in 1982 when Messrs Brooks & Dooley, a smaller underwriting agency, were accused of placing their syndicate reinsurances with a Bermuda-based company called Fidentia which they either owned or controlled. In this case £6.2 million was alleged to have been put into Fidentia from the Brooks & Dooley syndicates.

The Chairman of Lloyd's himself, Sir Peter Green, was also subject to critical attention. Allegations had been made in early 1982 about reinsurance arrangements made by Peter Cameron-Webb through a Monaco-based company called Unimar. Although no large sums of money had gone astray, the clandestine arrangements under which privately owned Unimar had received a 10 per cent overriding commission on outward reinsurances from the Cameron-Webb syndicates were suspect. Sir Peter's own largely private inquiry found no evidence of dishonesty – a conclusion that the press later found disquieting when Cameron-Webb's other actions came to light. A later Lloyd's inquiry by Simon Tuckey QC also reached the conclusion that there had been no dishonesty. The Department of Trade inspectors inquiring into Minet's had the power to question a wider circle of witnesses than the Lloyd's inquiry and they announced in July 1986 that they had found evidence of dishonest intent on the part of Cameron-Webb, Dixon and a Lloyd's broker, David d'Ambrumenil.[4] They reported that Sir Peter Green's conclusion that there was 'no dishonesty on the part of anyone connected with the transactions' went further than was justified by the evidence available to him.[5] However they agreed that further evidence would have been difficult to find given the limited circle of witnesses to which Sir Peter had access. They concluded: 'The conclusions expressed by Sir Peter in his letter of 26 February 1982 were his honest opinion of the matter. We reject the suggestion that he was guilty of a "cover-up".'[6]

Sir Peter was also under attack because of his personal shareholding in a Cayman-based insurance company called Imperial with which some of his syndicate reinsurances had been placed.

This catalogue of calamities brought strong reactions from a number of quarters. Lloyd's had for long been a closed book for the press, and relations between the committee and the press had never been easy. On the release of the *Savonita* report the committee had agreed to the report being made available to members of the press only if the journalists signed an indemnity undertaking not to libel the committee![7] Soon after I arrived at Lloyd's I was horrified to learn that it was the practice not to give the Lloyd's press office a copy of the monthly agenda of the council 'for fear of leaks'. In such a secretive climate moles flourished and as is usually the case when the press obtain stories from undercover sources the leaks tended to be incomplete and biased. The press leapt with delight upon the misfortunes of the lofty institution of Lloyd's. Front-page stories revealed increasingly detailed chapters of horror; the Bank of England, Whitehall and Parliament became concerned.

The Secretary of State for Trade and Industry was then Lord Cockfield, an energetic and single-minded individual whose fearsome command of detail I came to respect when I served as a member of the Price Commission under his chairmanship in 1977. Cockfield's concern to seek out the truth was confirmed by the promptness with which DTI inspectors were appointed into Howden's and Minet's.

Members of Parliament, who had been prevailed upon only six months earlier to pass the new Lloyd's Act, felt cheated and angry. They had tackled the question of divestment, at the prompting of Sir Henry Fisher, and achieved the separation of brokers and underwriters. But it now appeared that Sir Henry had shot the wrong horse. In pressing for divestment, in the name of avoiding conflicts of interest among brokers between their duties to their customers, the insured, and to the Names for whom they also acted as underwriting agents, he overlooked the much more serious abuses of conflicts of interest involved where agents put their own interests improperly ahead of their duties to their Names. Lloyd's had been given new powers by Parliament. But it was now revealed that among those who had argued so strongly for the granting of extended powers had been some who had cheated and even plundered the members of Lloyd's for whom they acted. Grob and Wallrock had been important witnesses before the Select Committee on the Bill. There can be little doubt that had Parliament known of the Howden, PCW, and Brooks & Dooley affairs before July 1982 the new Lloyd's Act would not have been passed and Lloyd's self-regulatory status would have been in grave doubt.

The reaction at Lloyd's was one of shock. Steps were taken to stem the damage. Those members of Lloyd's implicated in the scandals suspended themselves from the market, or were suspended by the committee. In order to allay the fears of Names, and no doubt influenced by Sir Peter Green's earlier unhappy inquiry into Unimar, independent inspectors were appointed by Lloyd's. Nigel Holland, a partner in accountants Ernst & Whinney, who was well versed in Lloyd's accounting, and Peter Millet QC, handled the Howden affair. Simon Tuckey QC assisted by Holland looked at PCW. Anthony Colman QC was teamed with Stephen Hailey FCA, a partner in Arthur Andersen & Co., to inquire into the Brooks & Dooley case. In each case staff and support were provided by investigatory staff of the Corporation of Lloyd's headed by the head of regulatory services,

Ken Randall. It was important for the inquiries to be seen as being carried out independently of the Lloyd's market professionals so that the public could be confident therefore that they would be thorough and fearless, even if members of the committee proved to be implicated. Although the Lloyd's inquiries were commonly seen as analogous to DTI inspections under Section 165 of the Companies Act 1948, this was not actually the case. After any prosecutions that may be called for as a result of the inspector's conclusions, DTI inquiries are always published so that the public may know the nature of the alleged wrongdoing. In the case of the Lloyd's inquiries the intention was different: to decide if there was a case to answer before a Lloyd's disciplinary tribunal for a breach of the rules, what that case was, what was the evidence for it, and what rules had been broken. The Lloyd's inquiries were similar to the inquisition carried out by an examining magistrate before a criminal case is brought in France.

Meanwhile steps were taken to place the management of the stricken agencies in fresh hands that would be charged with the job of recovering the missing funds on behalf of the Names. PCW underwriting agencies was a subsidiary of Minet's. It was therefore up to the board of Minet's, with the approval of the Committee of Lloyd's, to arrange the continuing management of the PCW syndicates and to recover the missing funds. Minet's invited a distinguished marine underwriter, Richard Beckett, formerly with Sedgwick's underwriting interests, to become Chairman of PCW; he was assisted by Graham White from Willis Faber as managing director. New underwriters were appointed and a start was made on unravelling the tangled accounting web at PCW and recovering for the Names the money of which they had been defrauded.[8]

The Brooks & Dooley agency had sprung off an older Lloyd's agency, Dugdale's, most of whose names were on the Brooks & Dooley syndicates. With the help of Jack Alston, from Lloyd's brokers Leslie and Godwin, as chairman, the board of Brooks & Dooley was recast. At the same time a new team was installed at Dugdale's under the direction of David Newton. Mark Farrar, a solicitor and a Brooks & Dooley Name, chaired a committee of defrauded Names and steered it towards an acceptable compromise of litigation with Messrs Brooks & Dooley which recovered a fair amount for the benefit of the Names.

Howden's, in whose syndicates almost a quarter of the Lloyd's members in 1982 were Names, needed a two-part recovery plan. A special agency was set up by Alexander & Alexander – Alexander Syndicate Management (ASM) – chaired by Jeremy Hardie, a chartered accountant. ASM were given carte blanche to take whatever steps were called for to recover missing funds for the benefit of the Names. If this involved litigation A&A would provide the necessary funds, even though their subsidiary, Howden's, would be a possible target of such litigation.

The second part concerned the Posgate syndicates whose management presented difficulties. Ian Posgate had established his own agency, Posgate and Denby, which was separate from Howden's. This agency ran a number of syndicates, including some for which Ian Posgate was the underwriter. In addition he was the active underwriter of the Howden syndicates. As the agency's managing director, principal shareholder and star underwriter had been suspended, new management had to be found. Colin Bramall stepped in as Chairman, with the approval of the Committee of Lloyd's, and led a long and arduous battle with Ian Posgate over the effective control of Posgate and Denby.

The Howden syndicates were trading at a profit. The task was to recover, through Howden's, the funds that had gone astray, and Jeremy Hardie was able to achieve an arrangement in which a fair proportion of the Names' claims, about 85 per cent, was recovered. The underwriters of the Brooks & Dooley syndicate called on the reinsurance funds in Bermuda to meet losses on the syndicate; the balance ultimately available to meet the claims of the Names was therefore somewhat depleted, but a reasonable bargain was struck in 1985. The case of PCW was much more difficult. Cameron-Webb and Dixon had been engaged in an elaborate series of devices to extract reinsurance funds from the syndicates, and to complicate the accounting records so that it would prove very difficult to unravel them. While this was going on their non-marine underwriters had written some disastrously unprofitable business. This was to show losses of over £235 million by 1986, so that the sums recovered from Gibraltar, Minet's and A&A (who had broked the questionable rein-surances) for the benefit of the Names were overtopped by the calls made upon them to meet these losses. The ultimate resolution of the problem of the PCW losses was to face the Society of Lloyd's with one of the most serious challenges in its history.

In all these scandals a common thread emerged. Lloyd's agents had breached the duty of trust that every agent owes to his Names under the law of agency. Any agent faced with a conflict between his own interests and those of his principals, the Names, has a clear legal duty to avoid that conflict if he possibly can. If he cannot avoid it, he must declare to his principal that there is a conflict, seek his principal's express informed permission to continue to act, and if this is granted he must then, at all times, put the interests of his principal before his own interests. A further rule of the law of agency provides that an agent who makes a profit with his principal's funds in secret is in breach of the law: he must disclose the profit to his principal and account for it in full. Thirdly, every agent has a duty to account regularly and in detail to his principal for his steward-ship. In each of the scandal cases, agents had breached the rules of the law of agency: principally those concerning conflicts of interest, the rule against secret profits, and the duty to account. In each case the arrange-ments had also secured dubious tax advantages.

In the three cases in question the agents responsible had plundered their Names; the sums involved totalled at least £55 million.[9] These were much the worst cases of outright plunder, but misunderstandings about the law of agency were widespread among the agents at Lloyd's. Insofar as the details of 'funding' reinsurance policies were withheld from Names the law of agency was breached. Such doubtful arrangements occurred among a majority of the major agencies and affected syndicates covering 92 per cent of the total membership of Lloyd's.

Baby or preferred syndicates were another problem. They had been brought into the open by the press towards the end of 1982. The worst case was in the PCW agency which operated two special syndicates for the benefit of a handful of insiders: the Principal Baby Syndicate and the Staff Baby Syndicate. The disciplinary report on the PCW affair[10] explained that the two syndicates participated in selected direct business, picked out by the underwriter, and also received premium by way of reinsurance from the main syndicates. From 1970 to 1979 the baby syndicates received payments and adjustments made for the purpose of engendering profits for the baby syndicates which to a very substantial extent would not have been made by underwriting the reinsurances which were there-fore bogus and dishonest.[11] Concluding their passage on this the Disci-plinary Committee said: 'The Baby Syndicates were ... operated in a manner which defrauded the members of the other syndicates managed by PCW and as a further means of dishonestly misappropriating substantial sums of money.'[12] No other underwriters went quite so far, but many, particularly in the marine market, adopted the practice of operating a preferred syndicate to reward agency directors or staff. Often an inner circle of brokers was included to encourage them to bring their business to the main marine syndicate. In adopting these practices the underwriters were not dealing fairly with their Names. Although it could be, and was, argued that the Names would benefit in the end from happier agency staff, or a better flow of business from brokers, the practice was not disclosed, so breaching the rules against secret profits and conflicts of interest.

By the end of 1982 the climate surrounding Lloyd's had become distinctly torrid. The press had found a cause célèbre, Parliament felt it had been cheated, the Tory Government was displeased at revelations of skulduggery in its own back yard the City, and the confidence of external Names in Lloyd's, its committee and chairman, was shaken. The Bank of England has a general responsibility for the regulation of City markets. It had taken an interest in recent developments at Lloyd's and had been influential in establishing the Fisher Inquiry. Under the new Lloyd's Act it had, for the first time, a formal role as sponsor of the nominated members of the new Council of Lloyd's. Now it was beginning to be seriously concerned that questions about Lloyd's might affect confidence in the entire City. It was decided to press Lloyd's to accept the appointment of an independent chief executive of public stature drawn from outside the circle of Lloyd's staff and from outside the membership.[13]

VII

The New Council of Lloyd's

The new Lloyd's Act took effect from 1 January 1983: the new Council of Lloyd's took office from the same day. In accordance with Fisher's recommendations the membership of Lloyd's was divided into two constituencies: the working members who elected sixteen members to the council; and the external members of whom eight joined the council. The election of external members presented a difficulty because unlike the working members of the society, external members did not know each other; it has always been contrary to the rules of Lloyd's for members to publicize their membership. The candidates were unknown to most of the external members so the election process was somewhat capricious. The winners were those who had the support of the principal agents whose Names wrote in for advice on how to vote. It had hardly been Fisher's intention, when he proposed that external members be included on the council to counterbalance the power of the working members – including the agents – that the agents should influence the choice. It is difficult, however, to see what other method of election would work. Nor did the external members' subsequent behaviour give any evidence of obligation to the agents who had sponsored them.

The new council held a preliminary meeting at Leeds Castle in December 1982. The first business was to appoint three nominated members who could not be members of Lloyd's. It was necessary to negotiate with the Bank of England on this point because the Act required that they be approved by the Governor of the Bank. Lloyd's was fortunate to obtain the services of Sir Kenneth Berrill, former head of the government Policy Review Board, Brandon Gough, Managing Partner of Coopers & Lybrand, the accounting firm, and Edward Walker-Arnott of City solicitors Herbert Smith & Co. These three were to serve for several years.[1]

The question of remuneration for council members came up at an early

64

stage. Members of the old Committee of Lloyd's, who now formed the sixteen working members of the council, had always served without pay. They had only to come up from the Room to attend a committee meeting on the second floor at Lloyd's and the business of the council was intimately connected with their day-to-day concerns as brokers, underwriters and agents. The 'chairs' – the chairman and the two elected deputy chairmen – served full time, but they were unpaid too. The working members on the council would look askance at any proposal to pay attendance fees to the external members of the council, who were regarded by the more conservative insiders as interlopers. Soon after my arrival at Lloyd's certain external members of the council were invited to accept outside directorships of agencies: clearly a connection with the ruling council would be useful to a growing agency. This caused grave offence to the working councillors and standing orders were drafted to forbid an external member of council benefiting financially from his office: he was precluded from drawing any salary from the market or changing his underwriting arrangements during his term of office in such a way that it might appear that he had benefited from inside knowledge. These provisions represented an injustice to the nominated members who had no financial interest in the success of Lloyd's. They remained unpaid until the beginning of 1987 when annual salaries of £8,000 were awarded to the three nominated members by bye-law.[2]

The Committee of Lloyd's is the second-oldest element in the structure of the society. In 1771 a committee was formed to launch the 'New Lloyd's' and it has had a continuous history of managing the society and regulating the business done in the Room. The 1982 Act transferred this responsibility to the new tri-partite Council of Lloyd's, but allowed the committee to live on. It was made up of the sixteen members of the council elected from the working membership. It continues its Wednesday morning meetings in traditional form: the committee stands when the chairman enters the room; members sit, and speak, in order of seniority; and subscribers (a category of members) are elected by secret ballot, using the ballot box. During the crises of 1982 the committee had frequently resumed work after its weekly lunch, but in early 1983 the new council began to feel its muscle, and take on an increased responsibility: the role of the committee began to diminish.

There was an early attempt to maintain the traditional status of the committee by the passage of a resolution delegating most of the new council's powers to the committee. This resolution would have had the effect of putting the general power to regulate Lloyd's back into the hands of the very body, the committee, that Parliament had just decided should surrender it to the new council. The external members did not like it and the resolution was given only four months' life. When the council returned to the matter in April 1983 a new power structure was proposed in which the committee would have a much smaller part to play. Over the next year new committees were formed by the council to be responsible for a number of matters formerly handled by the Committee of Lloyd's. These new committees included external and nominated members of the council who, in a number of important cases, provided the chairman. Committees were formed to deal with Finance, Investigations, Administrative Suspension, Rules, Accounting and Auditing Standards, Staff, Senior Appointments, Training, and External Relations. The formation of these committees had the effect of removing these responsibilities from the Committee of Lloyd's, since policy on these matters now came directly to the monthly council meeting for decision. Working members of the council played an important, but rarely dominant, role in these committees. Delegation by the council to the Committee of Lloyd's was in respect of specific matters rather than by granting a general authority.

The committee continued to have responsibility for the admission of members, brokers and agents, and for solvency. Two important sub-committees dealt with membership matters and with the annual solvency test, including recommendations on minimum solvency reserves: both these sub-committees were chaired by influential working members.

These developments, particularly the exclusion of finance and investigations, meant that the role of the Committee of Lloyd's changed and its weekly agenda, reflecting its diminished decision-making powers, looked increasingly thin. Attempts were made to reduce the frequency of meetings, fuelled by suspicions among external members of the council that the committee provided too good an opportunity for the working members to meet in caucus before the monthly council meeting. So far these attempts seem to have had little effect on the weekly ceremony on the eleventh floor in Lime Street.[3]

The Committee of Lloyd's remains, as it should, the principal forum for the expression of market opinion. Committee members are elected for four years at a time; one-quarter retire each year and must then take a sabbatical year away from committee duties before they can stand again for election. Because of the growth of the society the old system of voting in person on General Meeting Day in November has been replaced by a postal ballot – the only way external members could be effectively enfranchised. Although external members vote for a separate constituency – eight external members of the council – the same postal voting system is now used for the working members. The market associations are important in these elections because they provide a training ground for future committee talent. There are always marine and non-marine underwriters on the committee, and they have often been chairmen of their respective associations – the Lloyd's Underwriters Association and the Lloyd's Underwriters Non-Marine Association. Sometimes the fortunes of election give an opening for an aviation underwriter or a motor under-writer: both these markets are too small to ensure regular representation on the committee. The rest of the committee consists of brokers, often former chairmen of the Lloyd's Insurance Brokers Committee, and agents who have served their time on the committee of the Lloyd's Underwriting Agents Association. Although most leading agency figures are under-writers or ex-underwriters there is a cadre of professional agency men who have made their way up through handling the affairs of Names.

Because the working member electorate is small, so that candidates are usually widely known, and service on the committee is interrupted by sabbaticals, the electoral system is very democratic in the sense that it responds quickly to market attitudes. Time-servers on the committee do not, on the whole, last well because they have to secure re-election after an interval. This system of direct election gives the committee power and lends weight to its opinions on market questions. It has however one major disadvantage. There are under six thousand working members of Lloyd's, of whom two-thirds are at any time too junior or too old to be considered for elected office. The pool from which the committee members can be drawn is therefore small and the pressure on the more successful underwriters to avoid the commitment of elected duty is great.

Although the new Council of Lloyd's was drawn from the three con-stituencies of the working and external members of the society, and non-members co-opted by the council, it quickly cohered. Bye-laws must be approved at council meetings by a special resolution with separate majorities of the working members and of the external and nominated members voting together. This device was designed by Fisher to make sure that the working members' majority on the council could not be used to approve bye-laws against the wishes of the external members' representatives. In fact, special resolutions have always been supported from both sides of the council chamber and early fears that the council might become divided have proved groundless.[4]

The Leeds Castle council meeting decided two further matters. Sir Peter Green would continue as Chairman of Lloyd's for a fourth year, and the new post of Chief Executive would be created. I saw Sir Peter on 4 January 1983 and told him that I would accept that new position subject to certain conditions. I wanted to be a deputy chairman as well as Chief Executive.

I would be a nominated member of the council with the right to attend committee meetings – only working members can belong to the committee. Because I saw myself principally as an agent of change, I agreed to serve for a limited term only – a minimum of three and a maximum of five years. After that, the decision to continue the post or not was a matter for discussion by the council. I wanted certain staff to be available to me. I recognized that, in order to be free of any charge of partiality, I would have to retire from my firm. I would continue for the time being as Chairman of the Accounting Standards Committee (where my term of office ran out in June 1984) but I would give up my other public appointments. In concluding my discussions, I said that I would have to be free to make clear, if asked, that the post was not of my choosing but that I was doing it because the Governor of the Bank had approached me and that I considered I had a public duty to respond.

Sir Peter Green is a bluff man with considerable phlegm. He can be taciturn but has a strong will. There can be no doubt that he dominated the Council of Lloyd's in its early days. He certainly was not afraid of it. We did not discuss the details of my terms of reference, in the drafting of which I played little part.[5] He said that the job would be principally concerned with implementing the new self-regulatory regime envisaged by the 1982 Act. He saw the society as needing three things which the present chairs could not supply: continuity, because the constitution of the elected triumvirate of chairs changes each year; management skills, because underwriters have little management experience and neither do most brokers; and what he called a hard impartiality in the application of the society's rules. The proposal to appoint me as Deputy Chairman and Chief Executive was put to a somewhat startled Council of Lloyd's at the beginning of January 1983. A small sub-committee of councillors interviewed me. I can recall little of that hurried interview in the chairman's office at Lloyd's except for a comment by one of the group, Peter Miller: 'You do realize do you not,' he said, 'that your first duty is to the external members of the society?' This remark emphasized for me a significant aspect of my future job.

I began to get to know the top people in the Lloyd's market and among the council members. I was obviously something of an enigma to them. The paths of public accountants and Lloyd's underwriters don't often cross. To most I was 'the chap the Governor found'.

In 1983 Peter Rawlins was a senior manager (later a partner) with Arthur Andersen & Co. He came with me to Lloyd's as my personal assistant on secondment from Andersen's. He was the initiator of much good thinking at the early stages, especially in the area of rule-making.

He also drafted speeches, articles and papers and kept his finger on the pulse of the second floor, the market and, to a lesser degree because he too was an outsider, the staff. He was my trusted confidant and adviser and without him the job would have been ten times more difficult, especially at the early critical stages. Peter Rawlins returned to Andersen's in the spring of 1984 before leaving at the end of that year to take up the position of Managing Director of Lloyd's largest agent, R. W. Sturge & Co.

It was clear to me that the massive task of reforming the regulatory framework at Lloyd's would require high-level, professional competence. I had knowledge of standard setting in the accounting field and I had served as a member of the profession's Auditing Practices Committee. But I was not a lawyer and knew little about insurance and less about Lloyd's. I, therefore, proposed to my first council meeting that the council appoint three advisers on self-regulation. The first was David Stebbings. He was then the recently retired Senior Partner of Freshfields, the leading City law firm. He was one of the two non-Lloyd's members of the Higgins working party, appointed by the Committee of Lloyd's in 1982 to inquire into the agency system following an undertaking to Parliament during the debate on the Lloyd's Bill. He had had a baptism of fire at Lloyd's and knew about many of the problems. Before I took up office at Lloyd's he had talked to me about the iniquitous system of baby syndicates, which he described as 'daylight robbery', and the need to be rid of it. His input was particularly valuable on the law of agency so fundamental to Lloyd's. His lectures at seminars on the subject opened the eyes of many Lloyd's agents who were surprised to learn that trusteeship with its strict accountability, the very core of agency law, was as old as the Crusades and had long preceded the foundation of Lloyd's.

The second adviser was Philip Brown. Philip was a deputy secretary at the DTI. In a long civil service career he had acquired experience on the insurance regulatory side. Philip's initial brief was to advise on the investigatory and external relations areas, both of which were in need of attention. Later he joined the staff full time as head of external relations and then as head of regulatory services. He left Lloyd's just after I did.

Richard Wilkes was a former president of the Institute of Chartered Accountants and is a partner in Price Waterhouse & Co. I felt I needed advice on the accounting side as well as the legal and regulatory aspects of the job. Richard formed the third member of the team and his work on broker regulation was particularly useful.

The paper to council that approved the appointment of these three as advisers on self-regulation included some prophetic words: 'Council, Committee and market are all anxious to bring in necessary and appropriate regulations in order to lift the cloud of suspicion that hangs over Lloyd's and to render it free of future attack.... The advisers' overall mission will be to assure the Deputy Chairman and Chief Executive and through him the Council that the proposed arrangements meet necessary standards of quality in the public interest and are in the interests of assureds and Names.... They will report individually to the Deputy Chairman and Chief Executive and undertake tasks at his request.... Their independence of Lloyd's will help to stiffen his back against any tendency to temper the proper force of self-regulation.'

I started work at Lloyd's on 14 February 1983. On the very first day I had to focus on one of the issues which was to dominate my three years in Lloyd's and which lay behind all the major scandals – tax evasion. The Revenue had learnt from the papers about some of the dubious reinsurance practices at Lloyd's. This was the beginning of a course of inquiry into the reinsurance practices, described in Chapter V, which led to a settlement with the Revenue in October 1985. At this stage the Revenue was literally feeling its way. We explained the plans that had been developed within my working party on syndicate accounting to publish a register of underwriters' interests and suggested that this should give them the information they wanted.

When I started at Lloyd's I agreed a three-point plan with the chairman and the council. The first and most urgent thing was to restore confidence in Lloyd's as an institution. The press scandals did not appear to have had an adverse effect on the flow of business into Lloyd's: the insurance world knew the way that Lloyd's worked and were aware that the difficulties concerned relations between external Names and their agents. Policy holders were not affected because the security of the Lloyd's policy was not at risk. The proud boast that no valid claim on a Lloyd's policy had ever remained unpaid was still true. Business continued to flow in. Admittedly it was now accompanied by some snide comments from the American market; we no longer had an unimpeached record for integrity, but provided that Lloyd's cleaned up the mess there would be no lasting damage.

Reactions in the UK were more critical and the danger was that the confidence of Names as investors would be affected. In fact the volume of business written at Lloyd's doubled from 1983 to 1986 and the number of members rose by one-third over the three years, so any damage to confidence must have been marginal.

The second task was to write the rule book. Lloyd's bye-laws under the 1871 Act run to twenty-two pages. Most of the market's rules were unwritten, or embodied in the vague authority of letters from the chairman to the market. One of the principal reasons for the new Act was to furnish Lloyd's with a comprehensive legally enforceable rule book with which to regulate the business of insurance in the Room.

The third job was the most difficult. It was to alter the Society of Lloyd's so that it would be equipped with a regulatory framework appropriate to the world's largest insurance market. This meant not only managing the staff and finances of the Society of Lloyd's; it also meant changing the very structure of the society so that the application of the council's new rules to the market would be progressively transferred out of the hands of market insiders into those of independent professionally trained staff.

PART III

THE PATTERN OF REFORM

VIII

Cleaning up the Market

On top of the 1958 Lloyd's building in Lime Street stands a block of Portakabins erected to provide much-needed extra office space before the new building across the street was completed. It is approached by a draughty iron staircase across the roof. The block is isolated and cannot be overlooked. During the latter half of 1982 it was dedicated to the Lloyd's investigations and was known as Fort Knox. Here, remote from the Room six floors below, Ken Randall and his staff began to unravel the woeful deceit patterns spun by the scandals at Lloyd's. Ken had joined Lloyd's as an accountant at Lloyd's of London Press ten years earlier. Transferring to the regulatory staff of the corporation, his obvious skills had led him to the centre of power on the second floor and he was named to the new post of Head of Regulatory Services in March 1983.

The investigations staff at the end of 1982 numbered about fifty. A few were old-stagers borrowed from various Lloyd's departments; most were young lawyers and accountants, men and women newly recruited to the staff or seconded from City professional firms. The expense of the team, which itself co-ordinated the work of a number of firms of lawyers and accountants, was considerable. But the committee and the new council did not stint in providing the funds needed to do the job. The members of the team were either new to Lloyd's or new to investigatory work. They put in many hours of overtime. They were faced with the largest crisis in the history of Lloyd's.

My terms of reference had emphasized my special duties as far as investigations and discipline were concerned. Not being a member of the society and having resigned all other outside posts, I was the only member of the council who was in all respects and at all times completely independent of the matters under inquiry and had the time to give to the needs of the situation. Clearly the right policy was to back Ken Randall, a decision I never regretted; to replace the temporary staff arrangements by cheaper permanent ones and reduce the dependence on outside firms of solicitors and accountants; and to support the staff's efforts with the chairs and the committee. Allegations were then being made which ran close to leading figures in the market and even to the committee itself. Staff were justifiably nervous of their own jobs because they might find themselves investigating their masters.

The success of the Fort Knox team was urgent because the press was baying at our heels. The events of the autumn of 1982 had given Lloyd's a most unfavourable press. A great British institution, somewhat mysterious but none the less of the greatest economic importance, appeared to have soup stains down its tie and the press was not inclined to be generous in reporting Lloyd's.

Relations between the Committee of Lloyd's and the press had never been easy. Underwriters had always found it difficult to accept that journalists might have a legitimate right to inquire into the happenings at Lloyd's. The committee had always been reluctant to take the press into its confidence, although some years earlier the practice of an annual press conference was instituted at which the Chairman of Lloyd's, flanked by the chairmen of the market associations, presented the overall market results for the year. Lloyd's had a press department, but its principal role when I arrived was seen as that of keeping journalists away from the second floor.

Looking back at the headlines of autumn 1982, criticism fell into four categories.[1] First, it was alleged that Lloyd's would, as usual, cover up its scandals and sweep them under the carpet. Nothing would ever be heard of the outcome of the allegations being made, for that was the way things had always been done in the past. Lloyd's, it was said, had only one rule: 'Dog don't eat dog.' Any actions against the recently publicized miscreants would be confined to ensuring that they did not gain an unfair competitive advantage in the market. Moreover, it was said, the Committee of Lloyd's could never give a fair hearing to an accused who was himself a close competitor in a tightly knit market. Second, the press concentrated on the traditions of the place, its age and the conservatism of its attitudes and the unlikelihood that its members could ever be persuaded to alter their practices. Lloyd's was seen as an unchanging institution to which reform was inherently alien. Third, this conservative clannish club was founded on the maxim of privacy; secrecy was endemic at Lloyd's. 'Mind your own business' was the normal response to the press. The external Names and the public had scant chance of discovering what went on inside such a private, and some might say arrogant, society. Finally, Lloyd's was seen as essentially an elitist club in which the favoured few, the working members or 'market professionals' as the *Financial Times* had come to call them, would continue, as ever, to exclude the external members, the public interest and the professional staff from any power or influence over the affairs of the society.

These four points – the tendency to cover up, conservatism, natural secrecy and elitism – were the essence of the storm of criticism which Lloyd's was attracting from the press when I joined in early 1983. A contemporary quotation crystallizes these sentiments under the headline 'Lloyd's must regain its grip'. The passage reads: 'The essential problem at Lloyd's is that the market has failed to keep up with the standards of the times. To some extent this had been recognized by the passage of new legislation in Parliament to strengthen Lloyd's self-regulatory powers, but the whole approach to business needs to change. Much of the City has moved away from the old club-like approach; Lloyd's has lagged behind.'[2]

Our first task was to correct these impressions by improving relations with the press. My own past experience, my terms of reference and the promptings of the Bank of England all pointed me towards taking the initiative.

I had found over the years that the best posture with journalists was absolute frankness on matters where they had a legitimate right to know, and to say no and explain why if the matter was secret. The key was for the chief executive to handle the press personally. I therefore set to work to build better relations with the leading financial journalists by always making myself available to them on the telephone and by holding regular monthly press conferences after each council meeting. These were well attended at first, up to forty journalists came, but as the mystery was dispersed and interest fell the numbers came down to fifteen or sixteen. I boasted at the time that we had got Lloyd's off the front page and on to the back page, then into the inside pages, and finally we had disappeared from view. Because the press knew that they would be kept informed the search for leaks, which had so occupied them in 1982, flagged. Until the PCW problems emerged in all their seriousness in April 1985 we enjoyed a steadily improving press which lacked the carping tone that had been so noticeable before 1983.[3]

In handling the press it was always important to remember that the Chairman of Lloyd's is the chief ambassador for the market and its principal spokesman and figurehead; my appointment had attracted a good deal of press publicity; as far as possible I had to avoid my name and face prevailing in Lloyd's reportage. I therefore adopted the practice of speaking off the record to journalists other than at the monthly press conferences, and of ensuring that my many talks to market groups, external Names and public forums, were off the record.

In order to improve Lloyd's image, especially in the United States, arrangements were put in hand to publish the annual return of Lloyd's business to the DTI, which is called for under the Insurance Companies Act in a form similar to the annual report of a company. We added a statement setting out the financial resources that stand behind the Lloyd's policy. These documents were especially valuable in the USA because most of the leading American insurance companies reinsure with Lloyd's. New rules in the US required auditors of American insurance companies to check the financial status of those companies with whom their clients reinsured. But Lloyd's had never published accounts. The most useful way of meeting the need was to redraft the annual DTI return as 'Lloyd's Global Report and Accounts'. The figures were nothing but an amalgamation of returns submitted by each syndicate and they were not audited. But they served to give a clear picture of the size and scope of Lloyd's business and its relative profitability.

This process of opening up Lloyd's had the desired effect. The press coverage of Lloyd's, measured in column inches, fell steadily week by week, contrary to the expectations of the more conservative members of the committee who expected that the new policy would attract media attention. It was not however true, as was then alleged, that I had arranged to pay a bonus to the Lloyd's press department based on the reduction in the number of column inches achieved each month! But this relief was only a lull: the most convincing source of reviving confidence in Lloyd's would be evidence that the miscreants in the market would be dealt with properly. We had to show that there would be no sweeping under the carpet as had happened in the past.

I have already referred to defects in the disciplinary arrangements at Lloyd's under the 1871 legislation. Procedures to remove a member from the market were cumbersome and unwieldy.[4] Although the Lloyd's Act of 1911 provided that, instead of expulsion, the committee could suspend a member for up to two years, the procedures required were still so cumbersome that they were very rarely used. Instead the chairman of the day would, if the offence merited it, invite the miscreant to resign or accept such punishment by way of suspension or reprimand as was felt appropriate. This procedure depended upon the accused's willingness to accept his punishment, and upon the weight of the chairman's office being brought into play to secure this acceptance and execute the sentence. In the booming days of the 1970s, when a new breed of fortune hunter had entered Lloyd's, the old willingness to accept the rules of the club had withered and the committee felt, rightly in Sir Henry Fisher's view, that it lacked the powers it needed to discipline the market.

The new Act required the council to pass bye-laws establishing a Disciplinary Committee, a majority of which should be members of the society, and an Appeal Tribunal whose members could not be members of Lloyd's. Except for the council's power to confirm, modify or grant a dispensation in respect of any penalty or sanction awarded, all the disciplinary powers or functions of the council were to be exercised by the new Disciplinary Committee, and in respect of appeals, by the Appeal Tribunal.[5]

It was urgent to act promptly in respect of these new powers, and a comprehensive set of disciplinary bye-laws, which had been drafted before the Act had come into force, was passed by the council at its first meeting on 5 January 1983. The Disciplinary Committee consisted of senior members of the society with a minority of non-members, chiefly lawyers. Council members were excluded. The Appeal Tribunal was chaired by a distinguished Lord of Appeal, Richard Wilberforce: his deputy was David Calcutt QC who later became Chairman of the Bar Council. The range of penalties available to the Disciplinary Committee, which would sit in panels of three or five, now included the power to reprimand, censure, suspend and fine as well as to expel. There was a power frequently resorted to, to appoint an independent QC to chair a disciplinary committee in any particularly serious case.

The disciplinary and appeal bye-laws were buttressed by five others. The most important of these, the misconduct bye-law, laid down the matters which could constitute misconduct: breach of the Lloyd's Act or any bye-law, regulation or direction made thereunder; conduct detrimental to Lloyd's or those doing business there; conduct of any insurance business in a discreditable manner with a lack of good faith; or dishonourable, disgraceful or improper conduct. The range of penalties available to the Committee of Lloyd's was specified. The administrative suspension bye-law gave the council power temporarily to suspend the member if required to prevent the risk of serious damage to Lloyd's. The inquiries and investigations bye-law gave the council power to order inquiries into a member's conduct. Such inquiries could not be carried out by anyone having a financial interest in the matter or closely connected to the person involved. A committee of inquiry set up under this bye-law would have powers to obtain information from 'Lloyd's persons', that is to say all those within Lloyd's jurisdiction including members and the lesser categories of persons associated with Lloyd's: subscribers, associates and substitutes. The fourth bye-law made clear that any evidence obtained by such an inquiry was to be confidential and only to be used for the proper regulatory purposes of Lloyd's. Finally the council stage of the disciplinary process was set out, defining the council's power of clemency and giving it the power to publish the findings of disciplinary proceedings.[6]

This framework was a vast improvement on what had gone before. But everything turned on how the powers were to be used. Investigations and discipline had always been matters for the Chairman and the Committee of Lloyd's. In the current circumstances this was inappropriate because members of the committee were themselves under challenge. Further, the investigations bye-law now expressly forbade the involvement in this work of those having a financial interest in the matter or a connection with those involved. Lloyd's is such a small market, in terms of the numbers of leading figures actively involved, and cross-interests are so frequent (more than half the members of the council were members of Ian Posgate's syndicates), that great care must be taken to ensure that justice is properly done. We had to establish that investigations and any subsequent disciplinary proceedings would be impartial to avoid accusations of favouritism towards old friends, or antagonism towards hated competitors. This meant that any members involved in a decision to prosecute or sitting in judgment on a case had to have no connection with the defendant. Secondly, we had to ensure 'due process', as the Americans say. New bye-laws had to be applied punctiliously and correctly: there could be no repetition of the incident in November 1982 when Mr Posgate's proposed suspension from the market had been overturned in the High Court because of legal defects in the committee's action.

It was also necessary to apply John Locke's doctrine of the separation of powers. According to the letter of the law the Council of Lloyd's is supreme: it has full powers to regulate the business of insurance at Lloyd's. The council can bring charges against a member, it can hear those charges through the medium of the Disciplinary Committee, and it can exercise a power of clemency in respect of the sentence at the council stage of disciplinary proceedings. It had already been decided that no member of the council would serve on the Disciplinary Committee so there was no confusion when it came to hearing a case and bringing a verdict. But deciding whether or not to investigate alleged wrongdoing and then, having read the report of the investigation, to prosecute a member could not in my view properly be taken by the same council who would, later, decide if the sentence should be reduced. An Investigations Sub-committee of the Committee of Lloyd's had already been formed which reported regularly to the weekly meeting of the Committee of Lloyd's. We changed this by forming an Investigations Committee of the council chaired by one of the nominated members who was, by definition, not a member of the society. The membership was drawn from the working, non-working and nominated members of the council which delegated to the Investigations Committee two powers: that of ordering that matters be formally investigated under the investigations bye-law; and that of ordering that charges be brought against any member of the society alleged, by such an investigation, to have committed an offence. With the formation of this committee the Committee of Lloyd's ceased to have any role in the investigation and disciplinary field. When a matter reached the final disciplinary stage before the council, members of the Investigations Committee excused themselves from attendance on the footing that they already knew of the matter and were prejudiced because they had been involved in the decision to bring the original charges. In this way a proper separation of powers was achieved and Lloyd's was proof against allegations that members of the regulatory authority had been both judge and advocate in the same case.[7]

Similar considerations applied to administrative suspension. We had powers to suspend a member from the market for up to six months pending the completion of inquiries and disciplinary processes.[8] Such suspension was not meant to imply any pre-judgment of guilt: it was purely administrative, for the protection of the market. None the less, to suspend a member was to deny him the right to earn his living and gossips would make damaging remarks about his integrity. We had therefore to be very careful that such suspension was always judicially applied. An Administrative Suspension Committee of council members was established which excluded members of the Investigations Committee and represented all three constituencies of the council – working, external and nominated members. Cases for consideration were referred to this committee by the Investigations Committee who would advise, when considering charges, whether temporary administrative suspension was called for. The Administrative Suspension Committee was furnished with substitute members so that a quorum of members independent of the case would always be available. It sat in judgment on cases of administrative suspension, hearing the arguments advanced by the Investigations Committee and any defence advanced by the member affected.

The business of insurance at Lloyd's involves a lot of standing around. The Room is full of brokers queuing to get the attention of their chosen underwriter. While they are waiting they gossip and gossip travels fast. Allegations of misbehaviour travel fastest of all and in fairness to those accused we had to take steps to stop character assassination at the hands of the gossips in the Room and the press. The early investigations had been publicly announced, a necessary step at the time in order to restore confidence in the fair regulation of the Lloyd's market. But this had two unfortunate effects: those named as the subjects of inquiries were immediately and unfairly labelled as guilty; and the press and the members expected to read the resulting reports, even though the purpose of the inquiries was to see if any offences had been committed and to recommend what charges should be brought. We therefore took steps to withdraw the inquiry process from the public gaze both by using informal powers of inquiry where possible and by refusing to make any public comment on matters that might or might not be the subject of investigation. Lloyd's has a regular inquiry staff.[9] All investigations start in the Advisory Department. A few go further because it is necessary to report the matter to the Investigations Committee. Very few reach the stage of a formally announced investigation by a team of independent lawyers and account-ants.[10]

But we would not succeed in our mission to restore confidence in Lloyd's unless justice was seen to have been done. It was in my view unjust to publish reports of investigations while the wrongdoing portrayed in them was based on allegations, and had not been proved as facts. Once the matter had passed the disciplinary stage the case was different. The allegations had been proved or disproved in accordance with a criminal standard of proof as in a public court. The verdict had been judicially arrived at and the appropriate sentence passed. There then could be no injustice in publishing the facts within the jurisdiction of Lloyd's. The Council of Lloyd's adopted the daring and laudable policy of publishing the reports of disciplinary cases in full. These reports contain as full a recital of the facts of the matter as that in the investigation report on which the original case was brought. As a result Names and others directly affected had the evidence they needed to secure their civil rights based on the proven guilt of the defendants.

These new arrangements began slowly to prove their worth. We had to fight on two fronts. The press were determined that there should be no cover-up, and we could only assure them that, once the cases had been heard properly, they would have all the facts. Some of the defendants were eager to attack the disciplinary process through the courts or through public assertions that they would 'name names' if the matter came to a Lloyd's trial. The Lloyd's bye-laws provide that a disciplinary case may be heard in public at the option of the defendant, a provision inserted because of advice that the European Commission would expect it. This was used, without much effect, by one or two defendants who were anxious to embarrass Lloyd's. None succeeded in doing so because we had made our disciplinary processes impartial, fair, appropriately public and inexorable. Furthermore we had shown that they were to apply to all members of the market without fear or favour. Defendants who began by protesting their disdain of the Lloyd's process came in the end to accept that Lloyd's justice was unavoidable.

By the end of 1983 the inquiry reports commissioned in the autumn of 1982 began to come in. The first was the Fidentia report, named after the Bermudan insurance company formed by Raymond Brooks and Terence Dooley to receive and hold many of their syndicate reinsurance funds.[11] Under the Lloyd's inquiries bye-law inspectors are free to conduct their inquiries as they see fit, subject to any specific directions the council may give, and to the laws of natural justice, a breach of which could cause the inspectors to be challenged in the courts. Anthony Colman QC and Stephen Hailey FCA, the Fidentia inspectors, had decided to recommend that their first report be sent out immediately to the Names on the affected syndicates as it provided evidence which could help the Names to recover some of the missing funds. This proved to be the only exception to the rule that the subject matter of the reports would remain secret until disciplinary proceedings were at an end.

By early 1984 we were bringing charges against the first of the defendants in the main scandal cases, Brooks & Dooley. They challenged Lloyd's actions in the courts, arguing that the offences they were alleged to have committed ante-dated the new Act and that in effect Parliament had intended an amnesty in respect of past actions when they set up the new regulatory regime at Lloyd's. This case was brought despite Clause 10 of the Fourth Schedule of the Act which states that in preferring charges the council may have regard to acts committed before 1 January 1983. Lloyd's won, but had to undertake that the standard of conduct called for in respect of this and other disciplinary matters originating before the Act could be no higher than that prevailing at the time. In other words, the offences would have had to amount to discreditable conduct both at the time they were committed and by today's higher standards. In the event this rule proved to be of no hindrance to the serious cases with which we were dealing. Lloyd's is founded on the law of agency; gross breach of that civil law has always been discreditable conduct and today's codes and rules on the matter merely illustrate and clarify the basic principles of a law that ante-dates Lloyd's.

Alan Page and Jack Carpenter mounted a second challenge. Peter Cameron-Webb had left Lloyd's at the end of 1981. Towards the end of 1984, before charges had been laid against him, he applied to resign from the society. In accordance with the then current practice there was no alternative but to accept his resignation. Later, during 1984, Page and Carpenter sought to resign rather than face disciplinary charges. By this time the council had passed the membership bye-law, a critical clause of which deals with resignation.[12] A member of Lloyd's may submit his resignation at any time but will still be liable for his insurance obligations until the accounts are closed for the years during which he was a member by reinsurance into syndicates of which he is not a member. Until then he must leave his deposits with the corporation. Thereafter he will cease to be a member, but only if the committee exercises discretion in accepting his resignation. If there are inquiries afoot or charges pending the committee will not accept it. Again the judge upheld Lloyd's position. If he had not done so we would probably have been faced with a spate of resignations from those who would have preferred not to stay and face the music.

Challenges in the High Court were not the only reason that it took so long to clear up the cases: that against John Wallrock, for example, was settled only in July 1986, almost four years after the offences were discovered. In a number of cases defendants, as was their right, took the fullest advantage of the legal processes provided for by the Act and bye-laws.[13] We took care to be punctilious in ensuring that every defendant was granted his legal rights to the fullest degree. Arguably simpler proceedings should be arranged for simpler offences – for example, filing accounts late – but the present arrangements have stood the test of time well and produced acceptable justice in the face of profound scepticism and forceful legal attack by defendants.

The hurdles we had to overcome proved higher than we had at first assumed. It became accepted, and was confirmed by Lord Wilberforce in the Posgate appeal, that charges would have to be proved to a criminal standard of proof. He said: 'The Disciplinary Committee in my clear opinion correctly directed themselves as to the burden and standard of proof. Lloyd's must, they held, make good their case not merely on the balance of probability but on the criminal standard of proof so that the Disciplinary Committee could be sure as to their findings.'[14] This is a tighter regime than is called for by the civil courts. There are those who argue that a self-regulatory regime need not be so particular about excluding members from a club, but considering the sums at stake and the livelihoods that depend upon the decisions it is difficult to argue with Lord Wilberforce: he was, in any case, confirming the correctness of judgment of a number of the disciplinary tribunals, each of which had been chaired by a QC.

The success of the new regime is evident from the statistics. By 13

February 1987, four years after the new Act came into force, seventeen cases had been dealt with by the Disciplinary Committee involving forty-seven defendants. Charges had been withdrawn against eleven. Ten defendants had appealed. Of the thirty-six convicted, ten had been expelled, twelve suspended and three fined. Twenty-four had been given a censure or a reprimand. This record of achievement can hardly be matched by any other self-regulatory body, particularly considering the gravity of many of the cases and the fact that Lloyd's was initiating a new regime.

But there is one respect in which the support which had been hoped for was not forthcoming. From the earliest days it had been the rule at Lloyd's to co-operate closely with the authorities.[15] If fraud was afoot the police would be told, if gross tax irregularities came to light the Revenue would be advised. The new council endorsed the latter policy in June 1983: 'Those who work at Lloyd's must be punctilious about complying with all requirements of the tax laws. Furthermore if, after formal enquiry, cases of gross tax irregularity come to the attention of the Council they should be prepared to advise the Revenue.' As the Lloyd's inspectors continued their inquiries, evidence came to light, and when it concerned possible criminal activity the Director of Public Prosecutions (DPP) was advised. Initially we were concerned that the process of Lloyd's investigations and the subsequent hearing of disciplinary charges would be interrupted by criminal proceedings. Had such proceedings been brought we would then have had to wait years for these proceedings to be completed before taking action. However the decision was taken to press on hoping that, in the most serious cases where criminality was alleged, the DPP would follow closely on our heels. Had this been the case the authorities would have been seen to be actively supporting the actions of Lloyd's in publishing wrongdoers. It would put an official stamp of approval on our new disciplinary powers. There were those who suggested that the bringing of criminal charges against members of Lloyd's would damage the society. We did not agree, given the amount of publicity attracted by the scandals and the public way in which the council had decided to punish the transgressors. The matters were serious, Lloyd's had taken serious action, members had been expelled, and the market was stronger because it was evident that misbehaviour was not being condoned as might have been the case in the more secretive past. However as time passed the inaction by the DPP became an increasing source of embarrassment to Lloyd's. While I have no doubt that the DPP's delays were caused by genuine procedural reasons, there must be something wrong with a system of criminal justice in which a shoplifter goes to jail

85

for petty theft and a City fraudster, who may have stolen millions, gets off scot free.[16] Certainly there was no truth whatsoever in suggestions that Lloyd's had withheld evidence from the DPP or discouraged the authorities from pursuing their inquiries.[17]

Behind all these difficulties lay one major question. All those who had plundered the Names at Lloyd's had originally been motivated by a desire to reduce their, and the Names', tax liabilities. That had led to the tax improprieties described in Chapter IV. The resolution of Lloyd's difficulties with the Revenue would complete the task of cleaning up the market.

Reporting, in October 1985, that Lloyd's had settled its differences with the Revenue, the press stated that £43.5 million had been paid to clear the past tax problems of all but a handful of members, those few whose actions tended towards the criminal. The arguments, we have seen, turned on the tax deductibility of certain types of reinsurance policy.[18] The questionable arrangements were so widespread as to affect over 92 per cent of the then 26,000 members of Lloyd's. Individual members were directly affected by the issue of provisional assessments to reopen past years and the withholding of tax repayments in relation to their underwriting losses at Lloyd's. The Revenue had shown that its disfavour, expressed in this way, was capable of causing damage to the operations of Lloyd's as a whole. As it was not possible to allocate the tax liability fairly among individuals or sections, a global solution was adopted to clear Lloyd's name and purge past allegations with the sum being paid out of the central coffers of the society of Lloyd's.

The Revenue's interest in the scandals at Lloyd's no doubt followed the wide press publicity in the autumn of 1982. Initially their interest focused on the offshore aspects of reinsurance; later they asked about rollers, about time and distance policies by which an underwriter can reinsure a claim as to which the amount is known but not the date of settlement; finally they turned to the reinsurance to close itself which, aggregating by 1984 to £3.8 billion, raised serious questions for the Society of Lloyd's as a whole. Before serious negotiations could start it was necessary for both sides to go through a process of education. The Special Investigations Section (SIS) of the Revenue had to understand the complex workings of the Lloyd's insurance market. Some of the Lloyd's agents had to be brought to understand the serious peril in which their actions had placed themselves and their Names.

The essence of the Revenue's case was that reserving had been misdescribed as reinsurance and a whole framework of dubious arrangements set up to conceal the truth. As a result income had been shifted from a period of high tax rates to one of low rates: indeed in some cases, where the funds had been stolen, they had avoided tax altogether. The lack of clear rules at Lloyd's meant that there was no standard against which market practices could be judged, and it appeared that the committee's letter of December 1958 had been ignored. The calculation of the reinsurance to close, although probably fair in aggregate for the market as a whole was, in most cases, not properly evidenced by actuarial, statistical or accounting data, nor was it supported by an audit opinion. Consequently, in certainly individual cases, over-reserving had occurred. In order to achieve their purpose of reopening settled assessments the Revenue was forced to allege fraud, wilful default or neglect.

Lloyd's case was based on the commercial necessity of the arrangements made and on the fact that, in the vast majority of cases, no peculation had occurred. If the funds had been stolen, the agent's position was indefensible and Lloyd's had energetically pursued such miscreants. Further, the sheer complexity of reopening past tax assessments going back over ten to fifteen years and affecting up to thirty-five thousand taxpayers, a significant proportion of whom had died or resigned from Lloyd's, made the correct imposition of the tax liability literally impossible.

The Revenue's case was complicated by two facts. First, the agents who were alleged to have misled the tax authorities were not themselves taxpayers: the Names, in whose interest the arrangements had been made, were largely ignorant of them. It would be difficult to prove fraud or wilful default against a party who was totally ignorant of his offence. Second, when the funds were repatriated they flowed back into the Premiums Trust Funds which, by insurance law, could not properly be used for the settlement of tax liabilities. Lloyd's case was made more difficult because one of the foundations of the reform of Lloyd's, upon which the new council was engaged, was the reform of the agency system. All underwriting agents would have to re-register at Lloyd's and show that they were fit and proper persons – honest, competent and solvent. It might be difficult for an agent to meet such a test were he to be convicted of wilful default or neglect vis-à-vis the tax affairs of his Names.

The resolution of these difficulties was a long and tortuous process. The settlement, when it finally came in the latter half of 1985, was entirely fair and reasonable. But it made clear how pervasive the doubtful tax practices at Lloyd's had been.

The Revenue settlement was the major achievement in cleaning up the market. It capped three years of endeavour in which the chief villains had been caught. The cases of plunder, in which agents had bilked their Names, proved to have been very few. But misunderstandings about the law of agency were widespread. Many, indeed most, agents had infringed the law by their failure adequately to account for their stewardship, by their inadequate handling of conflicts of interest and (a smaller number) by their taking of secret profits. The infringements did not involve crimes, because the law of agency is civil law and a breach gives rise to a right of civil action by the principal, but close attention to the law of agency is fundamental to proper relations between Names and their underwriting agents and thus to the proper regulation of the Lloyd's market. A breach of the law of agency can thus be argued to be 'discreditable conduct' at Lloyd's because the whole system depends so heavily on that branch of the law. Sir Peter Green summed up the problem in his chairman's statement at the general meeting of members in June 1983: 'Our real problems have arisen due to a dichotomy. Whilst on the one hand the Society has scrupulously protected the interest of Lloyd's policy holders, we have failed to ensure that all those who make up the market fully comprehend the commercial and legal realities of the 1980s, especially in the area of accountability between agent and principal. The issues are almost all internal in the sense that members of the public are not involved. The main issues are conflicts of interest, to which Fisher drew attention, secret profits and failure to disclose.... The relationship between Name and agent is founded on mutual trust and we must ensure that nothing is done or not done which can undermine that trust.'

Agents advanced arguments in support of their actions: that the Names would have approved had they known, that the sums were trivial, that the Names would have refused to read accounts if they had been sent to them, that all the Names were interested in was a cheque, preferably a larger one than the year before, and that the doubtful arrangements had been in place for many years and no one had thought to challenge them. None of these were adequate to refute the basic thesis: there would have to be a change in the way in which relations between Names and agents were handled. The further argument – that such arrangements were regular practice in the market or that 'I didn't know it was wrong' – just revealed the scale and depth of the problem. The fact was that most underwriters had never had any form of business training in the field of agency law, company law or taxation: their training had been limited solely to underwriting. This was the essence of the problem.[19] Cleaning up the market, in the sense of removing fraudsters, was one thing. But it was not enough. By a process of education and regulation we would have to change the culture of Lloyd's. If this were not done the efforts of those in Fort Knox would have been wasted.

NOTE

The Taxation of Names at Lloyd's

Names at Lloyd's are taxed individually on their underwriting profits which are calculated on a calendar-year basis two years in arrears: thus the 1983 profit will be reported and distributed during 1986 when the accounts are closed at the end of 1985. The reinsurance to close contract transfers all outstanding liabilities to the next year of account, at a price. Once the price has been paid any balance remaining is profit. Tax is payable on this profit but, by a special concession applicable to Lloyd's, the tax assessment is deferred two years so as to coincide with the distribution of the profit. Where the underwriting account shows a loss then the taxpayer is entitled to reclaim tax in respect of the year in question on his other income. In addition, and separately, the Name will be liable to tax on the earnings of his premiums trust fund and any capital gains arising thereon.

A high-rate taxpayer who participates in loss-making syndicates which engage in long-tail business – business on which claims are not settled for many years and which therefore give rise to large balances in the premiums trust fund – will be able to reclaim substantial amounts of his tax on other income in respect of these losses. At the same time the large premiums trust fund, if appropriately managed, will generate substantial capital gains on which the Name will be liable to tax at 30 per cent rather than the 60 per cent applicable in respect of trading profits. It is this set of circumstances which gives rise to a most attractive tax position for the Lloyd's Name with a high income from elsewhere. A change introduced by the Chancellor in the spring of 1985 by which capital gains on premiums trust funds were less easy to obtain and more of the income on such funds was to be assessed as income had somewhat reduced this beneficial tax structure, but none the less it still represents an attractive arrangement for a wealthy member paying a high level of personal tax.

IX

The Rule Book

Schoolmasters were in short supply during the Second World War. As a boy at a London public school I got used to quite a few characters whose teaching skills were rather below the norm. One individual was notorious for his vagueness and inability to handle a class. In one of his lessons a boy lit a fire in his desk. The smoke billowed forth and the master rose from the dais and stalked down the aisle. 'Boy! What are you doing?' 'Please sir, I didn't know I wasn't allowed to.' 'Well in that case I clearly can't punish you, kindly put the fire out.' That tale epitomizes the rule problem at Lloyd's under the pre-1982 regime. Many of the rules were unwritten and those that were committed to paper were often vague and incapable of enforcement for lack of means. They were quite unsuited to new-style underwriters and brokers with big ideas and little respect for the past.

The bye-laws of Lloyd's, passed under the 1871 Act, fill a twenty-two-page octavo volume.[1] There are eighty-seven clauses. The margins are generous. The document looks like the rule book of a West End club. This impression is fortified by an examination of the contents: admission of members, fees, subscriptions, hours of opening, the allocation of seats, meetings, elections – and rules for determining the vital question of the seniority of committee members. Only at the end are there a handful of clauses touching on insurance, notably the power to refuse the renewal of a subscription by a broker, and the last clause, bye-law 87, which established a register of underwriting agents. The whole confirms the view of Lloyd's as a gentleman's club.

The difficulty faced by Lloyd's before 1982 in passing bye-laws has already been referred to as has the evidence that Lloyd's had outgrown its rule-making powers.[2] In a shift to cover the regulatory gap the old Committee of Lloyd's resorted to four devices.

The first was the use of undertakings. Lacking the power to make rules the breach of which could give rise to disciplinary sanctions, the committee sought to impose obligations on members, brokers and underwriting agents by requiring undertakings to be given on first admission and by imposing requirements on those admitted or by attaching conditions to admission.[3] These undertakings were contractual in nature: each party was bound in contract to the Society of Lloyd's. The difficulty was that, once the party had been admitted, the contract could not then be altered by Lloyd's unless the member, broker or agent agreed. As new requirements were introduced they could be enforced only on new applicants. This gave rise to anomalies, especially in the case of members' means. A member had only to comply with the means and premium income limit rules which he had undertaken to meet when he was admitted. Thereafter, although the rules might be tightened up, they could only be applied to new members or to those old members who wished to increase their premium income limits and had to show additional means in order to do so.

The second was the issue of manuals. For example the manual for underwriting agents was intended to provide the agent with a comprehensive guide to the workings of Lloyd's. Although useful as training material the volume was inadequate for regulatory purposes because it was too vague (the advice on reinsurance, which had to 'comply with the principles of honourable trading', has already been mentioned) and it was unenforceable. The only effective rules in the manual were self-enforcing regulations such as those prescribing what form to use for an application for membership. It was not possible to discipline an agent for not following the manual.

Rules for the market were more often, and more easily, promulgated in the form of the third device: letters from the chairman, a deputy chairman or the committee. The example of the committee's letter about rollers in 1958 has already been quoted.[4] The fact that it was widely ignored confirms the inadequacy of such methods of legislation: letters are fine for guidance but do not form an effective basis for disciplinary action.

Finally, there are market agreements, which continue to operate. These agreements govern the conduct of business among underwriters and brokers.[5] Some agreements which protect the market are appropriate for regulation; other market agreements could be seen as reducing competition among underwriters. The market agreements are the province of the market associations of underwriters. Although of use for the better operation of the market they are not essentially regulatory. Except for those covering binding authorities, they have been left alone during the recent spate of Lloyd's bye-legislation.

Breaches of market agreements are a matter for the market associations. Infringement of market letters or breaches of bye-law were a matter for the committee, which could under the 1911 Act suspend a member for up to two years; and more usually for the chairman, who could admonish a wrongdoer but could do little more without the consent of the culprit.

The new Lloyd's Act of 1982 totally changed this regime. Under Clause 6 the council is granted 'the management and superintendence of the affairs of the Society and the power to regulate and direct the business of insurance at Lloyd's'. The council may do this by passing bye-laws by a special resolution: which must secure separate majorities of the working members of the council and of the external and nominated members of the council voting together. A sixty-day period is stipulated during which a new bye-law may be challenged by a general meeting on the petition of not less than five hundred members. The council can delegate its powers and functions, other than bye-law making, to the chairman, a deputy chairman or to the committee. In particular the council can delegate to the committee, by special resolution, the power to make regulations regarding the business of insurance at Lloyd's. Finally, there is a power to make directions which the council may delegate to the committee or the chairs. Directions are rules applied to specific situations and are not, unlike bye-laws and regulations, of general application. For example, an underwriter may be directed to stop underwriting because he is in danger of breaching his premium income limits. Like bye-laws, regulations and directions are subject to challenge and if challenged may be ratified by a special resolution of the council.

This was the new legislative structure: bye-laws which only the council can pass; regulations, the province of the committee; and directions to be made by the chairs or the committee. Breach of any of these was made a subject for disciplinary action by Clause 7 of the Act.

Before the Act had been passed the Committee of Lloyd's had established a number of 'Fisher task groups' composed of committee members, representatives of the market, staff and outside professionals. Each was assigned a separate topic following the recommendations made in Sir Henry's report. A small central secretariat was established, 'The Fisher Implementation Office'. The establishment of the new self-regulatory regime at Lloyd's was the second of the three tasks with which I had been specifically charged by the council under the terms of my appointment. The Fisher task groups had, as I saw it, been engaged in a useful job of codifying existing practice. We would be making use of their work. It was first necessary for us to consider the regulatory philosophy to be applied.[6]

The term 'rules' embraces all means by which the conduct of the members of Lloyd's is governed in their capacity as members: it embraces bye-laws, regulations, directions, codes of conduct and practice, guidance and explanatory notes, manuals and market letters. Rules for any self-regulatory body must cover three aspects: to control admission, to govern conduct, and to provide for an effective disciplinary process for offenders. The rule book should have a dynamic capacity for re-examination and renewal of its structure.

It is important to distinguish between sanctionable rules, which may need to be enforced by disciplinary action, and non-sanctionable rules which are self-enforcing. For example, rules about membership quali-fications bear their own sanction in that if an applicant does not satisfy the qualifications laid down, he will not be admitted. Similarly, one might have a rule to the effect that certain business had to be submitted to the Lloyd's Policy Signing Office (LPSO) on a particular form only: if it were not submitted on such a form, it would simply not be accepted. Sanc-tionable rules are much more critical because they create offences; in the event all such rules were passed as bye-laws, the most powerful weapon in our legislative armoury.

Three special features distinguish Lloyd's from other self-regulatory bodies. The first is the importance of the law of agency which pervades all aspects of business at Lloyd's: the broker is the agent of the assured, the underwriter the agent of the Name.[7] Relations between principals and agents are governed by the civil law and it is not necessary for Lloyd's to legislate the law of agency: breach of agency law already gives rise to a right of civil action in tort and contract for damages by the principal against the agent. But the meticulous observation of the law of agency is fundamental to the effective working of the Lloyd's market. It follows that Lloyd's rules must be designed to bolster the law of agency and encourage its observance; a breach of the law of agency can be regarded as dis-creditable conduct in the Lloyd's context and would therefore be a quasi-criminal offence under Lloyd's rules.

The second peculiar feature of the self-regulatory regime at Lloyd's is the way in which the public interest is served. Lloyd's duties to its policy holders are supervised by the DTI whose solvency rules are designed to ensure that underwriters can meet their obligations when they fall due. Maintaining the security of the Lloyd's policy, in furtherance of this duty, must therefore be a special concern of the Council of Lloyd's. Additionally, there is the public interest in fair play between the external members and the agents, recognized in the presence on the council of external members and nominated members whose co-option has been approved by the

Governor of the Bank of England. As *Lloyd's Log* put it: 'Parliament accepted this interest by enshrining the right of external Names to substantial representation on the Council. Any previous atmosphere of caveat emptor has now been firmly dispelled. In formulating its self-regulatory policy the Council must have particular regard for the interests of the Names.'[8]

The third special feature of Lloyd's self-regulatory arrangements is the legislative framework in which it is set. Because Lloyd's is specially exempted from the detailed application of the Insurance Companies Act 1982 it must take particular care to be sure that its domestic arrangements for admitting and controlling those who trade in the market are at least as rigorous as those which prevail among insurance companies. Similarly, the new Lloyd's Act, which vests bye-law-making powers in the council and takes them away from the members in general meeting, provides challenge procedures for petitioning for a general meeting and also, and more importantly, for bye-laws to be passed by special resolution of the council. These unique checks and balances must be punctiliously observed.

During 1983 as the rule-making strategy developed four main issues emerged.

The first was the extent to which the market should be regulated by formal rules. Sir Henry Fisher had no doubt that, although Lloyd's had always depended on mutual trust between those actively involved in the transaction of insurance business in the market, the time had come when Lloyd's should have the power to penalize those who betrayed the trust of their fellows. He concluded: 'We do not believe that an institution such as Lloyd's can any longer operate without this sort of control over those whom it admits and over their conduct once admitted.' The general issue at stake was 'the extent to which Lloyd's can continue to base itself on mutual trust and confidence, unwritten but generally accepted standards of behaviour and personal relationships and the extent to which it has to accustom itself to more impersonal methods and written rules and codes of practice designed to govern those that are not prepared to abide by the old system or who cannot be trusted to behave properly unless compelled'.[9]

In recognizing this argument we adopted a policy we called minimalism.[10] Bye-laws would be confined to sanctionable matters. They would be brief and general. Details would be supplied by codes or guidance notes. And we would only legislate if there appeared to be a need for reform. In the event the bye-laws have proved to be longer and more detailed than had at first been hoped, usually because the lawyers required it so. The legislative powers of the Accounting Standards Committee, where I learnt about self-regulation, are limited to the production of statements of standard accounting practice for later adoption by the councils of the six accountancy institutes. They have no legal force. They are persuasive of best practice. They are also brief and to the point. It did not in the event prove possible to achieve such idyllic simplicity at Lloyd's, where the rules had to be capable of withstanding legal attack. Although the rule book therefore turned out rather differently from what had at first been intended it is probably the better for it.

Arising out of this was the second issue: the use of codes of practice or guidance notes. Lloyd's is a small self-regulatory community in which it should be possible to regulate as much by the spirit as by the letter of the law; there should be an atmosphere of compliance which should make unnecessary the sort of detailed prescriptive rule-making found in the tax law. In this context we intended to make use of codes of practice or explanatory notes. These were seen as helping the market professional to comply with the general prescriptions laid down in the bye-laws: if he follows the code he will comply with the governing bye-laws; if he departs from the code for a good reason he will still be in order; but if he departs from the code recklessly or heedless of the consequence he may have to answer for a breach of Lloyd's rules. This approach put the onus on the market to decide how the spirit of the rules is to be applied.

Although the policy of brief general bye-laws for sanctionable matters, supported by detailed codes to help the underwriter, agent or broker to comply, appears sensible and attractive, we did not in fact push it as far as had originally been intended. Our experiences in dealing with the miscreants, the realization that the key issue to be tackled was one that Fisher had not fully comprehended – relations between Names and agents – and the fact that misunderstandings by agents about their fiduciary duties to their Names was so widespread all conspired towards a more detailed prescriptive legal regime.[11]

The most effective way of dealing with breaches of agency law and at the same time of avoiding over-legislation was the use of disclosure. At my first press conference after my appointment I said that 'sunshine drives away the mists'. Although I used the phrase so often that it came to haunt me, the idea was correct and it was the basis of our policy at Lloyd's. Full and proper disclosure by agents to Names would itself correct many of the ills that had occurred. Agents would discontinue dubious practices if they were ashamed of explaining them to their Names. There would be a spate of cot-deaths among baby syndicates if agents were forced to explain why they existed and showed such attractive profits for their insider members.[12] Reinsurances with companies owned by the agents would be less likely if the financial details had to be exposed to the interested eyes of the Names whose money had been used. Secret profits are not offensive if they are no longer secret and the profits are accounted for; disclosed conflicts of interest invite the Names' approval which, if granted, purges the error; proper disclosure satisfies the agent's legal duty to account.

When I first came to Lloyd's it was still an amazingly secret place. Despite the recommendations of Cromer there was still no regulatory requirement that agents should send syndicate accounts to their Names. Many did so, but an important minority did not, and in the overwhelming majority of cases the figures were not audited. Despite bearing unlimited liability Names were far less well served in the matter of information than shareholders in limited liability companies incorporated under the Companies Act. My belief in the disinfectant value of disclosure has been vindicated by the disappearance of market practices that would have taken years to eradicate if the problem had been tackled solely by charging the individuals concerned one by one before the Disciplinary Committee. Soon after I came to Lloyd's I observed that the Room was loud with the susurration of collapsing arrangements – collapsing because their perpetrators were ashamed to expose them to the gaze of their principals.

The final issue faded into insignificance because the power structure of Lloyd's changed. Sir Henry had envisaged, and the Act provided, that the council could delegate its legislative powers to the committee, who could make 'regulations'. It also empowered the committee and the chairs to issue 'directions' regarding the business of insurance. The Fisher Report implies that the council would be lofty and detached and that the day-to-day business of making regulations for the market would lie with the committee. Parliament provided a framework so that this could happen. The scandals of autumn 1982 changed the scene at Lloyd's. The matters to be addressed most urgently concerned the agents and their proper role vis-à-vis the Names; although Fisher had concerned himself with these questions they were not the chief focus of his inquiry and the climate of the time did not dictate that very much attention would be paid to them. Now that climate had changed and it did not seem appropriate to the council that they should leave any substantive rule-making activity to a committee which consisted overwhelmingly of the very people who were to be legislated for – the agents. This issue gave our legal advisers some difficulty. They would say 'Parliament intended that the committee should issue regulations.' To which we would reply 'That's as may be, but the Council won't wear it.' In fairness it must be added that the Fisher Report suggests that the division of duties between the council and the committee should be a matter to be decided by those bodies themselves.

In summary, the conclusion was this: we would base our rule book on the use of bye-laws supplemented, where appropriate, by guidance notes, explanatory notes or codes of practice. Bye-laws would be as brief and general as possible. The council reserved to itself the principal legislative role. In the first three years of its existence the council passed forty bye-laws; the committee passed only three regulations, in each case under powers specifically delegated for the purpose by the council. The power to issue directions was not used until 1986 and then to direct an underwriter to cease underwriting because he had overwritten his premium limit. Guidance notes and codes were generally issued with the authority of the council although in some cases they were formulated by subsidiary committees. But the fundament of rule-making policy was disclosure, which would in many cases make unnecessary more detailed legislative steps.

This was the policy. How was it to be implemented? The first thing was to establish a committee of the council, the Rules Committee, to supervise the legislative programme. Our primary purpose in setting up this committee in June 1983 was to save the time of the council: rather than the council taking time to debate legislation line by line it would be better to leave the job to a sub-committee of councillors and others from the market who would recommend to the council legislation to be passed. It was the Rules Committee's job to reassure the council that the proposed bye-law would achieve the purpose the council had intended when it called for legislation. The Rules Committee had a facilitating and co-ordinating role. It did not recommend policy to the council: that was a matter for the Committee of Lloyd's or other committees, like the Accounting and Auditing Standards Committee, or ad hoc working parties set up for the purpose. In every case it was for the council to confirm the general policy to be followed.

Originally the drafting of bye-laws had been in the hands of the Fisher task groups. These were now wound up and the Fisher implementation office subsumed into the rules staff. Heavy use was made of outside legal skills at first but later an internal staff was developed, and we were able to make increasing use of in-house skills.

When it came to introducing legislation consultation was vital. The Accounting Standards Committee has a fifteen-year record of self-regulatory legislation and we adapted our practices from them. The policy under consideration – for example syndicate accounts or rules for members – would be exposed in a green-covered consultative document for public comment.[13] This openness did not find favour among some of the more traditional members of the council who felt that their authority might be undermined if, as a result of consultation, policy were changed. But the market welcomed the consultative process and the market associations in particular, who represent the views of the various sections of the market, became adept at marshalling their responses. We also frequently received submissions from people outside the market, like the DTI and the professional bodies. The consultative process gave a chance for the public to be involved.

Consultative documents were followed by exposure drafts of the proposed bye-laws. This stage gave an opportunity to consider and, if necessary, amend the original policy. More importantly it provided an opportunity to identify and deal with special situations which had not been considered before and in respect of which legislative exceptions could be made.

The second arrow to our bow was education. Underwriters and agents are busy men and they are not experts in legislation. Rules which stay in the rule book unread are of little use. The mere publication of the rules was not enough: it was necessary to explain and elucidate through a programme of seminars. The first of these was held in 1983 at the prompting of Sir Peter Green. He felt that agents did not know enough about the law of agency, the duties of directors under the Companies Acts and the effects of other legislation on the day-to-day work of the agent. It was also necessary to explain the new Lloyd's Act and how the regulatory regime arising from it was to be used. The seminar faculty was provided by my three advisers on self-regulation and myself. The chair was taken by a leading council member from the market and the response from agents was overwhelming. More than any amount of rule-making these seminars, which were continued and extended to cover additional topics as our regulatory framework developed, served to change the culture and attitudes of the market.

The various topics covered by the new council and its rule-making are best considered in relation to those affected: the underwriters, the agents, the brokers, the Names and the accountants. The order in which the various subjects were tackled by the council provides an interesting reflection of the priorities of the times. Most of 1983 was occupied with bye-laws establishing the disciplinary powers of the council described in Chapter VIII. Seventeen bye-laws covering these topics were passed by 7 February 1983. Then there was a pause until the heavier matters were ready for legislation. The busiest year was 1984, starting with interim rules for syndicate accounts and a bye-law requiring agents to disclose to their Names any financial interests they might have had in companies with which the syndicate had done business. This was followed by rules giving effect to the divestment provisions of the Act and requiring all underwriting agents to re-register. The autumn brought rules covering four vital matters: control of premium income levels, detailed rules for syndicate accounts, rules for members, and provisions for a new panel of syndicate auditors. The initial phase of Lloyd's legislation was completed in 1985 with the introduction of the new standard form of agreement between a Name and his agent, the rules for binding authorities, rules forbidding reinsurance by syndicates with related parties, and a rule banning baby syndicates.

Together with a number of procedural and amending bye-laws this is a considerable catalogue of achievement for a new council operating in an intensely conservative market place. Why did this happen? First, because the new council was eager to justify its existence and be seen to be cleaning up the market; in this the energy of Peter Miller who succeeded Sir Peter Green as Chairman at the beginning of 1984 had an influential part. Second, the resources and commitment were there. The money was available to get the job done and the staff were there to complete the necessary tasks in short order. But third, the continued pressure from the Names, the press, Whitehall, the Bank and Parliament all played a vital part.[14] It is unfortunate that proper public concerns about the constitution of Lloyd's regulatory framework and about the incidence and effect of fraud as seen in the PCW affair should have overshadowed a major self-regulatory accomplishment.

X

Syndicate Accounts

The Fisher Report had been firm about the need for better syndicate accounting at Lloyd's. One of its recommendations was the subject of a parliamentary undertaking by Lloyd's in 1981 when the Bill was before the House. It had promised to carry out Fisher's recommendation that the council should lay down rules as to the minimum information to be disclosed in syndicate accounts and the accounting standards and principles which shall apply. These would need to be specifically designed to meet the circumstances of Lloyd's and, although they would draw on the experience derived by the accountancy profession from application of the Second Schedule to the Companies Act 1967 and the various accounting and auditing standards which have been issued for the accounts of companies, they would recognize the special features of the Lloyd's system – for example, the three-year account period, the lapse of time between accepting a risk and the processing of the policy and premium through the Lloyd's Policy Signing Office (LPSO), the volume of reinsurance, and the central importance of the reinsurance to close.[1]

Ken Randall had been asked to chair a Fisher task group on this matter, and the first draft of an accounting manual for the guidance of agents and syndicate auditors was ready in December 1982. This followed the basic tenets of company law. It had to be assumed that most agents would be familiar with these as, except for the few who were partners in firms, they were themselves directors of companies incorporated under the Companies Act.[2] The accounting aspects of British companies legislation are based on the concept of disclosure: the Act lays down what should be disclosed, leaving to the author of the accounts the judgment as to how it shall be disclosed. Valuation rules for determining the figures to be shown in accounts are left to the accountancy profession and the statutes are vague and general on such matters. The Lloyd's Accounting Manual drafted by the Randall task group took the same line and stipulated what matters should be disclosed. In doing so it was guided by the current practices of the best agents, some of whom were already providing their Names with excellent accounts. However, details of such accounts were not easy to come by as the Corporation of Lloyd's had then no regular formal right to receive syndicate accounts.

This manual had largely been completed when I was appointed in November 1982 to chair a working party to consider, among other things, disclosure of interests by underwritings agents.[3] That working party had a different remit from the Randall task group: to prepare guidance on accounting by agents to Names for transactions in which the agents had been involved on their own account using funds belonging to the Names. The working party had been established following the scandals of 1982 which had revealed grave breaches of fiduciary duty by agents. The intention had been that all such breaches should be revealed by means of accounting guidance supported by revised instructions to Lloyd's auditors. When I became Deputy Chairman and Chief Executive of Lloyd's my former partner, Ian Plaistowe, took the chair of this group whose consultative document was released in August 1983.[4] It proposed that Lloyd's agents and those connected with them should disclose any interests in insurance companies or in companies which provided services to their syndicates. Two types of disclosure should be made: ownership interests; and transactions, transactions being those between the syndicates and companies in which the agent had an interest. Ownerships were to be disclosed to Lloyd's in a two-part register – the first, disclosing the fact of ownership, was to be made public; the second part, which would quantify the values involved, would remain secret. Transactions would be disclosed in syndicate accounts to be sent privately to Names.

This consultative document covered eighty pages and included elaborate diagrams illustrating the relationships that would have to be disclosed. It was not well received in the market because it was too complicated. But it triggered a far-reaching change at Lloyd's. Instead of the two-part register, said the agents, why not make the syndicate accounts themselves available on file at Lloyd's and permit the public access to them? Pressures from the press to come clean would be met, and the Names would be fully informed without the necessity of a bureaucratic register of interests.

This was a major step forward. The council adopted it towards the end of 1983 and the public filing of syndicate accounts became an important part of the reform programme at Lloyd's. The working members' enlightened view on this matter no doubt reflected, at least in part, a realization that with the growth of the society's membership and the increasing tendency for Names to be contentious, circulating accounts to Names would mean that they would in the end reach anyone who wanted to obtain a copy. The fact that Chatset, a company owned by a group of external Names then connected with the Association of Lloyd's Members, started to publish syndicate league tables based on those accounts that they could obtain from Names helped to confirm that the time had come to open up the books.

In the middle of 1983 guidance on matters of accounting policy provided by the Randall task group was taken over by a new committee of the council: the Accounting and Auditing Standards Committee. This was chaired by one of the nominated members of the Council, Brandon Gough, the Managing Partner of the large accounting firm of Coopers & Lybrand. His committee included council members, and accountants from the market familiar both with the ways of Lloyd's and wider professional practice. This committee was directly responsible for the policy behind the syndicate accounting bye-law and the syndicate audit legislation.

The provisional accounting manual for syndicates had been released for consultation in December 1982. This final version, containing a number of changes, was issued in November 1983 with a letter from the chairman which said that, although the document was still provisional pending a bye-law on the matter, it should be followed by agents as a guide to best practice in the market. The manual recited the fundamental elements of syndicate disclosures that were to be refined and reinforced, but not greatly changed, by subsequent bye-laws.[5] They were:

1. An underwriting account for the year just closed.
2. Underwriting accounts for the open years, normally two.
3. A balance sheet.
4. Notes to the accounts.
5. Disclosures of interests of agents in syndicate's transactions.
6. A personal account for each member, showing his interest in the syndicate result and any charges made to him personally.
7. A managing agent's report.
8. An underwriter's report.
9. A seven-year summary of syndicate results.
10. An audit report.

The first six items formed the accounts proper and would be subject to audit.

The third thread in the disclosure story emerged later but still found a place in the legislation to be passed in 1984. It concerned baby syndicates[6] – preferred underwriting arrangements (by which insiders on so-called baby syndicates get the best of the business) were in clear breach of the laws of agency. Parallel syndicates, on the other hand, under which the same underwriter runs two syndicates insuring different types of business but in which no Name is given an unfair advantage over another, can be legitimate. The matter had been discussed in a consultative document issued by a working party chaired by former deputy chairman Alec Higgins in September 1983.[7] Whatever legislation might be developed for resolving the problem it seemed that disclosure would, as for other matters, cure nine-tenths of the disease. Being required to disclose to their Names what was going on, agents would not wish to be involved in arrangements of which they would be ashamed.

These three elements: replication of the company accounting rules, disclosures of related party transactions (principally reinsurance) with agency-related companies, and baby syndicates came together in legislative form in 1984. In February a bye-law gave immediate effect to the accounting manual: this required agents to provide annual reports for syndicates comprising the first eight of the elements enumerated above. The accounts were to be audited and a central file of syndicate accounts, to be opened to public inspection, was established. This was followed in April by the Disclosure of Interests Bye-law which implemented the Plaistowe Report. Its provisions were quite different from his original proposals. It required every annual report in respect of a syndicate to include a fair presentation of all transactions entered into by the managing agent for the account of the syndicate in which the agent had, directly or indirectly, a material interest. If there were no such transactions or arrangements the annual report should state that fact.[8] This was one of the principal steps to avoid a repetition of the insider dealing associated with the scandals of 1982.

Both these rules were brief and short lived. The sufficed until they were overtaken by the principal legislation, the Syndicate Accounting Bye-law of 1984. This is a large document and one of the four principal foundation stones of the reform of Lloyd's.[9] The Syndicate Accounting Bye-law requires the agent to keep proper accounting records; it establishes the three-year accounts rule; it calls for syndicate reports containing the three elements described above; and it requires the accounts to be approved, signed and audited. They have to be circulated to Names and filed at Lloyd's. The schedules cover details about accounting records, accounting policies, the format and contents of accounts, including disclosures of interests, the contents of the managing agent's report, which is seen as corresponding to the director's report in a set of company accounts, and the contents of the underwriter's report, which is to be a discussion of the business of the syndicate for the year. The whole document is redolent of the corresponding sections of the Companies Act.

This regime took immediate effect. The first of the new-style accounts were prepared under the February 1984 bye-law and sent out to Names that summer. The central file of syndicate accounts opened to the public for the first time in August 1984.[10] The consolidating statute, passed in October 1984, governed the accounts produced in 1985 and subsequent years including those filed publicly in April 1985. An important element of these reforms, the requirement that the accounts should show a 'true and fair view', was deferred until 1986 to give auditors and agents time to prepare syndicate accounts able to match the standards of the company world in showing a true and fair view of the profit for the closed year.

For many years the Institute of Chartered Accountants has conducted an annual survey of company accounts. Each annual volume analyses the disclosure practices of the top three hundred or so companies and discusses critical accounting questions. The volume serves as an invaluable guide to best practice for company accountants and their auditors. We came up with the idea of carrying out a similar survey of Lloyd's syndicate accounts. In conjunction with the Research Department of the institute, Lloyd's financed a survey of syndicate accounts which was carried out by an eminent accounting academic, Professor Richard MacVe of Aberystwyth University. Based on a detailed examination of the accounts now placed on public file at Lloyd's, the book discusses each critical accounting question we faced in developing the syndicate accounting rules; it provides an excellent introduction to the subject of accounting for syndicates.[11]

Accounting legislation falls, in general, under two headings: rules about disclosure and rules about valuation. For companies, disclosure rules are the province of the Companies Act, while valuation rules are laid down by the accountancy profession through the medium of accounting standards which amplify the general statutory rule that accounts must show a true and fair view. These standards are, for the most part, directed at setting out valuation rules: how stocks, investments or fixed assets are to be valued, and how income is to be determined. In the Lloyd's context the valuation rules are generally simple because almost all syndicate transactions are for cash, and most of the assets are held in the form of short-term liquid investments which are carried at current market values. There are only two contentious accounting matters concerning valuation. The first is the reinsurance to close. The accurate estimate of this figure is vital to determining syndicate profit. It is essentially a matter of forecasting, in which the underwriter must form a view both as to the likely outcome of claims of which he has been notified and as to the expected development of claims of which he has not yet been advised – the IBNR or 'incurred but not reported' claims. This judgment is more likely to be fair if it is arrived at in a disciplined manner following a regular routine under which all the available evidence about the trend of claims is carefully sifted. From an accounting point of view the problem is no different from that which faces a building contractor estimating the cost of completing a building or an automobile manufacturer assessing future car warranty claims: in both these cases an accurate estimate is critical to the determination of annual profit. If the method is thoroughly and meticulously documented the auditor should be able to put his name to the result: not in the sense of warranting the accuracy of the estimate; but, as with the stock of a manufacturing company, in the sense that the figure for reinsurance to close is a fair estimate which a reasonable man might be expected to draw from the evidence before him, and that all the available evidence was considered.

As a result of the introduction of the true and fair requirement, and of pressure from the Revenue, improvements began to be made in accounting for the reinsurance to close, a matter in which the Revenue continues to take a close interest. The old secrecy with which the matter had been surrounded gave way to a regime of disclosure which no longer gave so much room for nudge and fudge. And the bias towards prudence which had always been present was increasingly overtaken by the concept of equity between Names. Although the practice of providing more than the circumstances required was admirable from the point of view of Lloyd's solvency and hence of the policy holder, it favoured tomorrow's Names at the expense of today's and provided the underwriter with hidden reserves with which to smooth over any future hiccups in his underwriting results.

Despite the introduction of the true and fair requirement, there are still valuation questions for discussion in connection with the reinsurance to close. A set of explanatory notes on this was issued in December 1985 to provide further guidance on the application of the syndicate accounting bye-law.[12] These notes consider whether the reinsurance to close should take account of the future costs of claims settlement, of future inflation on the size of claims, and of the effect of discounting claims by the time value of money when they are unlikely to be settled for many years ahead. At present this is not allowed, but an underwriter may purchase a time and distance reinsurance policy which has the same effect, save that the rate of discount is settled in the open market rather than in the syndicate's books.

The second valuation question remains unresolved. It turns on the market practice by which a risk is assigned by the Lloyd's Policy Signing Office to the year in which the completed slip is received from the broker rather than the year in which the risk starts. Provided that any delay in passing documents to the LPSO is the same from year to year, as claims will be matched to the year to which the premium is credited, no great harm may be done. But it will still be the case that Names may be liable in one year for claims arising in an earlier year because of the late filing of documents. As the Names on a syndicate will change from one year to another equity between Names is spoilt. The situation can be much worse than that when the broker deliberately delays the entry of risks because he wishes to delay handing the premiums on to the underwriter, or because the underwriter has exceeded his premium income limit and wishes to defer income to conceal that fact. Until Lloyd's introduces a strict rule that the risk is to be assigned to the year in which it incepts – inception-date accounting – it will not be possible to eradicate such practices.[13] Only then will it be possible to audit the LPSO and give syndicate auditors the comfort that they seek that the LPSO figures, on which the syndicate depends for important elements of its accounting input, are themselves true and fair.[14]

Four areas of disclosure proved to be contentious.

The first of these was reinsurance. The old practice had been to prepare accounts with premiums shown net of reinsurance so that the overall volume of the syndicate's business was not disclosed. Such a disclosure is important because premium income limits are set before reinsurance and, under Lloyd's rules, security must cover the gross business underwritten. No credit is given for reinsurance so that if the reinsurer fails to pay the policy holder does not suffer: the loss is a purely commercial one to be borne by the Names who should have sufficient means to meet it. There was some resistance in some quarters at Lloyd's to disclosing gross figures and the figures for outward reinsurance because it made it more difficult for the underwriter to conceal overwriting by quota share reinsurance which, in the case of PCW for example had been associated with irregularities.

There was much more resistance to making public details of the syndicate reinsurance programme as is required of insurance companies. The underwriters' reservations related to the competitive damage which a full disclosure of the secrets of their trade might cause.

The disclosure of pure year results is patchy too. To obtain a full picture of the performance of a syndicate from year to year it is necessary to see to which year developing claims relate. According to the strict letter of the accounting rules, all that must be shown is the total figure for the reinsurance to close covering all claims for all prior closed years. As these old claims come in they are charged to the account which has received the reinsurance to close premium regardless of the year to which the claim relates. MacVe argues that the pattern of claims development should be disclosed. He says, 'It would at least aid understanding of the kind of margin of error within which estimates have to be made. Although fewer syndicates gave this information in their 1984 accounts than in their 1983 accounts, I hope that the syndicates which have been giving this information will continue to do so and that others will choose to follow them.' [15]

More critical, and more difficult, is the disclosure of provisions on the open years. The open year accounts are nothing more than a record of premiums received and claims paid to date. No attempt is made until the third year to account for notified claims and the IBNR and hence to form a view of the profit.[16] For solvency purposes the open year liabilities must be estimated following the Lloyd's minimum percentages for reserving purposes, but the results of the solvency valuation do not appear in the syndicate accounts. MacVe suggests that a way forward, towards the more current accounting used by the insurance companies, would be to include in a note to the accounts the estimated deficiency on the open years and an explanation of the extent to which risks have been accepted that are not yet reflected in the accounts. It does not follow from this that Lloyd's would move away from three-year accounting when it comes to the distribution of profits. The ability to warn Names more precisely and earlier about the development of events would help to bolster their confidence in the Lloyd's system.[17]

The fourth area of argument was the underwriter's report. The accounting manual had proposed that the report would include a description of the business written including the reinsurance arrangements in force.[18] Schedule 8 of the syndicate accounting bye-law reflects the market's concern at the liberality of these proposals. It was finally decided that the comments were to be more general: no details of the reinsurance in force were called for nor were analyses of the source of business required. MacVe comments on this: 'The aim of the underwriter's report should be to assist understanding of the risks and returns of the syndicate's business. This requires a suitable blend of verbal explanation and quantified analysis. While the 1984 underwriters' reports show evidence of a greater degree of quantified analysis than was provided in those filed for 1983, the overall level was still low. Segmental analysis concentrated mainly on classes of business and currency. Underwriters generally need to give further consideration to how best to present useful statistics to provide performance indicators and guides to likely prospects, and how to strike a suitable balance between giving broad generalisations and swamping reasons with an uninterpreted mass of detailed figures.

'While there was an increase in the number of quantified forecasts in the 1984 reports, these were all in cases where losses were anticipated – there seems to be a general reluctance to provide quantified profit forecasts even for the open years, let alone future years. While uncertainty about exchange rate fluctuations and investment returns may contribute significantly to this reluctance, there is scope for giving forecasts on the basis of stated assumptions about these factors, or for giving a likely range of outcomes, which should be considered. Generally the question of how much further disclosure of segmental data, and of expectations and assumptions about future results, should be produced to Names (taking into account the nature of each market), and how much of this should be on public file, deserves further examination.'[19]

However, it should not be thought that the syndicate accounting reforms at Lloyd's are anything short of fundamental and valuable. As Professor MacVe concludes in his book, 'The developments that have taken place put Lloyd's syndicate accounts in many respects ahead of ordinary company accounts with respect to providing useful information. . . . One needs to promote further improvements in company accounts generally before turning again to Lloyd's.' Comparing this passage with the 1980 quotation from Fisher at the beginning of this chapter gives a fair measure of the progress made.[20]

XI

The Audit Panel

Accountants have been a part of the Lloyd's scene since at least 1908 when Cuthbert Heath's manifesto led to the establishment of the solvency audit.[1] The responsibility for this work became concentrated among a small coterie of accounting firms whose businesses largely depended upon Lloyd's. Contrary to the ethical guidance of the Institute of Chartered Accountants, they kept the books as well as doing the audit, thus in effect checking their own work. Furthermore their loyalty to their agent clients conflicted with their loyalty to the syndicates of Names, because most of the solvency auditors also acted as auditors of the managing agency companies that ran the syndicates.

The structure of the accounting profession in the UK changed considerably during the 1970s. A series of mergers between medium-sized and larger firms increased the relative size of the latter and greatly reduced the number of the former. Lloyd's was not immune from this trend, and although the number of member firms in the Lloyd's audit panel did not change their parentage did. Two of the largest three were taken over: Baker Sutton by Ernst & Whinney, and Angus Campbell by Josolyne Layton Bennett, which itself joined Arthur Young. Ernst & Whinney and Arthur Young are among the top eight international accounting firms and enjoy excellent reputations. When the 1982 scandals emerged Arthur Young took steps to apply their high standards to the Lloyd's clients that had joined their client list as a result of the Josolyne Layton Bennett takeover. Ernst & Whinney, who had not been responsible for any of the troubled syndicates, were heavily involved with their partner Nigel Holland in investigating the recent wrongdoings. The style of professional work at Lloyd's was therefore beginning to change before the 1984 reforms.

One of the principal problems the panel of auditors faced at Lloyd's was the misapprehension, on the part of the market, that they were responsible for auditing the syndicates. They were not: they merely signed annual solvency certificates confirming that each Name possessed the means to meet his obligations. The quantum of obligations was fixed by the Lloyd's minimum reserving rules plus such extra sums as the underwriter and the agent thought prudent; the means were measured by the premiums trust funds, deposits and personal reserves. In the usual case the premiums trust fund itself was large enough, and once the auditor saw that the obligations were covered he stopped counting. None the less the market called this an audit and allowed itself to believe that the fairness and equity of the annual syndicate results had been blessed by the auditors. It was urgent to correct this impression: a first step was taken in 1983 when the name of the committee responsible for supervising the annual solvency test was changed from the 'Audit Committee' to the 'Members Solvency and Security Committee'.

Fisher had called for the new syndicate accounts to be audited and this was provided for in the Syndicate Accounting Bye-law. But who was to do the audits and to what standards? The matter was discussed in a consultative paper issued by the council in July 1984 and prepared under the guidance of the Accounting and Auditing Standards Committee.[2]

As the consultative document says, the main reason for the audit of syndicate accounts is to provide an independent report to Names on the stewardship function undertaken by their agents. Having unlimited exposure to risk, the Names are in greater need of this protection than shareholders in companies. In addition the audit of annual reports would provide assurance to the Council of Lloyd's as to the effectiveness of reporting to Names and hence compliance with the standards and rules for accounting laid down as part of the regulatory framework at Lloyd's.[3]

Lloyd's did not wish to take upon itself the task of saying how syndicate audits were to be conducted. The accountancy profession already has this duty and all that was necessary was to hitch the Lloyd's wagon to the company audit train. This was done by means of the true and fair test: Lloyd's syndicate accounts had to give a true and fair view of the results for the closed year. The phrase 'true and fair' comes from the Companies Act and applies by law to the accounts of companies. The same Act lays down the duties of auditors who must report if the accounts show a true and fair view. The scope and nature of the audit work necessary to support this opinion is prescribed by a corpus of professional guidance issued under the aegis of the accountancy profession's Auditing Practices Committee. By requiring a true and fair audit Lloyd's was able to call upon the whole apparatus of professional guidance that sets the standards for company audits and apply it to the audit of syndicate accounts. Certain audit matters were peculiar to Lloyd's – foremost among them the reinsurance to close – but we looked to the Institute of Chartered Accountants to give guidance to auditors on this, just as they give guidance in other specialized audit fields. However, there were some aspects of syndicate auditing where it was appropriate for Lloyd's itself to lay down special rules.

The first related to the qualification of auditors. Experience had shown that a restricted panel of auditors, although perhaps ensuring that auditors understood the business, had attendant dangers of lack of independence and objectivity that proved more damaging in the end than any harm a lack of technical expertise might have done. In other fields the trend has been away from specialized audit panels: a proposal to provide for them in future legislation covering banking supervision has been dropped. Provided that the auditor is professionally qualified qua auditor it does not appear that there is much advantage in requiring him to be expert in a specific industry. An audit is an audit and the peculiarities of the client's trade are something the well-qualified auditor takes in his stride: compensating for any lack of technical knowledge with independence, detachment, objectivity and the ability to see the wood for the trees. It was tempting therefore to abolish the audit panel altogether and replace it with a simple requirement that syndicate auditors be professionally qualified. However, this was not possible. The Insurance Companies Act provides that the accounts of every underwriter shall be 'audited' annually by an accountant approved by the Committee of Lloyd's: the audit referred to is in fact the solvency test.[4] But the same auditors carry out the solvency test and audit the syndicate accounts and unnecessary duplication would be caused if the two separate tasks were carried out by different firms. Lloyd's would have to continue to license a panel of auditors for solvency purposes; it was decided to make the best of it and use the statutory provisions to ensure that auditors were better qualified.

It was therefore proposed to reconstruct the panel of auditors and require all those who wished to carry out syndicate audits to re-register. Those registering would have to show that they were qualified in two important respects: by their breadth of audit experience outside Lloyd's, including the audit of insurance companies; and by the resources they could bring to bear measured by their arrangements for recruiting, training and developing their staff. We wanted tough well-rounded auditors who could stand up to the agents, and to Lloyd's if need be; we didn't want poodles.

The second matter was independence. The auditors' lack of independence and the undue cosiness which existed between agents and panel auditors had been a critical source of weakness in the old arrangements.[5] The Companies Act and the ethical rules of the Institute of Chartered Accountants provide that the auditor should be independent of his client. He cannot be a director or a shareholder or keep the books. He should not earn more than 15 per cent of his fee income from any one client, so that if he needs to take a strong line on an audit point he is not tempted to trim his sails by fears for his own financial position. These general rules were specifically to be applied to Lloyd's by requiring that the auditor could not be a director or a shareholder of the agent, or a member of any syndicate managed by the agent.[6] Bookkeeping was dealt with specifically with the proposal that a complete prohibition on a bookkeeping firm from acting as auditor to its syndicate accounting clients is the best means of ensuring the independence of the audit of the syndicate annual report.[7]

The most significant change related to the conflict between the interests of the agent and those of the Names on the syndicate. As the consultative document puts it: 'There are, however, circumstances in the Lloyd's market where an auditor may face a conflict of reporting responsibility – i.e. where the same firm acts both for the managing agent and for its managed syndicates. It is apparent that the interests in each case (agency shareholders versus Names on the syndicates) are not mutually compatible. There is an increasingly held view in the market that there should be a separation of responsibilities and this has gained some support from existing panel auditors.... There should be a specific requirement for separate firms to act for an agency and for its managed syndicates as the introduction of a requirement along these lines will eliminate any appearance of a conflict of interest. This proposal is therefore considered to be more effective in protecting the independence of the auditor in each case.'[8]

A third question on which legislation was needed concerned the method of appointing syndicate auditors. Under the Companies Act the shareholders appoint the auditors, but usually at the instigation of the directors whose recommendation is rarely overturned. A syndicate is not a company. It is not even a legal entity – at law it is nothing more than a term of convenience. The members of the syndicate cannot vote because one cannot bind another, each has several liability and a direct relationship to the agent. Names owe no collective duty to fellow Names on the syndicate. Again, a syndicate is reconstituted after each year, and although many of the Names will continue some will change. Each year represents a different venture and could select a different auditor. There are therefore serious legal difficulties in the Names' appointing the auditor. Although the consultative document toyed with the idea that the Council of Lloyd's should appoint the auditors this was rejected. 'Appointment of auditors by the Council would compromise the operation of normal market forces not only as regards standards of service but also in terms of the costs involved, i.e. audit fee levels. These forces should be allowed to operate in respect of Lloyd's syndicate audits. However the major consideration under this heading lies in the conflict between the Council assuming responsibilities in respect of individual syndicates with its overriding duty to act on behalf of the membership of Lloyd's as a whole.'[9] Noting that in the case of most companies the directors appoint the auditors de facto although the shareholders appoint them de jure, the final proposal was that the managing agents should make the appointment. But safeguards were called for, 'in particular the responsibilities of the auditors to report to Names must be clearly defined notwithstanding the fact that the auditor is appointed on the Names' behalf by the agent',[10] and a resigning auditor was to have the right to make a statement as to the circumstances of his resignation like that provided for in the Companies Act. The council was to monitor appointments and removals.

The proposal that the agent should appoint the auditor drew strong protests from certain quarters. In particular chartered accountant John Rew of the Association of Lloyd's Members (ALM) argued strongly for the rights of Names to make the appointment. The judgment was a finely balanced one but the council, when passing the bye-law in 1984, agreed with the consultative document. Neill expressed some dissatisfaction with this conclusion, observing that the idea that Names should be able to appoint the auditors who report to them is attractive and urging the council to reopen the question if real problems emerge with the new recognition arrangements for auditors; but the Committee of Inquiry made no recommendation.[11]

The fourth and final matter which was peculiar to Lloyd's was the relationship between the Society of Lloyd's and the panel auditors. Auditors are not usually members of Lloyds, indeed some now have rules that their partners may not be members.[12] In general, therefore, panel auditors are not subject to Lloyd's jurisdiction and cannot be sanctioned by its bye-laws. Yet Lloyd's, as a regulatory authority, must have a relationship with each firm on the panel. The conundrum was solved by resorting to the regulatory device used for members, agents and brokers before the new Lloyd's Act was passed: panel auditors were asked to provide a written undertaking to the Council of Lloyd's as a means of defining the relationship between syndicate auditors and the council.[13] The undertaking would acknowledge the right of the council to appoint and remove auditors from the panel, and the auditor would undertake to comply with Lloyd's syndicate accounting rules and the new rules as to the auditors' independence. The undertaking also tackled the difficult question of client confidentiality, the preservation of which is regarded by many auditors as the touchstone of their relations with their clients. The consultative document explained the point: 'An auditor generally has a duty to his client to maintain confidentiality in relation to the affairs of that client; information would not normally be revealed to a third party without the express permission of the client. However, in order to regulate the market effectively in the interests of Names there are circumstances in which the Council of Lloyd's would need to seek information from syndicate auditors. In the past there has been some confusion as to the responsibility of an auditor to volunteer to Lloyd's information in respect of syndicate audit clients. For the avoidance of doubt it is not proposed that auditors should have such a responsibility, rather the intention is for syndicate auditors to be able to respond to specific requests for information after due observance of appropriate procedures provided for in Lloyd's rules.... It is important that both auditors and their clients appreciate that this proposal would override the conventional duty of confidentiality which an auditor owes to his client.'[14]

Neill had considerable difficulty with this conclusion because the undertaking lacks the statutory force that attaches to Section 109 of the Financial Services Act 1986 by which any duty of confidentiality owed by the auditor to his client is waived in respect of communications in good faith to the Secretary of State, whether or not in response to a request from him.[15] However, the general undertaking now to be signed by all members of Lloyd's waives in favour of the society any duty of confidentiality owed by a syndicate auditor to its Names.

The Syndicate Audit Arrangements bye-law, which was passed in December 1984, gave force to the provisions of the consultative document five months after it had been released for discussion. There was little variation from the council's original proposals. The new panel was to take effect from the end of 1986. A special committee of the council was set up – the Syndicate Auditor Registration Committee (SARC) – which began the task of registering the new panel of auditors. Although it was the general policy of the council to widen the circle of syndicate auditors it lacked the power to do this directly. The SARC therefore adopted the policy of encouraging new firms to apply. Lack of audit experience at Lloyd's was not seen as a bar to registration provided that the firm had adequate audit experience in related fields – insurance companies for example – and had taken steps to train its partners and staff in Lloyd's matters.

Considerable attention was paid to ensuring that those who took on syndicate audit responsibilities would have the resources to do the work; there had been bottlenecks in the past because too many syndicates were calling for the attention of too few auditors at the same time. It was an odd symptom of Lloyd's tradition of secrecy that the old list of panel auditors was confidential. Most of the audit panel firms re-registered, but not before they could satisfy the SARC that they were reorganized so as to meet the new more stringent standards. In certain cases SARC approval was given only after the receipt of assurances that individuals previously involved with syndicate work had been removed from that responsibility. The new list was to be published, but not until March 1986, by which time virtually all the firms which wished to do so had registered.

The new audit arrangements, at first sight, look little different from the old: the number of firms on the list is larger, nineteen as opposed to fifteen when Fisher reported, and the overwhelming bulk of the audits are still being carried out by four firms, which accounted for four-fifths of the syndicates.[16] While conceding that the new registration arrangements together with the enforced separation of agency and syndicate auditors adequately protects the auditor's independence, Neill admits that this continued concentration of audit work is unsatisfactory. He recommends that if there is no change by 1991 then Lloyd's should implement Fisher's proposal and limit the number of syndicates handled by any one audit firm.[17] There were important underlying changes however: the separation of agency auditors from syndicate auditors led to a large number of audit changes which gave agents the opportunity to reconsider carefully the quality of service being provided; the mergers with larger firms meant that by 1984 65 per cent of the syndicates were being audited by firms well known outside the Lloyd's community; and the requirement of registration including regular monitoring and recruiting, training and staffing arrangements, had caused all panel firms to look to improvements in these respects especially as registrations were in each case granted for a limited period varying between two and five years. One can only hope that the ring has been broken and that the forces of competition among firms for Lloyd's work will ensure that the complacency among accountants that served Lloyd's so ill in the past does not recur.

XII

Divestment and the Re-registration of Agents

The rules covering the re-registration of underwriting agents have two sources.

The first is divestment, imposed by Parliament as the price for granting the considerable self-regulatory powers given to the council by the Lloyd's Act 1982.[1] No doubt the ownership of a managing agent by a broker can present the underwriter with a difficult conflict of interest; no doubt too, that the broker's duty to his assured can conflict with his duty to the Names for which his agency acts. However, I came across no case where this conflict had led to objectionable abuse, and I am certain that such abuses as did occur were as nothing compared to those perpetrated by agents upon their Names. Fisher had said, 'The question is whether the undoubted difficulties, both of principle and practice, of a compulsory divestment by Lloyd's brokers of shares in managing agencies should be allowed to override this logic':[2] 'this logic' being the argument that broker-owned underwriting agencies created unacceptable conflicts of interest. The game may have been worth the candle as it frees Lloyd's of a set of conflicts that might be the source of abuse. But the question remains: Was it worth the disturbance to the market and the undoubted weakening of the agency system? This question was, however, academic. Parliament had decreed divestment and it was up to the Council of Lloyd's to make it work by the statutory deadline of July 1987.

The second thread was registration. In a paper in 1985 Peter Daniels, a leading Lloyd's agent and member of the council, outlined the history of agent registration.[3] Pointing out that Lloyd's agencies began to be acquired by public companies about 1950, he explained that the next major change to affect agents followed the publication of Lord Cromer's working party report in 1969. Among many other matters this report drew a distinction between an agent who attends to the affairs of the

Name and an agent who manages the syndicate, the former, as often as not, having been described in the past as an introductory agent. At about the same time another working party under the chairmanship of Mr Paul Dixey was asked to produce a code of conduct for underwriting agents. In November 1970 a bye-law was introduced for the maintenance of a register of agents, the main purpose of which was to give power to the Committee of Lloyd's to remove agents from the register. Following the Dixey working party report, an underwriting agents' manual was introduced.[4] This manual was the main source of guidance to agents when I arrived at Lloyd's.

In 1980 Sir Henry Fisher's working party discussed requiring agents to re-register with Lloyd's. It recommended that re-registration should be for a limited period only; that the committee should have the power to veto the employment of an active underwriter; that 'the Council should apply tests of suitability, standing and general market expertise when deciding whether to admit an underwriting agency to the register of approved Lloyd's underwriting agents'; and that 'the Council should have power, analogous to that possessed by the Department of Trade in relation to insurance companies, to ensure that only "fit and proper persons" have control over underwriting agency companies or firms, or are directors or senior employees of underwriting agency companies or firms'.[5] The Fisher Committee went on to recommend that minimum levels of capitalization for agencies be established and that agents be required to carry errors and omissions insurance. Turning to members' agencies Fisher recommended that boards of such agencies be encouraged to include an outside element and that at least one director be a member of every syndicate on which the agency placed Names.

During consideration of the Lloyd's Bill undertakings were given to Parliament that an inquiry would be set up into the underwriting agency system at Lloyd's with a view to implementing the divestment requirements of the Lloyd's Act. The committee of inquiry was established in March 1982 under the chairmanship of a former Deputy Chairman of Lloyd's – Alec Higgins. It was directed to have regard to the Fisher proposals as well as the divestment requirements of the Act. These two threads were to come together in a consultative document in March 1983.[6] This proposed that all agents re-register before July 1987 under rules that would give effect both to Parliament's wish to divest agents from brokers and to Fisher's proposals to tighten up the standards of underwriting agencies.

The reform proposals had two parts: those relating to the ownership and control of agencies, and those concerned with the minimum standards which agencies would have to achieve. Higgins concentrated on the first.

Lloyd's has always been anxious to retain supervisory powers over those who control underwriting agencies, fearing that if controllers were outside their jurisdiction it would be more difficult to supervise the market. As Higgins put it, 'The agency function is at the heart of the Lloyd's market. Although abuses have arisen in entities controlled by persons within the jurisdiction of the Committee of Lloyd's, for self-regulation to be effective it is necessary that those who have the ultimate control of the agency function should be able to feel: "We are all members of the same Society. This is our market place. We have a common interest in maintaining its quality and integrity." We doubt whether this sense of community would persist indefinitely if agencies became owned and controlled by persons outside the Lloyd's community. We would fear for self-regulation in that event.'[7]

Jurisdictional control was to be achieved by three measures. First, not less than two-thirds of the voting power of shares in agencies would have to be held by members of Lloyd's for whom the agent acted. Second, every holding of more than 10 per cent of shares, whether voting or non-voting, would require council approval which would not be given in the case of voting shares held by non-members. Third, not less than two-thirds of the directors would have to be Names for whom the agent acted.

The concept of the non-voting equity share, entitled to a full share of the company's profits but having no votes, is an unusual one and rarely found outside the Lloyd's community.[8] The idea goes back to 1954 when the Committee of Lloyd's required agencies to be in companies separated from their broker parents.[9] Since then there has been an increasing trend towards constructing 'Chinese walls' around agency companies at Lloyd's in order to protect the underwriter from outside interference. Commonly this was done by the use of non-voting shares held by the broker parent, which entitle the holder to all the profits and an equity interest in the capital, and voting shares generally held by the board members, which carry no rights to dividends but exercise the voting powers. The effect of these arrangements has been to discourage outside investors from owning agencies unless there is a collateral commercial reason, as there was for brokers. The unfortunate agency parent was prevented from exercising any effective control over its offspring, although it might ultimately be liable, legally or morally, or both, if things went wrong.[10]

The Higgins Report proposed two further safeguards on the ownership of agencies. In order to avoid agencies being dominated by one man, which has been a common situation at Lloyd's, not more than 40 per cent of the voting power of an agency could be held by any one person, save that a Lloyd's broker could own up to 100 per cent of a members' agent. The second aimed to meet Fisher's argument that brokers, although forbidden by statute from owning managing agencies, could none the less improperly influence underwriters by threatening to withdraw their Names from his syndicates, 'their Names' being those served by the members' agency under the broker's control. As the Higgins Report put it, 'It is in our reconsidered view either a case of forbidding Lloyd's brokers from controlling a members' agent while placing no restriction on supply of stamp capacity by the members' agent, or of limiting the supply of stamp capacity and permitting the Lloyd's broker to control the members' agent.'[11] A limit of 20 per cent was proposed and broker-controlled members' agents were to be given until 1992 to reduce their proportion of any syndicate's capacity to that level or below.

Debate at council and in the market concentrated principally on the question of the brokers' involvement in members' agencies. There were fears that the 20 per cent restriction of stamp capacity would be difficult to achieve and that those unfortunate Names who would be told to change syndicates would object to what they might see as an unwelcome change in their fortunes. The council decided to drop the proposals. The 40 per cent limitation on any one shareholder also went when it was pointed out that almost half of the Lloyd's agencies were affected. Instead the council proposed to rely on rules covering the collective character and suitability of the board to avoid too much idiosyncratic dominance by one underwriter.

During the summer of 1983 discussion on the divestment arrangements concentrated on the rules for the ownership and control of agencies. In the autumn a divestment sub-committee was set up to plan the detailed rules. It was chaired by Peter Miller, a marine broker with legal training; he continued to lead the sub-committee after he took over as Chairman of Lloyd's on 1 January 1984 although he later handed over the chair to the Senior Deputy Chairman, Murray Lawrence.

The re-registration proposals came before the council in bye-law form in May 1984. They reflected Higgins' plans for the ownership and control of agencies, except for the 40 per cent ownership and 20 per cent stamp capacity rules.

The bye-law also picked up Fisher's proposals concerning character and suitability. Directors would need to have adequate experience, be of good character and able to devote sufficient time to the position; boards collectively would have to show a balance of skills and contain an independent view. The board should contain an active underwriter from each market in which the agency manages a syndicate, and any syndicates which account for more than 10 per cent of the agency's total capacity should be represented on the board by the active underwriters. The Committee of Lloyd's would need to be satisfied that the agency had sufficient capital, staff, errors and omissions insurance and appropriate premises. The number of the syndicates managed would be controlled by the committee.[12]

The bye-law also gave specific effect to Sections 10 and 11 of the Act which require brokers and agencies to be divested. It directs: 'There should not exist any arrangement which might enable a managing agency to influence the policy or business of a Lloyd's broker or might enable a Lloyd's broker to influence the business of a managing agent unless such an arrangement is a normal commercial arrangement.'[13] The sections go on to exclude a profit-sharing arrangement between a broker and an agent unless this arises out of divestment negotiations and terminates no later than 1995. The effect of this part of the bye-law is to make undue influence involving an unacceptable conflict of interest between broker and underwriter a disciplinary offence at Lloyd's: such an improper arrangement would amount to a breach of a bye-law which is itself a sanctionable matter.

Within this legal framework the process of divestment began. The deadline laid down by Parliament was July 1987, but the bye-law said that any agency which had not made arrangements for divestment by May 1986 must write to its Names advising them of that fact so that the Names would know that there might be a possibility that their agency would cease activities in July 1987 and so that they would have time to make other arrangements.

An indication of the extent of the problem which divestment posed is provided in the appendix to a consultative paper put out by the Higgins Committee in September 1982. This reported that 114 of the 293 agencies at Lloyd's would be directly affected by divestment because they were then associated with brokers. These 114 agencies managed 308 of the 481 syndicates at Lloyd's – 71 per cent of the total, and in terms of volume of business the proportion was possibly higher. Divestment would mean that more than two-thirds of the capacity of the market would be under new management within a three-year period.[14]

In December 1986 with seven months to go before the parliamentary deadline Lloyd's gave a progress report on the registration process. The new agency structure was beginning to emerge; by July 1987 242 agencies were expected to have registered, a reduction of 20 per cent. It would be wrong to assume that most of those dropping out had failed to meet the new higher standards of management and capital; many represent the termination of shell agencies that had not traded for some years, the result of mergers, or a general tidying up of corporate structures. None the less the reduction must indicate some raising of standards and hence a greater degree of protection for Names.

The withdrawal of brokers from their connections with managing agents had no doubt contributed to the expected reduction in the proportion of combined managing/members' agencies from 54 per cent to 42 per cent. At the same time the number of pure managing agencies had grown from 35 (11 per cent) to 57 (24 per cent). The number of members' agencies had fallen from 105 (35 per cent) to 83 (34 per cent): no doubt the closure of a number of small members' agencies was to be balanced to some extent by the number of combined managing/members' agencies formerly owned by brokers becoming broker-owned members' agencies.[15]

An attempt was made in early 1984 to encourage institutions to invest in agencies by amending the bye-law proposals about non-voting shares, so that the holders of such shares could have the power to appoint directors with the consent of the Committee of Lloyd's and remove directors after consulting the committee. Despite this change it appears that the overwhelming majority of divestments have been carried out by means of a management buy-out. It is not only the strict, indeed arguably narrow, requirements of the council about the ownership and control of agencies that has led to this. Public investors are understandably chary about investing in companies where so much of the profit depends on the personal skills of the active underwriter. The risk has been highlighted by the recent scandals where errant agents have cost their broker parents dearly. Brokers have in general obtained lower prices for their agencies because of the prevalence of management buy-outs.[16]

Another consequence of the widespread use of management buy-outs has been to introduce weaknesses into the agency system in two respects: management and capital. The new reform programme at Lloyd's has quite properly imposed a considerably greater administrative burden on agencies and this has exposed the weakness of some of the smaller ones. Despite the formidable underwriting skills of working Names at Lloyd's, it does not follow that these are automatically accompanied by management expertise. By striking out on their own underwriters are discovering for themselves the scarcity of skills in agency management which were formerly provided, together with a whole range of back-up services, by their large broker parents. In the larger agencies the shortage is being met by introducing a new cadre of professional agency managers but the smaller agencies, with an average of less than one hundred Names each, cannot afford a full-time professional manager. In another respect the reforms have intensified the pressure on the smaller agencies because they have imposed higher capital standards. Not surprisingly, many agencies coming forward for registration had minimal capital no longer backed by that of the broker parent. Furthermore, in order to raise the capital, agents have had to take out loans which depend upon a high level of short-term profitability for their redemption. Agents must therefore take a shorter-term view of profits. This will be exacerbated by the new requirement to publish syndicate accounts; an important reform, but one which facilitates the production of syndicate league tables. These provide a spur to agents and underwriters to produce short-term results in order to maintain or improve their ratings in these tables.

These weaknesses of management and capital are likely to be more pronounced among the smaller agents. Lloyd's is quite a concentrated market. The ten largest agents are estimated to control over 36 per cent of the market and the two largest between them to control almost 16 per cent. This number has not changed much recently but there is a clear trend for the largest agencies to grow. Sturge and Merrett both have paper on the Stock Market and the path to future acquisitions must be regarded as open, especially as neither was directly affected by divestment and hence they are well capitalized and managed. There can be little doubt that the number of managing agencies would have fallen further had the bye-law incorporated the limitation of 40 per cent share ownership in one pair of hands, as Higgins had recommended. There have been a number of cases of agencies spawned under the wing of a larger managing agency but controlled by the underwriter in order to give him a share of the equity and the possibility of capital gain. Such agencies are frequently unable to offer a comprehensive service, being contractually dependent upon an associated company for support with accounting and investment management.

In October 1984 a consultative document on membership requirements recommended the ending of the one agent/one class rule.[17] This would have a much more profound effect on the structure of the agency system. It would mean that a Name could approach a profitable syndicate directly and would no longer be dependent upon the existence of a sub-agency agreement between his members' agent and the managing agent of the chosen syndicate. As a result Names would be able to move between syndicates more freely, provided that the underwriters were willing to take them on. An underwriter receiving such an approach would have the added incentive that he would not have to share his salary and profit commission with a members' agent. On the other hand, underwriters are jealous of their right to select Names for their syndicates and are not unaware that those who come easily in good times may leave quickly when times are hard.

In recent years there can be no doubt that brokers, as a result of divestment, are slowly distancing themselves from the underwriting side of Lloyd's, and the underwriters are beginning to realize that they are no longer literally in the pay of the brokers. As a consequence, brokers are reconsidering their attitude to the business of supplying Names to Lloyd's. Aware of the risks of suit by dissatisfied Names, one or two of the larger brokers have decided to get out of the members' agency game altogether. However, it is still estimated that seven out of the ten largest members' agencies at Lloyd's are broker-controlled and that those seven agencies account for one-fifth of the capacity of the market.

It appears, therefore, that divestment and its associated re-registration have not so far produced a drastic change in the structure of the Lloyd's agency system, but certain trends are clear. The number of agents is falling despite the doubling of Lloyd's capacity from 1983 to 1986 and the 33.3 per cent increase in the membership during that period. Divestment has clearly deprived a number of agents of resources that the brokers once provided, and institutional investors without Lloyd's broking interests, who could have replaced those resources, have not emerged. There is little evidence of divestment having led to the introduction of new capital into the Lloyd's agency system. The lack of management skills among the smaller agents is made more serious by the increased regulatory requirements. Against such a background a further con centration of underwriting power in the hands of a few large agencies must be a reasonable bet in the medium term.

Although formally separated from underwriting the brokers are not without influence. The rejection by the council of the Higgins proposal to limit the size of a broker-owned members' agent's share of any syndicate means that the threat to remove Names can be a potent one.

Furthermore, the relative financial weakness of some agents must mean that they will be less able to withstand broker pressure were it to be applied. As I have said, I neither saw nor heard of seriously improper pressure by brokers. It does now appear that Sir Henry Fisher may have shot the wrong horse in pressing for divestment in the name of avoiding conflicts of interest between brokers and agents while overlooking the much more serious abuses of conflicts of interest uncovered since 1982 where a few agents had plundered their Names, putting their own interest as agents improperly ahead of their duties to their Names. It must be said in mitigation of Sir Henry that the nature and extent of these abuses was not known at the time of his inquiry. Although divestment is, of itself, a perfectly proper policy it does not attack the real problem: the abuse of the interests of Names by their agents. It is fortunate that the Lloyd's Act 1982, which gave Lloyd's the powers that Fisher recommended, also enabled the council to look at these abuses and take steps to ensure that they will not recur.

However, a wider lesson may be drawn from Lloyd's experience with the ownership and control of agencies. One of the most notorious of the scandals is that of the PCW agency. This had been acquired in 1973 by the publicly quoted broker, Minet Holdings PLC, under conditions laid down by the committee of the day to ensure that there would be no improper interference by the broker parent with the underwriter subsidiary. The parent company was denied access to information about the subsidiary's activities, only one parent company nominee director was allowed, the agency auditors were different from those of the parent company, and the agency's errors and omissions insurance was severed from that of its broker parent. This is a perfect example of what the City calls a Chinese wall. Behind its protection £29 million was abstracted from the PCW Names. When the facts eventually emerged the broker parent was in a position to step in, take up the reins of power and perform a rescue. If divestment had been in place in 1982 there would have been no broker parent to step in, change the PCW board and shoulder the burden of resolving the problem. Broker power is not always malevolent.

XIII

Relations between Members and Lloyd's

The fourth foundation stone of the new regulatory edifice at Lloyd's was the corpus of rules governing relations between members, their agents and the society: the rules for members.[1] Before the 1982 Act most of these concerns were covered by contracts: a 'general undertaking' between the member and the Society of Lloyd's and an underwriting agency agreement between the member and his agent. These arrangements were now to be covered, as Fisher had recommended, by bye-laws.

The new structure was to involve a membership bye-law, and a number of lesser documents including a new form of premiums trust deed, and a brief general undertaking to abide by the rules of the society to be signed by each member. Having begun this codification of the membership rules the council set up the Bird working party on membership requirements which made its proposals for future changes in October 1984.[2]

A Fisher task group had been studying the question of rules for members since 1982. Its proposals were a prime example of codification: the consultative document reflected the then current practice in bye-law form, covering the admission and termination of membership, and the granting of permission to underwrite, a separate matter from membership.[3]

The rules for admission emphasize one of the most valuable features of Lloyd's. Despite the change from the old club atmosphere to an investing institution, good personal relations between the Name and his agent are fundamental. Agents are required to know their Names personally and the applicant must be sponsored by two members. The admission process takes up to a year and there is therefore little chance that a Name will be trapped unwittingly into an arrangement the nature of which he has not had an ample opportunity to consider in advance.

All applicants to join Lloyd's are interviewed by a member of the council, or a senior working member of the society at a 'Rota' interview. As over three thousand of these must be held in a busy year they take up a lot of time between July and November.[4] Each of these interviews follows a carefully prescribed form. The council member is accompanied by an officer from the membership department, the applicant by his agent. The surroundings are usually fairly impressive, given Lloyd's penchant for gilded plasterwork and chandeliers, and the applicant often somewhat overwhelmed. But the ten-minute interview has the great virtue that no one can become a member of Lloyd's without knowingly agreeing that he is willing to accept unlimited liability in respect of his insurance obligations.

The membership bye-law was brought before the council in November 1984 so that it would have effect for the 1985 membership year.[5] It introduced a novel and important change in relation to resignation. Hitherto a member could resign at any time 'at the discretion of the Committee'. Now a member could cease to underwrite with effect from the end of any year but would then become a non-underwriting member until a period of thirty months had elapsed.[6] The council would have the power to shorten or lengthen this notice period at any time before it expired.

The membership bye-law also incorporates two of the old fundamental rules of Lloyd's: that each member underwrites for his own part and not one for another – there is no liability by one member in respect of the underwriting of another; and that a member is not permitted to underwrite except at Lloyd's.[7]

Of more direct significance to the member is the agreement he signs with his members' agent, the underwriting agency agreement. This commits him to support, to the limit of his financial ability, the under-writing activities carried out by the agent on his behalf. At the same time he agrees to delegate powers to his agent. These underwriting activities may be carried out directly by the agent or by another managing agent to whom the member's agent may delegate his powers via a sub-agency agreement. There is therefore a contractual chain binding the member to those who actually underwrite the risks on his behalf. All members of Lloyd's sign such an underwriting agency agreement: the terms are onerous and the delegation of power by the Name to the agent extensive.

Cromer advocated a model form of agreement for the better protection of Names.[8] Having recommended that the council should introduce a mandatory form of agency agreement by bye-law, Fisher said, 'The relationship between a Name and his underwriting agent is governed by the terms of an agency agreement which both the Name and the agent sign. At present there is no rule which lays down which topics such agreements shall cover or lays down what terms they shall or shall not contain. The form and content of the agreement are left to the parties to determine, although they are in practice dictated by the agent, and the Name has no option but to accept them if he wishes that agent to act for him.'[9] The use of a standard form of agency agreement gives a new Name much comfort. He can be sure that the document he is asked to sign has been approved by an independent body on his behalf and is the same as that signed by all other members.

A task group of agents and Lloyd's staff chaired by Frank Barber, then a deputy chairman, considered these proposals in a consultative document published in July 1984.[10] This raised a number of contentious questions.

Accepting Fisher's main argument, the document proposes a standard form of underwriting agency agreement mandated by bye-laws. Rejecting the idea that there should be a direct contract between the Name and the underwriter of each syndicate to which he belongs, the proposals stick to the traditional Lloyd's rule of an agency agreement between a Name and his member's agent and sub-agency agreements between the member's agent and the managing agent of each syndicate.

The consultative document introduced certain reforms which improved the position of Names: the agent's liability under the agreement could not be restricted; agents were to pay interest on profits if they were distributed late; and the Name would have the right to notice if the active underwriter or a director of the agency came off the syndicate so that the Name would have time to withdraw too. It also strengthened the hand of agents in certain respects. The Name cannot summarily terminate the agreement, but has to settle his losses first and argue with the agent afterwards about any potential liability he may have to the Name – the 'pay now sue later' clause; the agent has the right to borrow to cover a Name's losses; and his duty to observe the syndicate premium income limits is not a strict duty but is confined to 'best efforts'. The apparently onerous 'pay now sue later' clause was approved by the council with surprisingly little debate; discussion concentrated on the other matters: deficit clauses and agent's charges.

Fisher had drawn attention to the offence caused to Names by the lack of a deficit clause: 'We have received complaints that a member with a line through the same agent on marine and non-marine syndicates can make an overall loss on his entire underwriting activities, yet pay a profit commission to the agent because there has been a small profit on, say, the marine syndicate.... We consider that it should be mandatory for every agreement to contain a deficit clause. But we consider that the matter requires further study and that the exact form of deficit clause would require careful consideration. It might prove difficult to arrive at a clause which was appropriate to every agency, but we think that the Council should make every effort to overcome the difficulties.'[11] This was a proposal on which a number of external Names focused, including committee members of the Association of Lloyd's Members.

Drawing attention to the inequity of penalizing the underwriter on a profitable syndicate by docking his profit commission because the underwriter on another syndicate on which the Name also had a line had made a loss, the task group said: 'If there is to be a deficit clause the task group recommends a vertical form of deficit clause under which a single syndicate's underwriting results in successive years would be taken into account.'[12] It was clear that the group did not like deficit clauses: 'Should the Council interpose between the Name and his agent, in the matter of the terms of business arrived at between them, by compelling the use of a deficit clause the result might well be the distortion and general re-negotiation of terms of business quite possibly to the ultimate disadvantage of some Names in a performance orientated market. It was also recognised that the members' agents' share of the profit commission represented a vital source of income to them.... Agents might therefore be moved to alter their rates and manner of charging their salaries and fees.'[13] Although the consultative document included an optional deficit clause, the standard agreement, introduced in March 1985, is silent on the matter. The council's conclusions in this regard brought out considerable press criticism which noted that the task group responsible for considering the matter was composed of agents, Lloyd's staff and a representative of Lloyd's solicitors. No external member was included. It must be said, however, that deficit clauses are permitted, some agents use them, and a Name who is keen on one can always seek out an agent who operates such a clause. The difficulty an innocent applicant to membership faces is that he may not be aware of his options.

The question of agent's charges was even more sensitive. In an average year half the profits of Lloyd's go to the agents in the form of salary and profit commission as a reward for the underwriting and management services they provide, and half to the Names as a reward for the risks they run. That is not to say that the rate of profit commission runs at 50 per cent. The overall effect is produced because Names bear all the losses and the agent's salary continues even if a loss is made. Cromer noted concerns about the level of agents' charges;[14] Fisher said: 'We consider that in principle agents should be free to compete with each other in the matter of charges, and that the varying circumstances of different agencies and different syndicates may justify some variations. But there is clearly a danger of abuse, particularly so long as the terms offered by different agents are not publicly known and Names are not in a good position to discuss whether relatively to others they are being overcharged.'[15] He recommended that agents give details of their terms and conditions of business, including rates of charges, to Lloyd's, which should keep them under review and take steps to check possible abuses. This proposal was accepted by Lloyd's when their counsel gave Parliament an undertaking during the passage of the Lloyd's Bill that it would be implemented by July 1984.[16]

The effective fee to be charged by an agent can be varied by adjusting the level of expenses charged to the syndicate as opposed to those borne by the agency itself. While the cost of finding and caring for new applicants for membership is clearly for the account of the agency, and LPSO charges and those of the syndicate auditor are for the syndicate to bear, there are a number of expenses that fall on the borderline and there were calls for a clear definition in the agency agreement of those matters which could be charged to Names and those which were to be borne by agents.

The scale of charges to be applied by the agent is laid down in the underwriting agency agreement. In order to assist Names in this respect the Higgins working party said:

'It is important to improve the conditions in which market forces can operate by making it easier for either prospective or existing names to compare remunerations of different agents. The disclosure requirements proposed ... will take care of much of this problem. It is recommended that consideration should be given to:
(a) writing into the proposed standard form of agency agreement principles laid down by the Council for the calculation of commission and the allocation of expenses;
(b) requiring the agreement to state any departure from those principles.'[17]

There were therefore three proposals before the council: the publication of a register of agent's charges, standard rules for calculating agent's charges in the agency agreement, and rules for the allocation of expenses.

The last two of these were matters for the underwriting agency agreement. The Barber task group considered the matter at some length, and proposed that the underwriting agreement should provide for the schedule of the business terms of the agreement to set out model terms to govern the calculation of the profit attracting the commission payable to agents; while at the same time allowing an agent to vary those terms provided that it was made clear that such variation had been made and how it had been made. The proposed model terms were set out in an attached specimen agreement. This represented a sound reaction to the problem. But the report added, darkly: 'It might be considered that the task group's solution represents an undue intrusion into the negotiation and settlement of the terms of business between Names and agents. This was acknowledged by the task group.' This footnote proved to be right. When the standard form of underwriting agency agreement was released the schedule covering salary and profit commission had no model clauses and the words in the agreement 'comprising the model terms as may be expressly varied (and shown to be varied) by agreement between Name and agent' had been deleted. Again the new Name's problem was not that the agent's charges were not fair, but that he lacked the means of knowing what alternatives might be in current use.

In dealing with the allocation of expenses the consultative document argues that it was wrong for the current regime, under which most underwriting agents had a relatively free hand, to continue. It says: 'The vital control over syndicate expenses that the task group has introduced into the underwriting agency agreement is the provision that, unless an expense is proper and reasonable, the agent has no contractual authority to charge the Name in respect of it.'[18]

It was also argued that the new disclosure provisions discussed in the previous chapter relating to syndicate accounts should solve the problem.

The fact of the public filing of the syndicate accounts has also been advanced as a reason for not proceeding with the parliamentary undertaking to publish a register of agent's charges. There had been promises but no progress when I left Lloyd's in February 1986. Professor MacVe devotes a chapter to this question.[19] In 1984 about 40 per cent of the agencies gave some explanation of how expenses had been allocated between managing agents and syndicates, an improvement on the 1983 accounts. In the matter of profit commission 67 per cent of the agents gave a note in the 1983 accounts, but only 27 per cent in the 1984 accounts, the recommended disclosures in this respect in the Provisional Accounting Manual having been deleted with the passage of the Syndicate Accounting Bye-law in 1984. But the seven-year summary of results, now required for all syndicates, disclosed the amount of profit commission in 58 per cent of the cases. The publication of syndicate results did not produce a regime which met the full demands of Fisher about disclosing agents' charges.

While it is arguable that the publication of syndicate reports puts the Name in possession of much more information, it does not meet the requirement to make public details of agents' charging rates for the consideration of prospective members, and those thinking of changing their agents. It is difficult to resist the conclusion that the reluctance of the committee to require this disclosure, and to incorporate in the standard underwriting agency agreement model charging clauses, is again related to the dominance of agents in the internal councils of Lloyd's. There are two points here. The first is the natural disinclination of any body of commercial men to encourage competition among their number, especially when the body consists of those who have succeeded in their chosen field and achieved the status of elected office. In this instance the agents' reluctance may have been fortified by the practice, identified by Fisher, of charging different rates of commission to different Names on the same syndicate. The second is the unfairness at law between the agent who has the power because he knows the ropes, and the Name who, lacking full knowledge, cannot be expected to rely upon the contractual doctrine of caveat emptor.[20]

In spite of criticisms about the disclosure of charges the new standard agency agreement was a major step forward in protecting the Names and was made mandatory by bye-law on 10 March 1985. This was expected to take effect on 1 January 1987 when a new form of premiums trust deed, approved by the Secretary of State for Trade and Industry under the Insurance Companies Act, together with a new abbreviated general undertaking, would also take effect. From that date all members of Lloyd's would have signed the same underwriting agency agreement. Differences would be confined to commercial matters such as salary, profit commission and expense allocations identified in the schedule to the agreement.

Given Sir Patrick Neill's remit to consider the regulatory arrangements at Lloyd's from the point of protecting the Names' interests, it is not surprising that he found much to condemn in the matters related above. In the view of the committee of inquiry things should have been better ordered, and Lloyd's failure to do so provides conclusive evidence that the constitutional structure was defective in being too concerned with protecting the self-interest of the agents who controlled the Committee and Council of Lloyd's. He condemns out of hand the failure to publish a register of agents' charges in accordance with the parliamentary undertaking and calls for standardizing the method of calculating charges. Like Fisher he considers that deficit clauses should be mandatory. He criticizes vagueness about the basis of allocating syndicate expenses. While recognizing the value of the 'pay now sue later' clause in protecting policy holders, he considers that its application is far too onerous: 'Lloyd's must take steps to temper the effect of this provision to deal with possible cases of abuse.' Finally he rejects the traditional arrangements at Lloyd's by which an indirect Name has a contract only with his member's agent who in turn contracts with the sub-agent who manages the syndicate. He points out the advantage of the Name having a direct contract with each active underwriter: the Name can then sue directly and the responsibilities of the managing agent are enhanced. He concludes that the standard agency agreement is written from the standpoint of an agent endeavouring to ensure the smooth running of his business and with too little regard for the interests of the Name.[21]

How is it that the Rules Committee of the council could have approved such an arrangement given the presence on that committee of external and nominated members? The answer lies in the terms of reference of that committee which was to propose rules 'to give effect to the policy decisions of the Council'. It was the council – guided by the chairs and the Committee of Lloyd's – which dictated the course of action which Neill rightly condemns.

The Bird working party[22] looked at the application of the new membership rules to the market and made proposals for change. Its report considered the required levels of means and deposits and their relationship to premium income. Minor but important changes were recommended both as to the amount and nature of qualifying assets. But the most important part was the revelation that over six and a half thousand members (approximately 30 per cent of the membership) were out of line with current security requirements, the total shortfall of deposits amounting to £350 million in a year when deposits totalled £1.2 billion. This had happened because under the old regime of written undertakings it was not possible to vary the deposit required of a member without his agreement. Members could only be made to come into line when they applied to increase their level of underwriting. As a result a few members were still accepting business on the basis of security laid down under rules twenty or thirty years earlier. Indeed there is a tiny handful of very elderly Names who still enjoy the pre-1920 regime in which there had been no limit on premium income in relation to deposits. Seventy-five per cent of the members who were below deposit requirements showed a shortfall of less than twenty thousand pounds, and the bulk of the cases concerned members elected in the mid-1970s when security requirements had been relaxed following the implementation of the Cromer Report. The ratio of deposits to net premiums was then 1:10 as opposed to 1:4 today. But the situation represented a hole in Lloyd's security which must be repaired now that the council has the powers under the 1982 Act.[23]

The working party confirmed the principle of unlimited liability of members. It urged regular certification of means, saying: 'Means should be positively confirmed every three years. ... Names who wish to increase their overall premium limits should be subject to a full means test at the time.'[24] It considered the touchy subject of Lloyd's vocational Names – working members of Lloyd's admitted on preferential terms to encourage those who work in the market to join the society. Frequently such a member's deposit will be financed by his employer. Bird recommends that such members should continue to be allowed, but on the footing that they show the same deposit-to-means to premium-income ratios as ordinary members, the only difference being that they are permitted a lower level of means and deposit and hence of premium income.

Finally, the Bird Report considered the question of market capacity. Whenever times are hard at Lloyd's and premium rates and underwriting profits are low the cry goes up for a limitation on the number of new members being admitted, the argument being that they are sharing in existing profits and diluting the interests of existing Names. When times are good, as in 1985 and 1986, the cry is the opposite: increase the premium-income to deposit ratio and provide more capacity from the existing security. At the same time members' agents are keen to encourage more members to join. In fact steps by the regulatory authorities at Lloyd's are both unnecessary and irrelevant to the question of capacity. If times are hard new Names will be unable to find places on syndicates and they will not willingly join Lloyd's, with a hefty entrance fee and annual subscription, if they see no return from syndicate memberships. In good times Names are attracted by high reported profits, and there should be no need to lower the barriers to membership. The potentially important recommendation that the limit on the individual's premium income be removed was not proceeded with. By retaining an individual maximum, now a premium income of £1.3 million, Lloyd's has ensured that it is still essentially a small man's market.[25]

XIV

Rules for Underwriters

Premium overwriting has been an endemic problem at Lloyd's. Although it tends to be particularly pressing at times during the insurance cycle when capacity is tight and there is a lot of good business around, it can happen at any time to a foolish underwriter.

Each Name contracts with each of his underwriters to accept business up to the limit of his line on that syndicate: that is up to his premium income limit. If the limit is exceeded further security will be called for by Lloyd's to back the additional risks undertaken. This may be provided by shortfalls on the Names' other syndicates, but if there are none the Name must put up an additional deposit. The active underwriter therefore has a duty to keep his syndicate's business within this overall limit or he will have difficulties with his Names – and Lloyd's. The difficulties are usually easy to overcome if the syndicate has made a profit because the Name will then be happy to provide the extra security. But if the syndicate has made a loss the Name will complain bitterly at being made to cover losses arising from trading beyond his or her contractual limit. A good agent will keep a close check on his underwriter's signings so that the flow of business can be cut off if there is a risk of overwriting. A sloppy agent may not keep good records and it may therefore be difficult to keep track of the underwriting for which he is responsible. But even a thorough and conscientious underwriter can be at risk for two reasons beyond his control. First, he may be writing risks in dollars – much of Lloyd's business is done in dollars – and a fall in the £/$ exchange rate will immediately increase sterling premium income for the same dollar risk. Second, he may have granted a binding authority to a cover holder who has written more business than expected.

Binding authorities are arrangements by which a non-Lloyd's cover holder, usually overseas, is empowered to accept risks on behalf of the syndicate; their incorrect use had been at the root of the traumatic Sasse affair.[1] The disciplinary report on Sasse illustrates the actions that a misguided underwriter can take when faced with premium limit excesses caused by a foreign binder going wrong. In a letter to the underwriter, Tim Sasse, dated 8 July 1976, the broker, John Newman, set the scene: 'I did intend to go on to generalise to some extent about the future, and also to give you a complete run-down on the American situation, which I do know that you have come to see as a mystery tour.'[2] There had been premium limit excesses. There were discussions between Mr Sasse and Mr Newman regarding the premium income problems which this increase posed for the syndicate. Mr Sasse instructed Mr Newman not to process premiums for the time being while he (Sasse) set about trying to find a way to 'lay off' premium income. The 'way' involved transferring premiums to other years of account.

The practice of concealing overwriting by reinsuring the excess into another syndicate or year is no longer possible because premium income is reckoned gross of reinsurance. Another strategy is for the broker to book the business late so that it appears in the next year of account;[3] this practice could only be fully prevented by the introduction of inception-date accounting which would lay down strict rules as to the accounting year to which a specific risk is to be credited.[4]

Sir Henry Fisher was concerned about underwriters exceeding their premium income limits: 'We consider that the importance of ensuring early detection of premium income excesses is so great that continued and unremitting efforts should be made to devise and introduce an effective scheme.'[5] Noting that the committee had already put in train an early-warning scheme for the 1980 account, he concluded: 'Any measures which the Council may take in the matter of premium income limits will incidentally be of benefit to Names, but the principal purpose of such measures would be the security of the Lloyd's policy'.[6]

Nothing causes greater annoyance to Names than being called upon to produce additional deposits to cover excessive underwriting which the Name has not authorized and on which the underwriter has made a loss. However, because the fault is not necessarily deliberate the committee has been extremely reluctant to make premium overwriting a 'strict offence': one in which the offence is the fact of exceeding the limit regardless of the reason. This attitude was reflected in the Syndicate Premium Income Bye-Law,[7] which gave effect to the Fisher recommendation. It laid a duty on the underwriting agent to take reasonable steps to ensure that the amount of insurance business underwritten through the syndicate is not such as would cause the syndicate's premium income to exceed the allocated capacity for that year of account.[8] The agent is required to have an effective system for monitoring premium income and to keep the development of premium income for every year of account under active review at all times. If monitoring shows a threat of excesses the committee is given power to step in and ask why. They may then direct the underwriter to stop underwriting: in which case the agent is required to tell his members.

The committee passed a regulation to coincide with this bye-law which requires each managing agent to supply a forecast of the expected development of each syndicate's premium income for each year of account, quarter by quarter. This forecast is compared with the actual figures as they come to the LPSO. If forecasts are exceeded the syndicate is placed on a 'watch list' by Lloyd's and the underwriter will be asked to explain his plans for avoiding a breach of his premium income limits. In serious cases the underwriter may volunteer to suspend business, or the committee may direct him to do so. The system is therefore based on the underwriter having a legal obligation 'to take reasonable steps'. If he fails to do so and is reckless or careless of his duties that will be a disciplinary offence.

An important effect of the new rules has been to improve agency records so that the build-up of business is tracked more closely. In this way the underwriter can reduce his margin of safety and make more money for his Names. The lesson is that better controls mean more profits.

Binding authorities have been described as a way of getting around the rule about writing business only in the Room. They are particularly favoured in the non-marine market, especially for US business. As Fisher says: 'Our evidence leaves us in no doubt that the use of binding authorities is essential for the success of Lloyd's.... Without the use of binding authorities Lloyd's syndicates, with their small staffs, could not have dealt with the volume of business which has over the years come to Lloyd's.'[9]

The marine market has rarely used binders, except when writing incidental non-marine business. A similar device, called a lineslip, is widely used in the marine market but there is a vital difference. While a binder is defined as 'an agreement between underwriters and a coverholder under which a coverholder is authorised to accept risks on behalf of underwriting members in accordance with the terms thereof and to issue documents without the specific prior approval of the underwriters'[10] a lineslip requires each risk to be approved by a leading underwriter who, by his approval, binds the other underwriters on the slip.

The regulation of binding authorities is an old story. A working party was chaired by Tim Brennan, a senior broker member of the committee who later became a deputy chairman of Lloyd's. This proposed in 1978 that all cover holders be approved by tribunals and that the tribunal procedure should be applied to all new applicants, that there should be a central register containing the salient features of all binding authorities granted and that a recommended binding authority agreement with standard general conditions should be introduced.[11] Fisher agreed that binders should be subject to regulation but conceded that Lloyd's might not yet have the necessary powers. A later working party finally converted these intentions into legislation in August 1985.[12] The binding authority bye-law briefly provides that every binding authority must be evidenced in writing and presented to the LPSO by the relevant Lloyd's broker. Only an approved cover holder can receive such an authority. A set of regulations, passed by the committee, lays down procedures for the registration of binding authorities and the approval of cover holders by panels of underwriters. A code of practice recommends, but does not enforce, standard conditions. The whole legislation puts heavy emphasis on the role of the Lloyd's broker as cover holder, or more commonly introducer of the cover holder to the underwriter.

The difficulties of this working party illustrated an important feature of the regulation of Lloyd's. Binding authorities are 'a market matter' – the interests of policy holders and Names are not directly involved. Underwriters therefore think it is unnecessary for the regulatory authorities to be involved, unless the security of the Lloyd's policy is at risk. The Non-Marine Association (NMA) had operated a system of 'tribunalization' for many years by which an underwriter could be advised of the bona fides of a proposed cover holder and told if the grant of a binding authority was inadvisable. A small staff was employed by the NMA to handle these approvals. However, the NMA freely admitted that it had no sanctions which could be brought to bear upon an underwriter who by-passed the tribunal system. At first there were many reservations about handing such a matter to the council for central regulation. Fisher observed: 'The Council of Lloyd's will have to decide as a question of principle whether any tribunal or tribunals which form part of the system of regulation should be run by the Committee of Lloyd's or by the market association. We are prepared to accept the view which seems to be fairly strongly held at Lloyd's that it should be the latter.'[13] In the end the council won. The tribunal staff were transferred from the NMA to the corporation within a regulatory framework laid down by the council.

It proved difficult to reach agreement among the market associations on the degree of rigidity to be incorporated into the new council-ordained regime. The non-marine market operates, in a rather buccaneering fashion, as a small element in the worldwide property and casualty insurance market. It explores new fields. It invents new covers. It encourages initiatives. On the other hand, the marine market, represented by the Lloyd's Underwriters Association (LUA), is a more stolid community. Their wordings and rates dominate the world market for marine insurance, of which they have a significant share. The mariners behave in an altogether more staid fashion; while not frowning on initiative they expect underwriters to follow market agreements, and by and large that is what happens. The LUA, who had little experience of binding authorities, asked for a strict set of rules, and in particular that there should be a standard form of binding authority laid down by Lloyd's and followed by all. The NMA was all for flexibility and freedom for the underwriter. A compromise was reached by which a code of practice was used to outline a standard binding authority. Not perhaps an ideal use of a device whose foreword says that it is 'to assist in establishing a recognised standard of professional conduct for all members of the Lloyd's community who should, in discharging their duties as such, bear in mind both this objective and the underlying spirit and intent of these codes'.[14] It was the non-mandatory nature of a code that appealed.

Lloyd's tries as far as possible not to interfere with the freedom of the underwriter to decide what risks to accept and how. It is felt that the best protection for the assured is provided by two facts: that the customer is represented by a skilled broker, and that the market is highly competitive. The regulators step in only where security is at risk, as with premium income limits, or there is a danger that outsiders might take advantage of the freedom of the market, as with binding authorities. There are a few strict rules, for example: against insuring war on land because of the danger of aggregation of claims,[15] or against insuring candidates' deposits in parliamentary elections.[16] As a matter of public policy Lloyd's now keeps away from elections. 'Tonner' policies were also banned on Fisher's recommendation. They have been described as a kind of insurance policy which is pure gambling. It started as a sort of excess of loss reinsurance for marine underwriters. They were afraid of the freak aggregation of loss that could arise if, for example, the *Queen Mary* were to ram the *Normandie*. They would cover themselves by taking out an insurance against two ships of more than 50,000 tonnes each being involved in a casualty in a given year.[17] Fisher points out that where the insured has no insurable interest a policy is regarded in law as a gaming or wagering contract and therefore unenforceable in the courts.[18] Since 1773 Lloyd's has been anxious to keep out gambling – the battle continues.

But there remained two important areas in which intervention in the practice of underwriting was necessary, both of which Fisher had overlooked – they emerged only during the revelations of autumn 1982. The first of these was related party reinsurance which was a feature of all three of the worst cases: Howden's, PCW and Fidentia. The problem is illustrated by a quotation from the Hart disciplinary case – Mr Hart, the defendant, was a Howden's underwriter. Mr Archer had been called in to put the affairs of the syndicate in order. 'In the summer of 1980 Mr Archer found a copy of the LPSO premium debit.... He thought it unusual and asked the Defendant to meet him. Mr Archer asked the Defendant for an explanation saying that he was very unhappy about it. The Defendant said that Mr Archer was not to worry, "there will never be a claim on the policy", and that it was a "dead reinsurance". Mr Archer asked what this meant and the Defendant said: "It's a means to get money to one of Jack's companies." Mr Archer understood this to be a reference to Mr Jack Carpenter. He told the Defendant that he would have to take the matter to Mr Grob (as the Chairman of the Alexander Howden Group) and the Defendant said: "There's no point in doing that because there are lots of policies like that at Howden's." '[19] However rare such extraordinary practices may have been their public discovery made preventive legislation inevitable.

In their first report of March 1983 the Higgins Committee pressed for each agent, its directors or partners and active underwriters, to disclose to Names the extent of their respective interests, whether direct or indirect, in insurance entities.[20] This requirement had been imposed by the Disclosure of Interests Bye-Law No. 3 of 1984 in April of that year and incorporated in the consolidating legislation – the Syndicate Accounting Bye-Law No. 7 of 1984 in October.

Despite the corrective effect of these disclosures the council felt that more should be done. The Committee of Inquiry report into the Fidentia affair, which was sent out to all Names on the affected syndicates, had recommended: 'As soon as possible Lloyd's should impose a comprehensive prohibition on all future related party reinsurance transactions. In particular we wish to record that, having regard to the fact that most syndicate members know very little indeed about reinsurance or the operation of the reinsurance market, disclosure to Names that such transactions have been entered into during the course of a given period is not an adequate substitute for an overall prohibition of related party reinsurance transactions.'[21]

This was advice which could not be rejected, and steps were taken to forbid a practice that could never be consonant with the proper application of the law of agency. However, there was a problem. Many related party reinsurance arrangements were made through the broker parent of the managing agency. The reinsurances might then be arranged with insurance company subsidiaries of such Lloyd's broker parents. Frequently the underwriter would have no say in where the insurance was placed, which would be decided by his broker colleagues. A syndicate's reinsurance arrangements are often long-term in nature and based on treaties: disturbing such treaties can be expensive, and can hardly be justified if it is only for a year or two. It would, therefore, be best to wait until divestment had severed links between managing agencies and Lloyd's brokers. Thereafter treaty arrangements could continue, and the reinsurances could not be characterized as related party reinsurance because the relationship would then have ceased. Meanwhile, with effect from the syndicate accounts produced during 1984, any such arrangements would have to be disclosed. Provided that the agent had made a full and fair disclosure in his account, the Names were on notice, and dubious reinsurance arrangements, of which the agent would be ashamed to tell his Names, would be unlikely to continue.

An exposure draft was therefore released in August 1985.[22] This forbade any reinsurances by a syndicate into an insurance company in which the agency had an interest. It also forbade the use of a broker related to the agency for the placing of outwards reinsurance. Not only were such transactions forbidden, so were significant ownerships by agents of insurance companies.

There was little opposition to these proposals. The proposed bye-law would take effect in July 1987 when divestment would be complete and therefore no transitional exceptions would be called for. The substantive bye-law was passed on 10 March 1986[23] and from that date, save for expiring arrangements that would be concluded by divestment, the sort of set-up that PCW and the Gang of Four had so greedily used became a disciplinary offence: now there would be no excuse for smoke billowing from the desks.

I doubt if many situations changed as a result of this legislation. Sunshine, present for two years before the related parties bye-law was passed, would have eliminated any dubious arrangements, provided that they had been fully and fairly disclosed in the agent's accounts as the law required. In a few cases there must be some doubt about the agents' candour in dealing with these matters despite the perusal of syndicate auditors independent of the agency: now there could be no reason for doubt that related reinsurance was wrong.[24]

The second necessary change in underwriting practice, also overlooked by Fisher, was the continued abuse of baby syndicates. While the PCW case was by far the most serious instance of plunder the potential for abuse was regarded so seriously by the Higgins working party that they devoted half their second report to it. 'Most people are concerned about those cases where an underwriter who writes for more than one syndicate intentionally prefers one syndicate by directing to it the better business or directing away from it the less good business. However, there are two other important areas of potential conflict of duty when a managing agent manages, or an active underwriter writes risks for, more than one syndicate. The one is the allocation of expenses between the syndicates, including particularly the cost of reinsurance protection. The other is the distribution of reinsurance recoveries between the syndicates.'[25] The working party went on to point out that there are many innocent situations where the same active underwriter can be managing more than one syndicate: for example, when the membership of the syndicate is identical – so-called mirror syndicates – because of an historical amalgamation of two syndicates; or, as is common in the marine market, because one of the syndicates writes incidental non-marine business; or because the underwriter wishes to handle two different classes of business, one low-risk and one high-risk and many Names do not want to be involved in underwriting risky insurances. Higgins said: 'We use the expression "preferred underwriting" where a managing agent through the active underwriter is in a position to prefer one syndicate over another where it is writing risks, allocating expenses or the cost or the benefit of reinsurance protection, or distributing reinsurance recoveries. We use the expression "parallel syndicates" where the managing agent manages two or more syndicates in the same class of business or the active underwriter writes risks for two or more syndicates (where they are not managed by the same managing agent) in the same class of business.' The report quotes examples of acceptable parallel syndicates: where participations in all risks are in a predetermined percentage; where the syndicates, although managed by the same agent, have different underwriters; or where the types of business are different enough to avoid conflicts of duty. However, three common cases are condemned because they give rise to unacceptable conflicts: a 'waiting syndicate' formed to accommodate new Names until there are places available on the main syndicate; 'broker syndicates' to give an incentive to a broker to bring business to the main syndicate; and a syndicate started for a deputy underwriter as an inducement: 'A deputy underwriter for one syndicate cannot in our view properly be an active underwriter for another syndicate in the same class of business.' Higgins recommended that these practices be regarded as unacceptable.

The report concluded that while preferred underwriting should be banned, parallel syndicates, under the same managing agent, could be permitted if there is a valid reason for a viable separate syndicate and the risks are divided on a predetermined declared percentage, or there is a separate underwriter, or the syndicate writes different categories of business in the same class. The onus would be on the underwriter to show that the parallel syndicate was permissible.

These recommendations ran into trouble because the use of baby syndicates had been widespread. Many leading figures in the market were involved. An estimate of the extent of the practice in 1982 can be formed from the ALM league tables published in September 1985.[26] If one categorizes a baby syndicate as one with less than 50 members and excludes those with a less than four-year history – starting syndicates – 27 of the 157 marine syndicates in 1982 were baby syndicates – 17 per cent of the number of syndicates. Of these 27 syndicates, 13 were among the most profitable fifth. A Name who belonged to one of them had a 2.5 times better chance of earning high profits than if he belonged to an average syndicate. The non-marine market showed the same effect but to a markedly smaller degree. Out of 143 syndicates 11 were babies: 4 of them were in the top 20 per cent for profitability. Thus a Name had a 1.5 times better chance of earning high profits on such a syndicate compared with the average. The motor and aviation markets gave no material evidence of the practice. It is not possible to form a clear view about how widespread preferred underwriting had been before 1982 because the ALM league tables for 1981 and earlier years rely on a sampling of the accounts obtained from external Names: accounts for the insider syndicates were not normally available to the ALM's investigators.

The Higgins Report was a consultative document. It proposed a policy which it was now up to the council to implement. This was done in two ways – by publicity and by regulation. The new syndicate accounting bye-law says: 'The managing agent's report shall include ... where the managing agent manages another syndicate which operates in the same market as the syndicate to which the managing agent's report relates, the basis on which insurance business is allocated between those syndicates.'[27] This disclosure, together with the public filing of all syndicate accounts, meant that the Names would soon become aware of preferred underwriting arrangements. Those involved knew that this would happen and many arrangements were wound up because they would not bear the light of day.[28]

But disclosure was not good enough. We had to go further.

The true extent of baby syndicates was not revealed publicly until the accounts of 1982 were filed in August 1985. During 1984 and 1985, while we considered how best to give legislative effect to the Higgins proposals, I had received more than one call from the Room, on the lines of 'We haven't heard much about baby syndicates recently. Are they permitted now? We're thinking of starting one up.' The revelations of the 1982 accounts, in which the league table was headed by a three-man syndicate whose underwriter was one of Lloyd's most respected figures, brought considerable press comment. Discussion of 'baby', 'staff' or 'broker' syndicates, all giving preference to insiders, added to the public concern about the substantial PCW losses and brought further coals of fire upon the heads of the unfortunate Council of Lloyd's. The matter of baby syndicates was raised in the House of Commons during the debate on the Financial Services Bill in 1986.

The two-year delay in legislating was caused by the complexity of the problem and the difficulty of producing a solution which was acceptable to the working members on the Committee of Lloyd's.[29] A ban on preferred underwriting was rejected because of the difficulty of prescribing in detail what was intended to be outlawed in practice. To control the size of the syndicate would be a crude and inefficient measure: there were many smaller syndicates having well over fifty members that were still confined to insiders. The most effective measure would have been a 'one underwriter one syndicate' rule with exceptions, if any, approved case by case by the council. With 30 per cent of the syndicates operating in parallel[30] this would have meant a major change in market practices and some parallel syndicates had a legitimate basis. But there is no doubt that the commercial damage caused to the market by the introduction of a 'one underwriter one syndicate' rule would have been far less than the political and public damage that was done by its rejection.

Because of the complexity of the problem a code of practice was preferred to a bye-law. It was felt that as preferred underwriting was already contrary to the law of agency a bye-law was unnecessary. Unhappily, a code of practice, although wider and more general in its application than a bye-law, does not give a Name such a ready right of action against his agent for breach, as Neill points out.[31] After rehearsing the principles of the law of agency the code, which confines itself to the case where an underwriter intentionally prefers one syndicate to another, sets out best practice.[32] First it recommends that the managing agent avoids the problem by confining himself to one syndicate for each class of business, or to managing mirror syndicates. If this is not possible the code advises that there must be a valid reason for each syndicate. 'The provision of incentive or remuneration to agency/box staff as a purpose or function of a syndicate will never be a valid reason for its existence.' Either there should be different underwriters for each syndicate, or the division of risks must be in accordance with a clearly stated policy. Reinsurances with different syndicates must be kept apart: the reinsurance programme should be arrived at independently and premiums and recoveries should be kept separate. Emphasizing the duty to disclose, the code says that the managing agent should 'make full fair and *prior* disclosure to all direct Names and members' agents as to its underwriting arrangements, to enable all Names to appreciate the nature of these arrangements and to make informed decisions as to whether or not to participate in them'.

This code was regarded by some critics as inadequate. It did not deal with the allocation of expenses, nor with 'waiting' or 'broker' syndicates. Neither did it deal with the tricky question of the allocation of Names to syndicates.[33] And it was felt by some that the use of a code was too weak: the council therefore linked the code with a bye-law which banned any syndicate 'which consists of less than 50 members unless at least 75 per cent of the capacity of the syndicate is provided by members who are not shareholders, directors, partners or employees of the managing agent or individuals who are connected with any of those persons'.[34] By the time it was passed, in December 1985, it seemed unlikely that many such syndicates still survived: the code of practice, because it should be following the spirit rather than the letter of the law, may well prove of more use in dealing with the offence.[35]

XV

Lloyd's Corporation Structure

The third part of the mission agreed by Lloyd's at the beginning of 1983 was to equip the society with up-to-date regulatory machinery.[1] The introduction of new disciplinary procedures and a new rule book would be largely pointless without the machinery to make them work. The chief executive's central role in this was clearly set out in his terms of reference:[2] overseeing the new self-regulatory regime; recommending proposed bye-laws; setting up and monitoring the progress of necessary task forces; consulting with the market and outside regulatory authorities on proposed rules; setting up machinery to implement new bye-laws; and taking responsibility for the quality of the new self-regulatory arrangements, particularly the disciplinary arrangements. This paragraph was supported by further clauses giving authority to manage the resources of the society, appoint and direct the staff and maintain proper channels of communication. These executive powers were in addition to his role as a policy adviser to the chairs and the council.[3]

The chief executive's responsibility to the council for the quality of the new rules and their application made it essential for him to have staff capable of doing the job and committed to the better regulation of the market. When the new council took office the staff were ill prepared for this new role: not because they lacked the necessary qualities, although some did, but because they lacked the necessary authority and standing vis-à-vis the elected members. The curiously deferential style of the corporation staff is the product of Lloyd's peculiar history.

In the second half of the nineteenth century the practice of having an active underwriter as chairman had been dropped. The committee decided to look outside Lloyd's for a chairman with influential connections, although that would mean a man who was not available for the day-to-day work of the society. Thomas Baring, of the banking family, was chosen. He had been a member for twenty years and was a Tory MP who could have had a cabinet post had he wished. He held the chairmanship for eighteen years, and was succeeded in 1869 by G. J. Goschen, a young Liberal MP who had already held cabinet rank and was subsequently to occupy a string of official posts, culminating in Chancellor of the Exchequer under Lord Salisbury. Goschen was chairman from 1869 to 1886 and again from 1893 to 1901 when he reached the age of seventy. In the years between, Lord Revelstoke of the Baring family occupied the chair.[4]

This arrangement meant that the day-to-day leadership of the society devolved on the committee and its secretary.[5] The committee supervised the affairs of the society through the 'member in attendance', one of the committee appointed to stand by for a month at a time who for that short period acted as the absentee chairman's vice-regent.[6] In such a regime the power and influence of the permanent secretary was considerable. The needs of the situation appear to have been met in Sir Henry Hozier, 1874–1906, and Rear-Admiral Sir Gilbert Englefield Bart, 1906–22. Pensioners' letters in Lloyd's staff magazine, *Triangle*, relate the tartar-like character of the autocratic rear-admiral who ruled the staff until 1922.

This concentration of power became too much for the committee and after Sir Gilbert's abrupt enforced retirement, with a generous golden handshake, there was a major change. Reversing the policy followed for 120 years, Englefield's successor was called 'Principal Clerk to the Committee'. The message was clear. Elected members, and elected chairmen who had been chosen from the working members since Goschen retired, were determined to be masters in their own house. After 1922 the senior member of Lloyd's staff was called the Principal Clerk and the title was changed to Secretary General only in 1975 because American members found difficulty in accepting the authority of an office holder bearing the title of 'clerk'.

The title changed: the role and attitudes did not. Soon after his arrival at Lloyd's one of my most senior and highly paid colleagues asked a waiter if he was required to attend the committee lunch that day. He was amazed to be told: 'No sir, no clerks at lunch today.' The green-baize door syndrome, keeping the servants firmly in their place behind it, was deeply ingrained in the culture of Lloyd's.

Reinforcing this attitude, the three elected chairs were responsible for the direct day-to-day management of the staff. An organization chart of the corporation in 1970 shows the principal clerk as one among a number of committee clerks or departmental managers, none of whom reported to him and for whose work he had no direct responsibility. Until 1983 the arrangement was that each of the seventeen major departments of the corporation reported directly to the chairman or one of the two elected deputy chairmen.[7]

Over the years, as new market-support activities developed, the tendency had been for these activities to be established independently of the Corporation of Lloyd's and then to be adopted by the corporation as the market made increasing use of their services. The tribunalization department of the Non-Marine Association for example, which was responsible for the registration of binding authorities, was the last of a long line of such activities to come under corporation control.[8] The same thing had happened sixty years earlier with the LPSO.[9] Given the history of these departments, it was not surprising that each of the boards of underwriters who supervised their affairs saw themselves as a board of directors responsible for the day-to-day management of the department and its staff. This approach, although suitable for departments whose activities served the market, was not at all appropriate for those whose job it was to regulate the market.[10]

The appointment of a chief executive in 1983 put heart into an important element of the staff – the investigators working in Fort Knox on the roof of the Lloyd's building.[11] Now they had someone to whom they could turn to protect them against the real fears that some had for their careers as their inquiries brought them nearer to the leading figures in the society. Regulation which is anything more than the minimum which everyone is voluntarily prepared to agree upon is inherently unpopular to a greater or lesser extent. It involves saying 'no' and stopping people doing what they would otherwise want to do. It also involves making them do things they would not otherwise want to do. Regulation can seem offensive by appearing to impute to people's actions and 'market practices' a degree of impropriety. The difficulties which this might pose can be described in extreme terms. Would the elected chairs support the abolition of practices which the market thinks are okay or, more extremely, in which the chairs themselves are heavily involved? Drawing from recent history the answer must be 'no'. In this context the need to introduce an independent voice among the chairs was clear, but the confusion of loyalties which such an introduction would produce could have serious implications on the regulatory side.

This was the background to the situation at the beginning of 1983. Seventeen departments reported to the Chairman of Lloyd's either directly or through a 'policy board' in the case of activities that had once been autonomous. The chairman of the day had adopted the practice of assigning responsibility for certain departments to one or other of the deputy chairmen. The secretary general was not seen as having anything other than a co-ordinating role exercised through the supervision of the agenda for the weekly committee meeting and a daily management meeting, called O Group, presided over by the chairman at which a lengthy agenda of decisions was taken. Lacking authority themselves, departmental managers were used to turning directly to the chairs and enjoyed the opportunity it afforded them of walking the corridors of power.

In May 1983 the committee received my proposals for a new approach. Staff would report through an organizational structure of six group heads to the chief executive. This would ensure that departmental managers would be accountable for the quality of their work to their group heads and through them to the chief executive. Policy guidance for certain departments would be provided by policy boards of elected members who should not see themselves as having a management role. Although they could be consulted on staff appointments, promotions and salaries, these were essentially matters to be settled by the chief executive on the advice of the Staff Policy Committee, or the Senior Appointments Committee in the case of the most senior posts. These changes were designed to weld the staff into one organization, owing allegiance through the chief executive to the council and taking responsibility for the execution of policy decisions, but leaving the determination of policy in the hands of elected members. Sir Kenneth Berrill, who chaired an inquiry into Lloyd's Corporation structure which reported in March 1986, recognized the importance of these structural changes. 'The appointment of the Chief Executive clearly had major implications for the relationships between senior Corporation Staff and the elected chairs.'[12]

Sir Kenneth's report also comments on the role of policy boards or committees: 'In our view it should be a cardinal principle that, except where they are specifically fulfilling a task assigned to them by bye-law, committees should be non-executive. . . . While committees retain so many executive functions, the staff reporting lines remain divided between their executive supervisors and their committees. This crucially reduces the ability of the Chief Executive to fulfil his role as the person responsible for all staff and inhibits him from welding the activities of the corporation into an effective instrument for implementing Council policy.'[13]

But as Berrill points out the 1983 organizational changes had still to be implemented effectively: 'The practice of staff relating to a particular Deputy Chairman and expecting him to take most executive decisions fails to recognise the change brought about by the establishment of a Chief Executive and a number of high quality group heads.'[14]

The reshaping of the corporation staff took place against this background of divided loyalties. New high-level talent was brought in to head finance, external relations, data processing and the corporation's legal services.

By the beginning of 1986 four of the six group heads had been appointed since the new council took office. At the lower level, of the twenty-four posts reporting to those group heads, ten had arrived at Lloyd's since 1983 and a further nine had been promoted from the corporation staff. This wholesale strengthening of the staff brought inevitable tensions, and new personnel policies had to be developed to match Lloyd's needs. A job-evaluation study established proper gradings and salary bands for each staff post; a new system for performance assessment was introduced, together with a more rigorous and fairer system of job evaluation and salary administration. Better graduate recruiting and training for new entrants and managers would have to wait until new heads of personnel and training were appointed in 1985 and 1986 respectively.

In two respects staffing the corporation has its own particular difficulties. Corporation staff and their wives or husbands cannot be members of Lloyd's. Many of the staff see membership as a road to riches that is being taken by their friends in the market, many of whom are less well qualified than they are. But the incorruptibility of the staff is essential to Lloyd's: it would be quite wrong for members of staff or their partners, having access as they do to insider information about syndicate affairs, to be members of the society. Berrill cites the opinion ' "that the member of Lloyd's is the core of Lloyd's and if the Corporation staff are not members they are in the important sense not members of the central community". We have sympathy with this view but are persuaded by the force of the argument that a potential conflict could so easily arise from full underwriting membership.'[15]

A second difficulty is caused by the regular loss of staff from the Corporation of Lloyd's to the market. As divestment proceeded newly independent agencies cast about for management expertise and their eyes all too frequently fell on members of the corporation staff who had received a basic training in Lloyd's at the expense of the society. They were thus ideally equipped to act as agency staff. With better planning and a longer time scale it would have been possible to recruit a number of graduates for the corporation each year in the expectation that in five years' time many would have left to work in the market: the market would be strengthened by such trained recruits and the balance, left for the corporation, would fill the needs of the regulatory authority.

The Corporation of Lloyd's had a good budgetary system and proper financial controls: they were made even stronger. An internal audit department was set up and regular audit checks of corporation activities became the rule. The work of the external auditors was extended to cover the members' deposits and the trust funds and the systems in use at the LPSO. These activities were funded by the boom in membership which generated substantial cash flows from entrance fees and subscriptions.[16] As a result Lloyd's was able to erect a new building, paid for through subscription income, remodel the data-processing systems which support the market, and carry through a plethora of regulatory changes including an extensive series of disciplinary investigations at the same time. Funds were always available when needed for regulatory work.

The process of reform is inevitably largely one of education, or re-education. New rule books are academic unless they are understood and followed. Management and staff cannot adopt new practices unless they know what they are and why they are needed. Better training at Lloyd's was vital: a series of market seminars did much to change the attitudes of the underwriting agents.[17]

Reflecting on the reforms in the management of Lloyd's during the last three years, it now seems that the fundamental necessity was a change in the culture of the staff: a change in the way in which they looked at themselves, their jobs and those in the market with whom they worked. The green-baize door, with its forelock-tugging attitudes, had to go: not just in the name of modern democracy, or to achieve the abolition of outdated class distinctions, but because the admiration and respect of staff for their 'betters' – the working members of Lloyd's – had been destroyed by the speculation and wrongdoing exposed in 1982; they had seen through the green-baize door.

The old attitude had been one of respect for a fine old institution and the Lloyd's men who had led it down the years: the chairmen, the deputy chairmen and the committee members. Lloyd's was steeped in tradition and the staff had been made to feel part of a large family in which devotion and faithful long service were the most desirable virtues. The events of 1982 changed that: the staff could no longer feel respect for a committee which included members who had been involved in discreditable practices. The older and more traditional members of the staff felt disillusioned and cynical. What was needed was to rebuild the staff in a new ethos: more detached, more professional, relying more on good pay and conditions than security and long service, but above all being aware of the importance of their independent responsibility for regulating the society on behalf of its members, four-fifths of whom were not working in the market.

The introduction and expansion of modern management methods – budgetary controls, financial planning, value for money, job re-grading –

was all very well, and certainly helped to improve the efficiency and effectiveness of the staff. But the fundamental need was for a change in the corporate culture. The change could not succeed unless there was also a change in the culture and attitudes of the second floor: the servants could not change unless the family changed too.

XVI

The Position of the Chief Executive

The necessary change in the culture of the corporation and in the attitudes of the staff turned upon the relative positions of the Chairman of Lloyd's and the Chief Executive.[1] The proper establishment of these roles would lay the foundations for a Lloyd's in which new rules, developed under the aegis of the self-regulating Council of Lloyd's, would be applied to the market by impartial, independent professionals, rather than by partisan insiders taken for a brief period from the ranks of brokers and underwriters to play monitor and amateur policeman.

The Chairman of Lloyd's had functioned since 1901 as the executive head of the corporation. In this role he had been supported by the two deputy chairmen, who, like him, had to be drawn from among the working members of the council.[2] The chairman had four principal duties: to act as figurehead, spokesman and ambassador for the society; to chair the council and the committee; to lead the society in policy matters, proposing the line to be followed by the council; and to set the tone for Lloyd's — sleepy or bustling, formal or informal, hard driving or laid back.

In addition the chairman had an executive role: directing the work of the departments, assigning duties, and dealing with the plethora of day-to-day regulatory matters affecting agents, brokers and underwriters to whom the chairman's office door was always open. The Room enjoyed the privilege of direct access to the chairman, a fact of which the regulatory staff were frequently made aware. Chairmen sometimes found it difficult to back the staff against the working members, being well aware that they held office thanks to members' votes.

The appointment of a chief executive was clearly intended to lead to a change in the role of the chairman and his two elected colleagues. While the elected chairs would continue to play a dominant role in policy matters, on which the chief executive would act as an adviser, the execution of policy should be left to the chief executive and his professional staff, given his responsibilities in that respect to the council.

When I was appointed as Chief Executive of Lloyd's, with a nominated seat on the council, I asked for the additional title of Deputy Chairman, because of problems in the past about the status of Lloyd's staff. A certain mystique attached to 'the chairs' and it was essential to be one of them to have authority in the market and, more importantly, among the staff who needed to feel that they had a representative on the council. It was also necessary to make clear that the chief executive had a position as a member of the policy team, with a particular responsibility for representing the voice and interests of the external members and the public. The role was a dual one: policy adviser, as a member of the policy-formulating team of the four chairs; and executive responsible directly to the council for the execution of policy decisions. In policy formulation he was to have particular responsibility for supporting the chairman in external relations: the other two deputy chairmen, by the nature of their previous experience, would be less well qualified for this. In the execution of policy he was to be particularly concerned with the regulatory and disciplinary arrangements.[3]

The appointment had been made at the insistence of the Bank of England and the DTI. There can be no doubt that it was strongly resisted within Lloyd's, where the market professionals saw it as an unwarranted interference in their internal affairs. But the gravity of the 1982 crisis made such an appointment essential. Not only had leading market members been taking advantage of their Names, but those responsible had enjoyed the confidence, respect and company of the ruling circles within Lloyd's: no less than three members of the 1982 committee were later to face charges before Lloyd's disciplinary committees. Lloyd's was presented with two alternatives: to accept the imposition of an external chief executive or to suffer the discontinuance of its self-regulatory status. The former was seen as the lesser of two evils. Given the circumstances of the appointment the authorities drafted the terms of reference of the chief executive with considerable care: their prescience was to prove significant when these terms of reference became a critical point of attention.

There were, however, weaknesses in the terms. Hope was offered to the Lloyd's traditionalists by the last clause: 'The appointment is seen as a temporary one with a term of three to five years. Whether there is to be a successor and what his duties might be remains to be considered.' It might therefore be possible, one day, to revert to the status quo ante.

A legal difficulty was dealt with by clause 6 which began: 'The Deputy Chairman and Chief Executive will not make directions to the Market.'

This referred to the fact that under the Lloyd's Act 1982 only a chairman and deputy chairman, who must be elected from among the working members of the council, could receive delegated power from the council to give 'directions regarding the business of insurance at Lloyd's to any member of the Society'.[4] It was made clear at the time of my appointment that I could not be empowered to deal directly with market matters, a reservation which fatally weakened the post. The weakness could only be overcome by a change in the Lloyd's Act: such a change would be seen by many at Lloyd's as removing the keystone of their self-regulation. Given that legal obstacle the chief executive could only proceed by persuasion and by the fact that, through control of the staff, he would in effect command the resources of the society.

But the greatest problem was caused by the fact that there were no terms of reference laid down for the chairman and the elected deputy chairmen.[5] The potential for ambiguity was particularly dangerous in the regulatory area, where the clear and unchallenged authority of an established chief executive was needed in order to resist the pressures that were frequently brought to bear on regulatory questions from the market. Further confusion was caused by the fact that the system by which deputy chairmen are assigned departmental duties continued.[6] Managers saw themselves as having divided loyalties: to their group head and through him to the chief executive; and to the deputy chairman who monitored the department for which they were responsible.

The arrival of a chief executive should have meant a major shift in the traditional role of the chairman. He would no longer be the executive head of the corporation. The staff reported to the chief executive who had the authority to decide questions of appointment, promotion, remuneration and dismissal. Also, and importantly, it was his job to decide who does what among the staff: to settle the organizational duties and responsibilities. This was not an authority to be exercised out of hand. I made it my practice to discuss organizational matters with my three fellow chairs and to seek their advice and opinion before reaching decisions. My terms of reference gave me the power to appoint staff, but in the case of senior appointments this was subject to the approval of the council: a Senior Appointments Committee was formed, with the chairs as members.[7]

When I started at Lloyd's in February 1983, Sir Peter Green had no alternative but to back me up and support my authority. The lack of a clear demarcation between the roles of the chairman and the chief executive did not then matter. But to many of the traditional members of the committee the presence of a chief executive was a standing slight upon Lloyd's. He was a constant reminder of the shameful events of 1982 and the sooner he went the sooner the bad times would be behind them. They accepted the need for the medicine, at the time, but once it had done its work the prescription could be discontinued. This school of thought was anxious for Lloyd's to be master once more in its own house: it saw the chief executive's presence as the denial of that principle.

The election in November 1983 of Peter Miller as Chairman in succession to Sir Peter Green signalled a change. By that time confidence had been restored in Lloyd's. Business continued to flood in. The investigatory and disciplinary processes were clearly working. Relations with the press had been transformed: in the new climate of openness they were coming to accept that the old Lloyd's practice of sweeping matters under the carpet had gone for ever.

In this context recidivism emerged: the market professionals were feeling their oats again. Asked at his inaugural press conference how he saw our mutual roles Peter Miller replied: 'I am the Prime Minister, Mr Davison is the head of the Civil Service.'[8] This suggested a fundamental misunderstanding of the nature of the role of the Chief Executive of Lloyd's. A civil servant's job is to support his minister, through thick and thin, and to carry out his policy. He should advise on policy certainly, but should never allow his own views, especially his own political views, to appear. But that is not how the role of the Chief Executive of Lloyd's should be seen. He must have the independence to make value judgments about the situations that face Lloyd's, and must be free to express a view that is not coloured by self-interest. He has to be able to differ from the chairman, publicly if necessary. Above all he is the voice of the external Names and the public in the inner councils of the society.

The new chairman's inaugural statement introduced a period of steady erosion of the authority of the chief executive. Early in 1984 there were arguments about the right of the chief executive to enjoy the same status within the society as the other deputy chairmen to whom, it was made quite clear, he was junior. Emphasis was placed upon using the chief executive's expertise in the rule-making area on which it was suggested he should concentrate most of his energies. The new chairman was keen to take an active role in the two major crises then facing the society – the Revenue settlement and the PCW affair – and was anxious to exclude the chief executive from both, which would in my view have left the responsible staff in an impossible position.

Peter Miller is an extremely energetic man and this translated itself into a mood of bustle which accelerated the reform programme. But at the same time confusion over the executive role of the chairman, and conflict between that and the role of the chief executive, made my task increasingly difficult, especially in relation to staff appointments and organization.

I had never at any time seen myself in a career position as Chief Executive of Lloyd's. I was an agent of change brought in at the instance of the Bank to introduce a programme of reforms, which included reforming the structure of the society. I realized that the latter, which would involve a fundamental change in the power structure of the corporation, would take longer than my three-to-five-year span and would call for outside intervention. My successor would be critical to these developments. But the question was posed by my terms of reference: would there be a successor? I was sure that the continuation of the post, with undiminished powers, was essential if the new reforms were to stick. Meanwhile the chief executive's authority vis-à-vis the staff was being eaten away by confusion over two centres of power.

By June 1985 I had begun to consider suitable dates for my departure. According to my contract of employment the earliest possible date would be February 1986, the latest February 1988. If Mr Miller were to go at the end of 1986 I might have a duty to stay on and see in a new chairman, but if he were to stay in office in 1987 I could leave sooner rather than later. By the summer of 1985 the structure question was the most important single issue remaining on the reform agenda. The other tasks we had begun to tackle in 1983 were well on the way to completion: the major miscreants would have been disciplined by the end of 1985, the bulk of the rule book was completed and the rest of the work was well in hand. But the difficulties caused by the defective constitution remained. This was the key issue to be tackled and I decided that as I could not resolve it myself, having neither the time in office nor the necessary powers, I should use my resignation to force the issue into the open in the hope that it would thereby be resolved.

On 12 July I set out my concerns in a lengthy letter to the Bank of England. I concluded: 'First, that the system of having unwritten terms of reference for the Chairman could only work in a climate of self-restraint which we now know cannot always be guaranteed. The experiment of yoking a full-time Chairman to a full-time Chief Executive cannot work without detailed written responsibilities for both, and this must be done for my successor.

'Second, there is a profound misunderstanding between the Committee of Lloyd's and the outside world about the meaning of the phrase "Self-regulation". To most informed observers, and no doubt to most Names at Lloyd's, it means that the rules are made by those to whom they are to be applied. The application of rules, on a case by case basis, would be the duty of the staff [vide Fisher above].[9] The traditional Lloyd's man sees it differently. He has never known a written rule book, but has relied upon the precepts of the Chairs. To him self-regulation is consonant with self-government. The Chairs decide, case by case, what shall be done. This approach suffers from the lack of clear policy direction, or, at the least, from the lack of proper segregation of policy from execution. Further, those deciding are frequently parti-pris, often concerned themselves, may have a conflict of interest, and usually suffer from knowing the individuals socially. The correct answer must be to relieve the elected Chairs from any responsibility for the day to day regulation of the Market, which should be handled by the professionals, expert in the topic, dispassionate and experienced. Rule-making itself, however, should remain in the hands of the elected Council. This would produce a much more effective regime which would still be properly described as self-regulation.

'Third, given the experiences of the last two and a half years, it is necessary for me to be succeeded by a forceful public figure capable of dealing with a climate of Committee opinion that is still largely unaltered despite the experiences of the last three years. He must be a Deputy Chairman because of the status that brings here, and should be appointed for a five-year term, renewable once. He must be independent and must, therefore, come from outside the Society. His appointment must be publicly endorsed by the Bank. And, if self-regulation is to work, he must be supported by a powerful staff of senior colleagues who apply the rules.'

At the council meeting on 11 November 1985 the new office holders for 1986 were confirmed. The recently developing pattern of governing the society was thus set for the near term. At the end of the meeting, having told the chairman beforehand of my decision, I read out my letter of resignation.

Two matters made me choose the council meeting on 11 November 1985 to submit my resignation: the Berrill Inquiry and the Financial Services Bill.

At the end of the council meeting on 9 September 1985 Sir Kenneth Berrill intervened with criticisms about the administration of the society's affairs. The meeting had started with a discussion of the reasons for an error in the global accounts which had emerged at the last moment.[10] The chairman seized eagerly upon Sir Kenneth's intervention to propose a committee of inquiry into the administration. I took it as a reflection upon my position that such an inquiry should have been launched without any advance notice to me.

I welcomed the fact of the inquiry insofar as it addressed the structure question – the relative roles of the elected chairs and the chief executive.

157

But it also considered the organizational structure of the staff reporting to me. The process of developing evidence on that point would, as the chairman insisted despite my objections, involve round-table discussions at O Group among the chairs and the group heads. This I found damaging to my authority with my colleagues, who saw that the chairman now intended to take a direct hand in the assignment of responsibilities. The staff saw this as a return to the old ways: I saw it as a fundamental threat to the authority of the chief executive, who must be responsible for the corporation carrying out efficiently and effectively all functions required of it. To do so he must be able to organize the staff and obtain and allocate resources as needed: staff must report and be accountable to him. Ambiguity in reporting could lead to conflict and the undermining of authority. It would also be difficult to retain high-quality senior staff if the chief executive's authority were diminished. I felt that my usefulness and effectiveness had been substantially reduced by the diminution of my authority in the eyes of the staff: a diminution which would make the achievement of changes in staff attitudes that much more difficult.

The report of the Berrill Inquiry was published in March 1986, by which time I had left Lloyd's. Pointing out that 'the appointment of a Chief Executive clearly had major implications for the relationships between the senior Corporation staff and the elected chairs'[11] the report went on to say: 'Our main and basic conclusion on the structure of the Corporation of Lloyd's is that the organisational changes instituted in 1983 have still to be implemented effectively.'[12] It continued: 'The work of the elected chairs has not changed to the extent it should.... The pre-1983 practice of staff relating to a particular deputy chairman and expecting him to take most executive decisions fails to recognise the change brought about by the establishment of a chief executive and a number of high-quality group heads.'[13]

The central conclusion of the Berrill Inquiry was the confusion of roles. ' "O" Group in its submission to the working party, accepted that under the present working arrangements there is at least a potential source of difficulty in that the Chairman and Chief Executive can be viewed as "two centres of power".... This is indeed the central issue as Mr Davison's letter demonstrated.[14] Until 1982 the role of Chief Executive was undertaken by the Chairman (assisted by the Deputy Chairmen). The appointment of a Chief Executive should have meant a complete change from that system. ... Lloyd's is unusual among City institutions in having a full-time Chairman, a full-time Chief Executive, and two Deputy Chairmen who devote the bulk of their working time to their office.... We believe that in this situation there is a danger that the elected Chairs will remain involved in matters which should be left to the permanent staff.'[15] Regrettably, the report did not carry the argument to its logical conclusion, contained in my letter to the Bank of England in July: 'The correct answer must be to relieve the elected chairs from any responsibility for the day to day regulation of the market, which should be handled by the professionals, expert in the topic, dispassionate and experienced.'

The Berrill Inquiry was useful. But I objected most strongly to the fashion in which the collective evidence of O Group was developed. In my letter of resignation submitted to the council at its meeting on 11 November 1985, I said: 'My conclusion that now is the time to resign is prompted by the Council's recent initiation of an internal inquiry into the structure of Lloyd's, which has started discussions about changing the Terms of Reference and status of the post of Chief Executive. The preparation of the Corporation's evidence for this inquiry has revealed divergent opinions about the continuing need for the Chief Executive to be independent and responsible directly to the Council.

'My own views on the paramount necessity of an independent Chief Executive, with appropriate terms of reference, responsible directly to the Council, have not changed and, therefore, I would find it impossible to continue in office were those terms to be significantly altered. At the same time, the argument is a perfectly proper one for a self-regulatory body and, by resigning at this time, I remove an obstacle to the Council's freedom of discussion and to my freedom to argue for the retention of the position of Chief Executive with independent powers without any suggestion of self-interest.'

The second factor affecting the timing was just as compelling. The Financial Services Bill reforming the regulation of financial institutions in the City was about to be published. Lloyd's might or might not be within its proposals. But, in or out, Lloyd's would be a lively topic at Westminster, because the announcement of heavy losses in the PCW non-marine syndicates in summer 1985 had produced a spate of letters to MPs from aggrieved members of the syndicates. This had been exacerbated by discussions and concern about baby syndicates, the pervasiveness of which had become apparent when the 1984 accounts of syndicates had been published at the beginning of August 1985. Had I continued as chief executive it would have been impossible for me to speak out on the issue of fundamental importance – the defective constitution of the society. I was in any case intending to leave. It would be better to have the matter done with before parliamentary debate started rather than to resign during the debates and, perhaps, be accused of trying to influence the result or, at the least, of embarrassing the Government.

My resignation, the PCW losses and baby syndicates all contributed to parliamentary concerns about Lloyd's. There was widespread pressure to bring Lloyd's within the scope of the new Financial Services Bill. The Tory back benches were placated by the launching of an inquiry into self-regulation at Lloyd's to be chaired by Sir Patrick Neill. It would address the question whether or not Names at Lloyd's enjoyed protection analogous to that afforded to investors under the Financial Services Bill.

In concluding this chapter about my resignation it may be helpful to recall the words I used in a speech to the Tory Back Bench Finance Committee at the House of Commons just after my resignation. I said then that when I was appointed, with the backing of the Governor of the Bank of England and the approval of the then Secretary of State for Trade and Industry, my contract made it clear that I was appointed by the Council of Lloyd's and that I was to be accountable to the council for the organization and management of the corporation staff. These principles were vital for the continued success and acceptability of self-regulation – and particularly, the staff and management responsibility. First, the Chairmanship of Lloyd's is a temporary position and office holders have varying characters and interests. The chief executive must have the necessary security and independence from today's incumbent to maintain a proper course until the arrival of tomorrow's.

Second, the chief executive has a particular duty to represent among his fellow office holders the interests of the external members of the society and the public at large. He must be able to report on a contentious issue to the whole council – directly to, amongst others, the external and nominated members. This power may never need to be used, but it is an essential part of the chief executive's armoury if the system of self-regulation and the Lloyd's Act are to be seen by the Names and the outside world to be secure.

More important is the chief executive's sole responsibility to the council for the appointment, organization and direction of the staff. Much of the regulatory work of the corporation staff involves the exercise of judgment over activities, actual or proposed, of members of the market who are enterprising businessmen. Someone, and it has to be the corporation staff, must supply a wider vigilance. That needs a degree of self-confidence in the relevant staff members, self-confidence which can only be given by a position deliberately insulated from any pressures brought by members of the market. If a chairman of the future were able to give orders to individual members of the staff, or, even more seriously to be in a position to affect their postings and future careers, or, most seriously of all, to reorganize the structure of the staff – all things which a succeeding chairman might reorder differently in a short space of time – the staff would be unable to exercise the essential regulatory vigilance.

To argue that there is an analogy between the structure of Lloyd's and that of the Civil Service, as I have said, is quite wrong. Civil servants are the servants of the Government. The staff of Lloyd's are not the servants of the elected chairman of the day, nor indeed of the committee, but of the Council of Lloyd's representing the three constituencies of working, external and nominated members. It is also false to argue that Lloyd's is like a large corporation with a chairman and a chief executive. Constitutionally Lloyd's is a more complex animal, and John Locke's analysis of the separation of powers – legislative, judicial and executive – is more apt.[16] Lloyd's is unique, and requires a unique solution. Given the possibilities of regression which must exist, I believe that a separation of powers, rather than some kind of constitutional subordination, is the only secure guarantee which members of Lloyd's, and the wider public, can have that recidivism can never be a danger.

Given these firm convictions, I was naturally perturbed to find developing at Lloyd's a clear alternative view and an inclination so to change the position of the chief executive that independence from the chairman, in the particular respects that I have described, would be largely eliminated. The development of evidence for the Berrill Committee showed the range of different ideas that by then existed within Lloyd's about the future role of the chief executive. I must emphasize that those who wanted to change the role of the chief executive did not do so for any sinister or improper reason. They did not, however, realize the implications of the constitutional position. My purpose in giving notice as I did was to ensure that full consideration was given to a question which I believed to be vital for the future of the society, and which deeply concerns all the members of it, as well as all external authorities with an interest in its continued success.

PART IV

THE FUTURE OF
SELF-REGULATION
AT LLOYD'S

XVII

Unfinished Rule-making

By the end of 1984 the four main foundations of Lloyd's new rule book were in place. Bye-laws covered disciplinary matters, the re-registration of agents, syndicate accounting and auditing, and membership rules. During 1985 and 1986 the structure was elaborated with a number of measures designed to cope with inadequacies revealed by the scandals: binding authorities and bans on related party reinsurance and preferred underwriting. By the summer of 1986 there remained one major area for regulation, and a number of less important ones.

The major area was the regulation of Lloyd's brokers. The 1982 Act gave formal statutory recognition for the first time to Lloyd's brokers[1] and Schedule II of the Act invites the Council of Lloyd's to regulate their admission and continuing right to broke business in the Room. The brokers are the marketing arm of Lloyd's. They develop new policies and forms of insurance as well as meeting the existing needs of their customers: companies or individuals, for insurance; and underwriters for reinsurance. These functions are performed by all insurance intermediaries – Lloyd's brokers, non-Lloyd's brokers or unregistered insurance consultants. Only brokers at Lloyd's have the additional duties of preparing policy documents, handling claims, and providing financial and accounting services for underwriters in conjunction with the LPSO. In Fisher's eyes, the existence of these duties justified the maintenance of a restricted class of Lloyd's brokers.[2] The right to belong to this restrictive class, and to carry on the company's letterhead the subscript 'and at Lloyd's', has come to acquire a considerable value in terms of commercial goodwill.

As with other parts of the Lloyd's market brokers have traditionally been regulated by means of contractual undertakings between each Lloyd's broker and the Society of Lloyd's. As these are obtained on admission, changes in the rules cannot be applied retrospectively. Current undertakings require brokers to meet minimum standards of solvency and financial standing, to provide audited accounts to Lloyd's, and to give information about their business to the corporation if asked. Applicants for admission to the register of Lloyd's brokers must show that they have a good commercial record and adequate management expertise and office facilities, and are not overly dependent on one source or type of business. The disciplinary sanction for the enforcement of these rules is provided by Bye-law 72 under the 1871 Act which empowers the committee to refuse a broker's subscription 'whenever they see fit'. This bye-law remains in force under the 1982 Act pending new legislation.

This quaint set of arrangements continues to regulate a field of business which has changed beyond all recognition over the last twenty years. Lloyd's brokers are now giants in the insurance world and the majority of their business is no longer placed in the Room. Although the number of Lloyd's brokers may have changed little since the Second World War there has been an increased concentration of business furthered by a number of recent mergers. Many have involved overseas groups, notably Americans, thus rendering a dead letter the old committee rule that not more than 20 per cent of the shares of a Lloyd's broker could be held by non-Lloyd's insurance interests.[3] Fisher noted that in 1978 two-fifths of the business at Lloyd's was placed by three broker groups and two-thirds was placed by twelve.[4] This concentration has not yet proved sufficiently significant to attract the attentions of the Office of Fair Trading, but a greater concentration might do so.

Early in the 1970s the broking community discovered that the benefits of holding premiums and claims money, in terms of the interest earned on such funds before they are passed on to the underwriter or assured, could provide a handsome supplement to normal brokerage income. Increasingly, brokers developed skills in controlling the cash that passed through their hands, skills which bore great fruit when falling inflation in the 1980s produced positive real interest rates and a period of rising stock markets. Aggressive policies of cash management generated greatly increased broker earnings; but they also generated friction with under-writers who saw their own earnings eroded by the late settlement of premium payments; and their reputation as underwriters damaged as assureds complained about the late settlement of claims.

These tensions were augmented by the unforeseen advent of divestment. While the underwriter was an employee of the broker he could not complain about his cash flow as vigorously as he could when he found himself independent. Complaints about late settlement of claims and cases of delayed preparation of insurance documents increased. While Lloyd's brokers remain an integral and essential part of the Lloyd's market there is no doubt that they feel further from the underwriters than in pre-divestment days: even more do newly divested underwriters feel independent of their former broker parents.

In this context there has been talk among underwriters of increasing direct business. Not all business is brought into Lloyd's by Lloyd's brokers. The Lloyd's Act allows for '... a Lloyd's broker or such other persons as the Council may from time to time by bye-law permit'.[5] Bye-law 12 of January 1983[6] applies this proviso to the motor market where underwriters deal directly with high-street brokers: policies are issued by the underwriters' own organizations, which also handle claims. Lloyd's brokers are still included in the chain: as guarantors of the credit of the retail brokers; but they do not have an active business role. Some motor underwriters argue that the guarantee by the Lloyd's broker is unnecessary and could readily, and more cheaply, be replaced by credit insurance.

Aware of the dwindling share of the total business of the large Lloyd's brokers that now comes to them, underwriters are arguing the case for relaxing the direct dealing rules further so that such covers as yachts, livestock and householders' comprehensive insurance could be handled without going through a Lloyd's broker. Although many Lloyd's brokers object to such developments for the obvious reason that it erodes their commercial advantages, the retail business in which underwriters are interested is not the sort that brings a large broker much profit.

The Insurance Brokers' Registration Act 1977 brought in statutory regulation of insurance brokers by restricting the use of the title 'Insurance Broker' to those registered with the Insurance Brokers' Registration Council (IBRC). It is designed to protect the public when dealing with insurance intermediaries, and registered brokers must meet standards of solvency and show that they are 'fit and proper persons'. They must comply with a statutory code of conduct the essence of which is that they must display the utmost good faith in their dealings, they must always act in the interests of their clients, and they must never mislead or exaggerate.[7] Lloyd's brokers were automatically admitted to the new register on the footing that they already complied with standards required by Lloyd's that were at least as rigorous as those laid down by the new Act. Lloyd's brokers are therefore regulated both by Lloyd's, through contractual undertakings, and by the Insurance Brokers' Registration Council in which they play a significant role: the Chairman of the IBRC is a senior Lloyd's broker.[8]

Following the passage of the Insurance Brokers' Registration Act the Committee of Lloyd's set up a working party to review all pre-admission requirements and post-admission conditions for Lloyd's brokers.[9] This recommended measures, endorsed in the report of the Fisher Committee,[10] to regulate brokers by bye-law which would subject all brokers to the same rules. These would cover the admission of brokers, when the Council of Lloyd's should have regard to the suitability, standing and general market expertise of the applicant for whom minimum standards of capital, solvency, staff, facilities and range and scope of business would be required. Controllers, directors and senior employees of brokers would have to show that they were 'fit and proper persons'. All Lloyd's brokers would have to re-register.

Lloyd's brokers have traditionally handled claims on behalf of under-writers. In doing so they place themselves in a position of conflict with their duties to their customers. In two High Court decisions in 1969 and 1970 it was held that it was in law inconsistent with a broker's duty to the assured for the broker to act as agent for Lloyd's underwriters without the consent of the assured.[11] Because, except for reinsurance business, this consent is not easy to obtain, Fisher recommended that Lloyd's should discourage reliance by underwriters on the services of brokers in settling claims. It is not clear what real effect this recommendation, which is well known in the Lloyd's broking community, has had on claims settlement practices.[12]

Fisher also considered the position of insurance creditors when the broker becomes insolvent. He urged the council to develop a scheme which would achieve 'trust' status for all monies held by Lloyd's brokers in their IBAS[13] so that in the event of insolvency this money would be available only to insurance creditors.[14]

From this background the regulatory requirements were clear. Our objectives in regulating Lloyd's brokers would be three: to discharge our duty under the Act to regulate Lloyd's brokers; to raise the standards of brokers; and at the same time to widen the source of Lloyd's revenues by allowing for the admission of new brokers and for the approval of direct dealing arrangements for classes of business where the full rigour of the standards applicable to Lloyd's brokers was not required. There would be three parts to the regulatory framework: rules covering accounting and financial requirements, including if possible preferred creditor status for insurance funds; rules covering experience and competence, including the character and suitability of controllers, directors and senior employees; and a code of conduct for brokers at Lloyd's extending the IBRC Code to matters particular to Lloyd's, that is to dealings between brokers and underwriters including completion of the slip, documentation, claims settlement, cash flow, disclosure of fees, binding authorities, etc. The principal purpose of the code would be to define 'discreditable conduct' in broking at Lloyd's.[15]

However, these plans remain in draft. No consultative document has yet been issued and no bye-laws passed. Why is this?

There are three principal reasons. The first is that there has been more urgent business. The crux of the problems at Lloyd's lay in relations between Names and agents: most of the urgent reforms were addressed to this matter. Such was the pressure for action, compounded by the fact that re-registration of agents arising out of divestment had to be achieved by July 1987, that brokers had to wait. Secondly, there are no major problems with the present arrangements. Only two aspects of broking conduct have caused offence: binding authorities, which had been separately dealt with;[16] and umbrella brokers to which I shall turn next. Under these circumstances there was a case for putting the regulation of brokers on one side.

There was a third and more subtle reason for delay. The broker scene was changing. The Americans had arrived: Marsh McLellan, Alexander & Alexander and others acquired Lloyd's brokers. Divestment was tearing apart the old fabric of agency/broker relationships. Had we legislated over-hastily we would have been in danger of setting in stone a framework that was becoming out of date. Self-regulatory legislation should always follow commercial relationships and never precede them. We had to wait for the new post-divestment pattern of commercial relationships to emerge.

The Multigarantee case about extended product warranty insurance, had brought to light two major lacunae in the Lloyd's regulatory set-up. Confusion had arisen about who precisely was insuring the warranty risk: customers were led to believe it was Lloyd's, while Lloyd's underwriters believed they were insuring the guarantee company. A working party chaired by Sir Kenneth Clucas, formerly Permanent Secretary at the Department of Trade, reported to the Council of Lloyd's in November 1985. It recommended that it should be the purchaser and not the manufacturer/retailer who is the insured, i.e. individual certificates of insurance must be issued off binding authorities.[17] It recommended a code of practice for extended warranty business to be introduced by the Council of Lloyd's.

The second problem was more widespread; the offending brokers in the Multigarantee case had not been Lloyd's brokers at all: they had been operating in the Room under the umbrella of a Lloyd's broker who had allowed them to use his name but had taken little interest in their work. The practice of umbrella broking, which gave access to Lloyd's for non-

Lloyd's brokers, was investigated by a working party who reported that there were at least one hundred and twenty-five umbrella arrangements, which increased the numbers of broking companies working at Lloyd's by 50 per cent and produced about 5 per cent of the total premium income. The practice was unregulated and had led to abuse: underwriters had been gulled by unethical and unscrupulous brokers. The practice had originated when former employees of a Lloyd's broker wished to set up in business pending their application to become a Lloyd's broker, or a non-Lloyd's broker wanted to save brokerage commission on a piece of business, or a Lloyd's broker wanted access to the specialized skills of a particular non-Lloyd's broker. The working party recommended that such arrangements be restricted to a broker who intended to apply to be a Lloyd's broker within three years. Meanwhile the sponsoring Lloyd's broker whose name was used should take full responsibility for all the business of the umbrella broker. These proposals, having been put out for consultation in May 1984, are waiting for the formulation of a general set of rules for brokers into which they will fit.[18]

Besides the major problems of brokers, five lesser matters are still waiting for legislative attention by the Council of Lloyd's – excluding the long list of matters proposed by Neill.

The first is the disciplinary rules described in detail in Chapter VIII. The package of disciplinary bye-laws was passed in January 1983. It was put to immediate use and has on the whole proved effective, as the disciplinary statistics show. It has weaknesses: proceedings are very legalistic, the criminal standard of proof is a heavy burden for a self-regulatory society to carry, and defendants are given considerable scope to delay proceedings. On the other hand it has been supported in the courts and complimented publicly by Lord Wilberforce in the House of Lords.[19]

Two steps could be taken to simplify and accelerate disciplinary proceedings. The first would be to limit the use of the council. After the imposition of a penalty by a disciplinary committee, and an appeal, if there is one, every case comes before a specially convened meeting of the full council.[20] The council can confirm, modify or waive the sentence and decides about publication: its policy is always to publish the report of the disciplinary and appeal proceedings. This stage takes time, brings about delays and increases legal costs. It could be abolished without any loss of natural justice: the defendant has already had the right of appeal to a tribunal presided over by an ex-judge or senior lawyer from outside the Lloyd's community and any miscarriage of justice at this stage could be remedied by the High Court. If not abolished the council stage could at least be restricted to cases where the defendant wishes to exercise his right to be heard by the full council; it should not be compulsory.

A second step would be to develop a form of summary jurisdiction offering quicker and cheaper justice for minor misdemeanours. To provide an alternative system offering lesser penalties would make it too easy for the Investigations Committee to choose a soft option when the circumstances of the case may not justify it. The introduction of fixed penalties into bye-laws should achieve the aim of quicker and cheaper justice without that defect. At present the defendant has no means of knowing how seriously a disciplinary committee will view his offence. He therefore fears the worst and mounts a full and often over-elaborate defence. If he knew that the worst penalty he could face would be a reprimand, censure or limited fine, he might well be willing to approach his defence more simply, saving his time and that of Lloyd's.

The Fisher Report looked at the information available to prospective Names. 'Many of the Names who submitted evidence to us complained about the limited evidence which was available to a prospective Name to enable him to decide which agency to join and to compare the results of different syndicates so that he can make a rational choice.'[21] During the passage of the Lloyd's Bill, Lloyd's gave an undertaking to Parliament that the Fisher recommendations about this would be legislated within two years of the passage of the Act, that is by July 1984.[22] This was not done.

Fisher recommended that there should be a bye-law laying down mandatory requirements for disclosure to prospective Names; that there should be a council brochure for applicants; that there should be a register, available to serious applicants, of the terms and conditions of business offered by each agent; that audited syndicate accounts for the last seven years should be made available; that agents should disclose their other business interests; and that the same information should be shown to all prospective Names.[23]

The Fisher recommendations focus on two matters: information about syndicate results, and information about agents. Since the syndicate accounting bye-law and the introduction of the public register of accounts, analyses of syndicate results are produced in tabular form by a number of organizations, including Chatset and the Association of Lloyd's Members. Any prospective Name therefore can obtain most of the information he might need about syndicate results, and about the related party interests of his prospective agent.

None the less Neill concentrates attention on these matters.[24] Lloyd's produced a new and greatly improved membership brochure while the inquiry was in progress.[25] Neill states, 'Our overall impression is that the proposed content is much more suited to its purpose than the existing one.... There are clear references to the existence of comparative syndicate results, resignation procedures and stop loss insurance, and applicants are advised to consider visiting more than one members' agent.'

But more needs to be done: an explanation of the advantages and disadvantages of joining one type of agent rather than another; publishing details of agents' charges, the absence of which occasioned so much criticism of Lloyd's;[26] and the publication of comparisons of the relative performance of members' agents. On the last point Neill suggests that members' agents should submit to Lloyd's for entry in a central register an analysis of their aggregate underwriting on a standardized basis. This information would then be used by the organizations that currently publish league tables of syndicate results. These steps represent a significant loosening of the anti-competitive practices at Lloyd's. So far has this gone that the Association of Lloyd's Members, once the pariah of the Committee of Lloyd's, is to be consulted on further editions of the membership brochure.

There is also unfinished business on preferred underwriting, discussed in Chapter XIV. The allocation of Names to syndicates must, if the underwriter is popular and the syndicate profitable, involve some element of discrimination. The underwriter may favour a certain type of Name: a wealthy man, or one with a taste for high risks, or one who is not likely to worry him, or a broker who brings him lots of business. The opportunities of exercising preference are manifold; some preferences may be fair, others may be prejudicial to the agent's other Names. The underwriter should be required to publish his criteria for selecting the risks that he prefers to write and the type of Name that he will accept. If more Names apply than there is room for the new members of the syndicate should be chosen by a ballot. There are parallels in issuing shares in companies: they provide appropriate guidance for Lloyd's. Certainly it is wrong for insiders, such as fellow underwriters or brokers, to obtain favourable syndicate memberships at the expense of external Names.[27]

For many years Names have been able to buy personal stop loss policies which insure them against an overall underwriting loss.[28] Such policies usually have a minimal loss to be borne by the Name, £10,000 or £20,000, and an upward limit, £100,000 or £200,000, above which the Name is still liable. They appealed originally to the faint-hearted and some agents had a policy of discouraging their Names from taking out such policies, arguing – as did the PCW agencies – that the syndicate's reinsurance programmes provided all the protection a Name could want. Whereas five years ago perhaps 10 per cent of the Names took out such policies, recent events at Lloyd's, most notably the PCW losses, have greatly increased the popularity of stop loss policies to the point where about 50 per cent of members have them. The practice should be examined. Two regulatory issues arise here: Names have in a few cases been misled into believing that they had adequate stop loss cover when they did not; and the practice of reinsuring stop loss within Lloyd's means that the same security is being used twice over to back the same risk. These problems must be dealt with by regulatory measures to lay down wordings of stop loss policies, because in this instance the buyer and the seller are not on an equal footing; and to resolve the security conundrum, perhaps by requiring such insurances to be placed outside Lloyd's.

With the major exception of regulations for brokers the Lloyd's rule book as originally proposed by Fisher is now largely written. However the recommendations of the Neill Inquiry, which total seventy, will require a considerable further effort of rule-making, given the great pressure to which Lloyd's is now subject.

Lloyd's must also consider how to apply its new bye-laws. Monitoring of compliance is not a new matter for the corporation: the LPSO ensures that policies do not break the rules; the deposits department ensures that deposits are in order; and the annual solvency test requires a complete check of syndicate reserves against members' assets. But the new framework at Lloyd's will require much more monitoring. Agents, brokers and panel auditors must be re-registered regularly, so that standards are maintained. Four-yearly or more frequent certification of means will require a considerable effort with a membership of over thirty-two thousand. The newly filed syndicate accounts must be reviewed for compliance with the bye-law. Binders, multiple syndicates, direct motor business, underwriting agency agreements, and premium income limits all require continuous attention. There is no point in the new rule book unless resources are put into ensuring that it is applied even-handedly and rigorously across the market.

The Review Powers Bye-Law, No. 5 of 1986, was passed by the Council of Lloyd's on 13 October 1986 to give effect to the monitoring function. It gives an authorized person power to review the affairs of any broker or underwriter. It is significant that this power is vested not in the elected chairs, who are themselves invariably brokers or agents or both, but in the independent office of the chief executive.[29] This is a major step towards the impartial independent and professional regulation of the market advocated in Chapter XV.

XVIII

PCW and the Names

Anyone who has read as far as this will realize that the reform of Lloyd's is not complete. One of the purposes of this book is to permit the author, freed from the ties of office at Lloyd's, to present his own ideas for the further reform of the market born of his experiences there. The proposals fall under four headings: relations between Lloyd's and its Names, relations with Parliament, with worldwide insurance markets, and finally the question of who works in and around the Room.

The history of the PCW affair involves all the principal issues which affect Names on troubled syndicates.[1] The origins of the problem lay in quota share reinsurance arrangements which placed syndicate funds offshore – in Guernsey, the Isle of Man, Gibraltar and Geneva – where they escaped UK taxation and were used in part to line the pockets of the principal directors of the agency. In addition, baby syndicates were operated with the avowed purpose of providing additional remuneration for the agency's directors and underwriters. These actions involved dishonesty and serious breaches of the civil law of agency, including the taking of secret profits, failure to handle conflicts of interest properly, and inadequate accounting by the agents to their principals, the Names. The Syndicate Accounting Bye-law[2] requires proper syndicate accounts to be prepared incorporating disclosures of related party interests; it requires the accounts to be audited to full professional standards, and it calls for the accounts to be placed on public record. These measures go a long way to prevent the recurrence of such iniquities and provide better protection for Names.

After the PCW agency finally ceased trading in July 1985 Lloyd's appointed a fact-finding inquiry under John Davis[3] to review the management of the PCW syndicates from December 1982 to July 1985 – the period when the agency was under the chairmanship of Richard Beckett.[4]

The Davis Report was published in July 1986: it found no evidence of fraud or gross negligence by the management of the agency during the period of Richard Beckett's chairmanship.[5] Peter Dixon voluntarily suspended himself from Lloyd's on 1 November 1982. Thereafter the agency's parent company, Minet Holdings PLC, chaired by Ray Pettit after John Wallrock's enforced resignation on 21 November 1982, took steps to run the agency directly until Richard Beckett was appointed as Chairman of PCW on 6 December 1982. After Dixon's suspension investigations were started by Lloyd's, the DTI and Minet's, who commissioned Neville Russell & Co, chartered accountants and members of the Lloyd's audit panel, to prepare a report.

PCW, a large managing agency, operated a stable of syndicates – covering marine, non-marine, and aviation. There were underwriting problems, especially with the non-marine syndicates. The account was unusually dominated by long-tail classes of business, particularly general liability business emanating from the USA.[6] This type of business was giving continuing problems for the market as a whole: the 1983 results showed that although general casualty business contributed only 12 per cent of Lloyd's premium income it accounted for all the market's losses in that year.[7]

The problem was made worse by the fact that PCW operated a group reinsurance programme covering syndicates with different constitutions. As Davis explained, 'The syndicates which submitted claims earlier would "burn up" the retentions so that later claims for different syndicates could be reimbursed in full. If some underwriters deliberately held back claims their syndicates would benefit because they could make full recoveries from the programme.'[8] In practice reinsurance recoveries had been on a 'needs basis', which had helped the non-marine syndicates. Later the recoveries were reassigned on a basis proportional to the premiums paid, disadvantaging the non-marine syndicates which had no other significant reinsurance protection.

The early efforts of the new agency management were directed to chasing the funds moved improperly overseas. Substantial recoveries were made from Gibraltar in particular, and these were supplemented by contributions from the brokers who had helped to make the original reinsurance arrangements: Howden's and Minet's. In all about forty million pounds were recovered in this way. It was only just in time. The losses on the syndicates were mounting. As Ray Pettit said, 'To our horror, the underwriting losses were really beginning to emerge as a very serious issue. To be looking into the jaws of death and knowing ... that a big figure was going to be announced to the Names at the end of April, and that on top of what was missing, we could not get the money released in Gibraltar: all hell was going to break loose!'⁹ An offer of repayment was made to the Names on 21 June 1984. The recoveries made by individual Names under the offer were dependent mainly on the accuracy of the underwriter's reserving. In total however the sum offered equalled the losses announced in 1984. The Davis Report assures us that this was a coincidence.

In deciding whether or not to accept the PCW offer Names were under considerable pressure: if they refused the offer they would have to put up funds to meet their reported underwriting losses or else cease underwriting and forego the possibility of future profits with which to recoup their losses; if they accepted the offer they would have to sign away their rights to any further recoveries from those responsible until Howden's or Minet's had recovered the £13 million they had contributed to the settlement. Further pressure was provided by the approach of the Lloyd's solvency deadline, deferred to mid-July and, later, to 5 August. This was seen by many Names as an attempt by Lloyd's to persuade them to accept the offer. There was mistrust by some Names both of the agency which, although independently managed, was owned by Minet's; and of the second floor at Lloyd's because of the influence of agents and those involved with the syndicates before 1982 on the Committee of Lloyd's. Many of the Names came to the PCW syndicates through members' agents who were liable at law to their Names for any misdemeanours committed by their sub-agent, PCW. Agents in such a position were faced with a difficult conflict of interest in which their errors and omissions insurers might require them to protect their own position even if it meant being less helpful to their Names than they would otherwise wish.¹⁰

The outcome was that the offer was accepted and the solvency test completed. In April 1985 it came to light that the non-marine syndicates were showing an even worse position. A new underwriter, Ralph Bailey, took a different and much more rigorous view of the probable outcome of the non-marine business and used a statistical forecasting approach to reserving instead of the method used by his predecessor which involved adding a 'loading' to notified claims. But the significant deterioriation largely resulted from entirely new claims. The Davis Report quotes the underwriter, Ron Pateman: '1984 brought forward in the non-marine market a major deterioration in known outstanding claims and also a lot of new outstanding claims going back many, many years. They were mostly to do with product liabilities. Certainly some of the asbestosis reserves went up. But the main thing was product liabilities and medical malpractice.'¹¹

The effect was to produce losses on the non-marine syndicates far larger than the previous year's but the impact on the Names was moderated by the use of discounting. Where claims are likely to be deferred discounting can be considered. In the PCW case losses arose because of the need to reserve against expected future claims. The business of the syndicate being long-tail, many of the claims would not settle for years. Meanwhile, the money in the premiums trust fund would earn interest. It was argued that the expected settlement value of claims could be discounted by a suitable rate of interest to recognize the earnings that would accrue on the funds pending settlement. If solvency means, as the lawyers define it, 'meeting your debts as they fall due', then it is correct to say that what is required is to show that you will be in a position to meet your debts in the future even though you may not have the funds now.

This argument prevailed at the time because there were no Lloyd's rules about it. Since then guidance has been issued which precludes discounting for solvency purposes[12] because, firstly, of the difficulty of estimating the timing of payments of liabilities and of estimating the correct future rate of interest, secondly, of the difficulty in segregating the funds to ensure that the earnings on those funds can not be diverted to other purposes, and thirdly, because discounting would have the effect of increasing profits, and taxes, on the profitable syndicates. The Revenue could not be expected to accept that discounting should apply only to loss-making syndicates. Instead of discounting, an underwriter who wishes to take a view on a claim the settlement of which is a long way off can take out a 'time and distance' reinsurance policy which has the similar effect of paying out a smaller sum now against the receipt of a larger sum later, but which also has the advantage that the appropriate rate of interest is determined in the open market by an arm's length transaction between the broker acting for the reinsured and the reinsuring underwriter.

The facts, therefore, were these: The non-marine syndicates had a high concentration of long-tail American product liability business the exposure on which had been aggravated by a policy of writing a 100 per cent line on the slip, thus losing the advantage of second, third or fourth opinions on the risk from following underwriters. This business was showing mounting claims losses, and thanks to the group reinsurance programme whose benefits had been reallocated away from the non-marine syndicates, the losses were largely unreinsured. During 1985 the losses had been made worse by a markedly more conservative reserving policy, although this had been mitigated somewhat by discounting the claims provision. The overall effect on the Names concerned was horrendous. Some two hundred Names faced losses of over a hundred thousand pounds each; for the first time many at Lloyd's realized what unlimited liability really meant.

I had many conversations with PCW Names at that time. All accepted that they had a liability and that they knew it was unlimited. The direct Names had a number of particular grievances: Cameron-Webb had a policy of advising his Names to concentrate their underwriting on his own agency's syndicates so they lacked any chance of covering their losses with profits elsewhere; he had strongly discouraged his Names from taking out stop-loss policies and when they did the cover provided was inadequate; many Names suspected that the new losses had arisen through fraud – certainly the lack of adequate reinsurance was suspect; Lloyd's itself had been less than helpful, as they saw it, with the solvency deadline and they were not sure that Lloyd's was on their side rather than that of the members' agents or brokers concerned; and they were extremely suspicious of the fact that the losses had emerged so late and seemed to some extent to be attributable to a different method of reserving rather than to a deteriorating experience of claims. The Names in question faced losses of up to five times the premium income they had written on the syndicates. Not surprisingly, in view of the uncertainty, they refused to pay, and a large number of them were suspended in August and September 1985.[13]

At this stage Minet's announced that they were pulling out of the agency business, and Lloyd's was invited, under its bye-law powers, to appoint a substitute agent. A company was formed – Additional Underwriting Agencies No. 3 Limited or AUA 3 – in which Lloyd's owned the shares but for whose actions it took no management responsibility. Sir Ian Morrow[14] agreed to chair an independent board. He insisted that AUA 3 must be free to pursue the interests of the Names, even against the Society of Lloyd's itself. Lloyd's would have to provide the finance, some of which could be recovered from Minet's, who were saving themselves overhead costs by ceasing to back the defunct Richard Beckett Agency.

A process of negotiation then started which was accompanied by even higher reported losses in 1986. It has not been concluded at the time of writing. Speaking at a general meeting of members on 26 June 1985, just after the vast losses had become known, Peter Miller referred to his speech the preceding year and said: 'I made it clear then that the hard fact remains that the incompetent or even wrongdoing agent is still the agent of the Name.' Going on to describe the help provided by Lloyd's to Names on damaged syndicates he concluded: 'The one thing the Council cannot do is to provide some sort of so-called financial lifeboat and thus depart from the principle that we each individually have to respond for our share of losses if, unhappily, they occur.' His speech at the November general meeting had a more emollient tone: 'In summary, the Council is determined that the Names on these syndicates should receive justice; in particular the Names' interests and rights against any third parties will be vigorously pursued without cost to the Names. Clearly one hopes that reasonable solutions can be found. I and the Council will, of course, be using our best endeavours to bring this about.' By the June 1986 meeting the message was clear: 'It must be that Names respond to losses justly and properly established, however they may have arisen. At the same time, it must be the wish of us all to see a fair and early settlement of this matter. The alternative could be five or more years of litigation here and perhaps in the United States, which would be expensive, of no assistance to our good name, and might well cast doubt on our ability to deal with our own problems within the framework of the Society.'

It therefore seems likely that the PCW affair will be resolved by a market-wide solution. This was done in 1979 for the Sasse syndicates, referred to in Chapter V. It was also done in 1923 in the Harrison case where the underwriter got out of his depth with credit insurance.[15] The exercise was repeated in 1954 when a fraudulent underwriter and his auditor conspired to cheat their assureds and their Names. It was decided that in the special circumstances of the case the Names should be relieved from their underwriting liability and have the value of their debts discharged for them.[16]

At intervals, when the seriousness of the case demands it, Lloyd's does not eschew a mutual solution to such a problem, despite the rule of each for his own account, not one for another. What lessons for the future of Lloyd's and its relations with its members can be drawn from the PCW saga?

The first is that Lloyd's must get away from the annual solvency test deadline. The Insurance Companies Act requires Lloyd's to furnish a certificate each year to the Secretary of State that all members have assets sufficient to meet their insurance liabilities.[17] No deadline is laid down in the Act for this and the DTI are usually very understanding when difficulties arise. An annual deadline is actually imposed by the fact that the New York State Insurance Commissioner requires, by 1 September each year, a certificate to the effect that Lloyd's has complied with current UK regulatory requirements with regard to solvency. Failure to meet this deadline would mean the suspension of Lloyd's in New York, America's leading insurance market: such a suspension would be devastating for Lloyd's American business.

This problem could be avoided if the solvency test were recast. In manufacturing industry the calculation of closing inventory for accounting purposes no longer depends upon an annual stock take. Continuous inventory-taking on a cycle basis, allied with careful record-keeping and tight internal controls and audit, ensure that the closing stock figure is available promptly and accurately. If similar thinking were applied to Lloyd's there could be a continuous audit of members' assets and deposits, with the liability figures calculated currently and audited on a continuous rotating cycle. Assuming all syndicates continue to operate on calendar-year accounts, there would still have to be a cut-off at year end, but the calculation of the annual outcome could be much quicker. The annual report to the DTI and to the New York commissioner and other regulatory authorities around the world would confirm that Lloyd's has in place a system of checking solvency continuously and that reviews and audit of the system show that it is functioning well. It would follow that regulators could reasonably rely upon the figures produced by the system.

The second lesson is that Lloyd's must have better accounting and auditing. The PCW affair highlights the importance of proper reserving. At the time of their Lloyd's inquiry the Revenue had doubts about the reinsurance to close: they felt that in too many cases the figures were subjective and unsupported. The existence of 'waiting' syndicates in the PCW agency shows that there was a considerable endowment element in the premiums trust funds of the main old-established syndicates; so that a Name had to wait, and build up his own 'dowry', before joining a profitable and well-funded syndicate. There should really be no such endowment effect: it can only arise because the underwriter sets aside more funds to meet expected claims than is justified by a strict examination of the evidence. This may be done in the name of prudence, to protect the policy holder, or to reduce the burden of tax, but it is neither true nor fair in accounting terms.

The new guidance issued in December 1985 on reinsurance to close urges the underwriter and his auditor to be careful and thorough in their calculations and checks.[18] The evidence must be set out and examined. The conclusion must be properly documented. The more openness there is in these calculations the less the chance that rogue or errant solutions will be arrived at. The more the market shares its experiences and skills through the publication of details in the syndicate accounts the better for the Names.

The third question concerns the level of help provided by Lloyd's to Names when agents get into difficulties. It has been pointed out that in the circumstances of the Brooks and Dooley and Howden cases the members' agents were in an equivocal position and could not help, and Lloyd's was unwilling to help, even by providing addresses so that a committee of Names could send a circular out to those affected.[19] In these circumstances the independent position of the deputy chairman and chief executive is especially important. The Names, knowing that the Committee of Lloyd's consists usually of agents and that the chairs are almost always agents too, presume that they cannot expect a fair hearing on the second floor. The chief executive, with his independent remit and powers, can be relied on to give that fair hearing and should take steps to facilitate, by every means in his power, the exercise by the Names of their proper rights. This would include calling a meeting of Names and acting, rather like the official receiver with an insolvent company, as interim locum tenens until the Names appoint their own committee. Meanwhile he should see that the Names are provided with legal and accounting advice, at the corporation's expense, until a committee of Names can make their own arrangements.

The Neill Report adapts and elaborates this proposal in its chapter on complaints and disputes. Neill proposes that the chief executive should operate an investigatory service for Names with a complaint against their agent. Compulsory arbitration would be available to settle money claims. The service would be supervised by a Names Interests Committee, chaired by a nominated member of the council with a majority of external and nominated members. The report also proposes the appointment of an ombudsman chosen by the nominated members of the council to investigate and make recommendations on Names' complaints against the corporation. Such an arrangement is seen as particularly appropriate in view of the statutory immunity against suit by members enjoyed by the corporation under S.14 of the Lloyd's Act.[20]

The importance of a truly independent committee or agency is seen in the cases of Brooks and Dooley and Howden's. In the first instance the committee was financed by a subscription from the Names, and in the second Alexander Syndicate Management was formed by Alexander & Alexander as an independent company owned by the broker but provided with independent finance to pursue claims independently against anyone, including its parent and paymaster. The history of PCW might have been different if the rescue agency had been chaired by a figure independent of Lloyd's, and if the agency had been independent of its parent, Minet, so that there could be no grounds for suspicions, on the Names' part, that the interests of Minet's public shareholders might be preferred to their own.

The PCW case brought calls for a fraud compensation fund to protect Names against defalcations by their agents. It was argued that the Stock Exchange Investors Protection Fund performs a similar function for investors in shares. The Central Fund at Lloyd's has a different role: it exists to ensure that every valid claim on a Lloyd's policy will be met regardless of the insolvency of any Name on that policy. It is intended to be a policy-holders' protection fund and does not exist to protect the Names: they must be declared in default and suspended from underwriting before the fund can be used to cover their liabilities. The society then has a right to sue the Name to recover any disbursements made against valid claims on his behalf.

There have been recent attempts to change this role, with the argument that the Central Fund could also be used for other purposes in the general interests of the society – as by bye-law it can.[21]

It is argued that a separate fund should be established to protect Names against the fraudulent acts of their agents. Such a proposal would surely be impractical because of the difficulties of defining fraud. Fraud is only provable in a court of law, and until the case is proven, fraud can only be alleged. None of the recent cases at Lloyd's involve fraud, strictly speaking, because none have been brought to criminal trial. The line between fraud and gross negligence is indistinct. It is not clear by any means that all the losses in the PCW cases are fraudulent. No doubt the lack of reinsurance is dubious, and the books were not well kept, but the losses appear to be related to valid contracts of insurance validly arrived at. A fraud fund would be likely to fail for the lack of a clear definition of the offence.[22]

A better solution might be to dispense with the doctrine of unlimited liability. Lloyd's has shown on several occasions that when push comes to shove it will abandon its principles and accept a mutual solution. Each case is attended by protestations of undying commitment to the principle of 'each for his own' on the part of the society and endless sleepless nights on the part of the unhappy Names. During 1985 it was clear that while PCW Names objected strongly to paying the alleged losses, they objected even more to the fact that they could not be certain where the liabilities would end. The lack of certainty is the most cruel thing.

The secret of the financing of Lloyd's is not unlimited liability: it is uncalled capital. It is worth being a Name at Lloyd's because your money works for you twice: it backs your underwriting and at the same time you have the use of the funds – not because of unlimited liability but because of the concept of uncalled capital. A security statement produced by Lloyd's identifies the members' certified means among the reserves of the society. In the statement at 31 December 1985 these amounted to £2,591 million, an important element in Lloyd's total reserves.[23] But in fact members were liable beyond this – to the very limits of their means whatever they might be.

If the liability of a member of Lloyd's were to be limited to his or her certified means it would make no difference to the figures in the financial statements. Nor would it affect the security of the Lloyd's policy in the eyes of the average American risk manager, who takes a pretty sceptical view of the financial worth of the rolling green acres behind the ladies and gentlemen of England who are members of Lloyd's. On the other hand the attitude of the Name would be transformed by the certainty that there was a limit to the financial misfortunes that could befall him.

Suppose that limit were to be breached? Members on average write on ten syndicates and, notionally and on average, put one-tenth of their means behind each syndicate of which they are a member. The number of cases in which a syndicate's losses have exceeded the certified means of its members must be very very few. It would mean losses of five times the premium income if the member had a spread across other syndicates – which could be a requirement of membership – and the other syndicates on average broke even. The cases where a Name's limit would be breached would be few, just as PCW cases have been very few. But if it happened there is a mechanism already available to resolve the problem: the Central Fund. It would not then be necessary to go through the drama and palaver and anguish for those involved.

Many Names already take steps to transfer assets in excess of their certified means out of their own names into those of their wives, children or trustees. Why should it be necessary for a Name to do this? How much simpler to cover the matter by limiting liability to certified means. How much more comforting to Names and, what may be important in the future, to new applicants.[24]

XIX

Lloyd's and the Legislators

Lloyd's has had a relationship with Parliament since first coming to public prominence during the Napoleonic Wars. In the nineteenth century this relationship had two dimensions: Lloyd's marine intelligence services were an important national resource that deserved support in the Parliament of the world's largest maritime nation; and, because Lloyd's is an important part of the network of financial activities which make up the City, a number of leading MPs, generally on the Tory side, were Names. Later, in this century, the insurance role of Lloyd's became increasingly important. Parliamentary regulation of the business of insurance was strengthened after the Vehicle and General Insurance collapse in 1971, when many motor policy holders suffered. As the direct regulation of insurance companies tightened, questions began to be asked about the unique isolation of Lloyd's. These questions were, to some extent, answered by tighter solvency returns from Lloyd's which have provided exemplary protection for the policy holder. But relations between underwriters and their backers, the Names, continued to be entirely self-administered under the Lloyd's Act 1871 and its subsequent amending statutes.

With the Sasse affair the problem of regulation became public: essentially Lloyd's had outgrown its old constitution, but there was no parliamentary pressure for reform. Early in my career at Lloyd's I tackled a leading Labour front bench MP on this point. I asserted that the difficulties were all the fault of his party who had left Lloyd's alone too long. Had they harried it over the years, as they had harried the Stock Exchange, Lloyd's would have been forced to put its house in order. He replied: 'It's quite simple. There are four reasons why we have left Lloyd's alone: first, we don't understand it; second, you don't kill the goose that lays the golden eggs; third, there are no votes for us in reforming it; and fourth, whenever things go wrong it's only the rich stealing from the rich anyway.' Although this sounds like a simplistic answer, it was politically shrewd. Lloyd's had never been in the political limelight until the 1980s.

The Fisher Report was instituted by Lloyd's, although there is no doubt that the Bank of England encouraged the inquiry. Fisher's major conclusion was the need for a new Act of Parliament, and like its 1871 predecessor this was to be a private Bill. A private Bill should not be confused with a private Member's Bill. It is brought forward by a petitioner, in this case Lloyd's, under arrangements that are based today on those provided in the 1840s for the promotion of railway companies which, because of their need for compulsory land purchase rights needed parliamentary assistance. A private Bill does not take government time, or need government intervention. A select committee of the House scrutinizes the Bill and, provided that the measure is in the public interest, will recommend the granting of appropriate statutory powers to the petitioner. The procedure is most frequently used by local authorities seeking additional powers.

Backed by the powerful and wide-ranging recommendations of Fisher the Lloyd's Bill was, by and large, given support in Parliament. Some critics were opposed to Lloyd's on principle because of the alleged arrogance of the committee.[1] But most of the debate centred on the question of the conflicts of interest, highlighted by Fisher, between brokers and broker-owned underwriting agents. The new Act imposed divestment directly on Lloyd's and did not leave it to the council to deal with by subordinate legislation, as Fisher had recommended. Parliamentary pressure to impose divorce between the syndicate management functions and the members' service functions of agents was defeated after a poll of the members of the society. There was also a fierce debate about Clause 14 which grants immunity to the Council of Lloyd's against suit by members of the society. In this field the opposition was led by those who doubted that it was right to grant Lloyd's such sweeping powers of self-government; parliamentary approval for the Lloyd's Bill was secured only after Lloyd's undertook to provide more information to and protection for Names.[2]

Events since 1982 have undoubtedly hardened parliamentary attitudes towards Lloyd's – it now seems most unlikely that the 1982 Act would be passed were it put before the House today. There are a number of reasons for this change of view. The revelations of autumn 1982 which disclosed how dishonest agents had milked their Names brought out a point that Fisher had missed: conflicts of interest between Names and their agents were a much more serious problem than those between brokers and broker-owned agents. Salt was rubbed into the wound when it became clear that some of the leading witnesses before the select committee had themselves been involved in improprieties.[3] Later revelations about the size of the PCW losses and the prevalence of baby syndicates made matters worse.

There was a common view that Parliament had been misled, whether intentionally or not. Although the offences committed at Lloyd's antedated the passage of the Act they did not become a matter of public knowledge until after the Act. Had they been known in 1980 and 1981 Parliament would undoubtedly have taken a different view. Indeed the imposition of an independent chief executive by the authorities could be viewed as an admission, by the Bank and Whitehall, that more needed to be done than was provided for under the 1982 Act. The view was taken that Lloyd's could not be counted on to implement the new Act fully and fairly without some outside intervention.

In January 1984 Professor Gower's *Review of Investor Protection* was published.[4] This review had been commissioned by the Secretary of State for Trade in 1981 to consider the statutory protection required by investors in securities. Since the Prevention of Fraud (Investments) Act 1958 there had been no major piece of legislation covering the entire field of City investment markets and a new statute was needed: Professor Gower was to provide proposals to form the basis of a Financial Services Bill. At the time Gower was appointed the scandals at Lloyd's had not emerged: he was not, therefore, directly concerned with tightening the regulation of Lloyd's which, in any case, was granted new and additional powers by the 1982 Act during the course of his inquiry. However, there can be no doubt that Gower thought that Lloyd's would be covered by the new regulatory arrangements for City markets. He said: 'I assume, too, that Lloyd's would wish to become recognised as a self-regulatory agency through which registration could be obtained by its underwriting agents who clearly undertake investment business of some magnitude in seeking and advising investors in underwriting syndicates and in managing their investment.'[5]

This passage betrays a lack of clarity about the functioning of Lloyd's. Clearly Gower sees the Name as an investor, not as a sole trader in the business of insurance which, in strict legal terms, he is. He refers to the business of the agent as managing the Name's investment in the singular. Clearly and rightly Gower felt that the Lloyd's Name was as deserving of protection as any other investor. The Financial Services Act, however, left Lloyd's out. It deals with investment activities. And investments are defined as shares, debentures, warrants, options etc. The Act lists the activities which it seeks to regulate and clearly membership of a Lloyd's syndicate is not among them.[6] Underwriting agents do, however, deal in one type of investment activity on the part of their Names. They manage the premiums trust funds. Here they are strictly limited to trustee-type investments by the Insurance Companies Act[7] and, quite reasonably in my view, the Act excludes such investment activities by managing agents from the new regulatory arrangements.[8]

Parliament was faced, therefore, with a Government Bill to create a totally new self-regulatory regime in the City, in which despite the scandals and public opprobrium that had fallen upon Lloyd's and despite Gower's assumptions, it appeared likely that it alone of the larger City markets would be excluded. Furthermore the exclusion was seen as being on legalistic rather than policy grounds. This situation generated considerable concern on the government back benches, led by a recent Secretary of State for Trade and Industry, the Rt Hon. Patrick Jenkin MP. The concern was measurably increased by my resignation on a point of principle. In response to this pressure, Sir Patrick Neill, Warden of All Souls College, Oxford and former Chairman of the Council for the Securities Industry, was appointed by the Secretary of State to inquire into the self-regulatory arrangements at Lloyd's, and the extent to which they provided protection for Names analogous to that to be provided for investors under the provisions of the new Financial Services Act. If the protection of Names were deficient reforms would be proposed.

There can be no doubt that the 1982 Act has been put to good use by the Council of Lloyd's. Measures have been introduced that transform the protection of Names. Miscreants have been dealt with thoroughly and publicly and, while many things are still to be done, the achievement has been considerable. There have been three reasons for this: the introduction of competent and energetic talent to the corporation staff led by the chief executive; the willingness of the Council of Lloyd's, presiding as they do over an extremely rich institution, to provide very considerable resources to get the job done quickly;[9] and continuous pressure from the press and the authorities.

But the constitutional arrangements of Lloyd's remained defective. Lloyd's is today a society of external investors: four out of five members have never worked in the market. Yet the constitutional power remained in the hands of working members, almost all of whose representatives on the council are agents. This power was exercised through the Committee of Lloyd's, made up of the sixteen working members of the council, and the executive Chairman of the Society and his two elected deputies, who by the Lloyd's Act must be chosen from among the working members of the council. Almost all are agents. Being human they lack the capacity to be totally impartial over questions involving relations between Names

187

and agents – questions which lie at the root of so many of the problem cases at Lloyd's. These difficulties were compounded by the fact that there had been close associations between some of those charged at Lloyd's with disciplinary offences and the ruling insiders on the committee.

The Neill Report, when it was published in January 1987, concentrated on this very point. Complimenting the council on the progress made since 1982 the report said: 'We know of no profession or equivalent organisation which has accomplished such a major programme of reform in such a short time scale.'[10] Notwithstanding this progress the arrangements at Lloyd's did not match those called for under the Financial Services Act. A number of detailed changes were needed but, 'more fundamentally, the constitution of Lloyd's does not currently provide for that degree of involvement of independent outsiders and that degree of detached scrutiny of the activities of market practitioners that will be a feature of the regime under the Financial Services Act. The checks and balances at Lloyd's are not, in our view, so firmly in place. The balance of initiative rests too much with the working members.'[11]

Rejecting the argument that Lloyd's should be brought, as Gower had recommended, within the ambit of the Financial Services Act and under the supervision of the Securities and Investments Board established by that Act, Neill proposed instead that the Council of Lloyd's could itself be the supervisory body provided that its balance was altered by the addition of a further four nominated members and the deletion of four working members. The majority would then be held by the nominated and external members who would number sixteen to the working members' twelve. This solution had the advantage that it would not require legislation. As Neill says: 'It is directed at the specific weakness we have identified in the Lloyd's regulatory structure. This is that the balance of the initiative lies with the insiders, the working members who up to now have remained dominant in the policy making of the Society. We believe that a change in the composition of the governing body, together with a somewhat more extensive involvement of nominated members in the committee work that supports it will provide independent oversight no less effective than the board members of any external supervisory authority could be expected to provide.'[12] The more extensive involvement of nominated members would involve reserving for them the chairmanships of the Investigations, Disciplinary, Rules and Names Interests committees, and requiring their participation in the work of the Administrative Suspension, and Registration of Underwriting Agents committees.

Sir Patrick's inquiry took a year, six months more than had at first been expected. During this period Lloyd's took steps to put its house in order by announcing the publication of a register of agent's charges; passing a Review Powers bye-law[13] which gave the chief executive the authority to review the affairs of any Lloyd's registered agency; and, just before the Neill Report was published, releasing a detailed brochure for the information of new Names, which not only went into details about the financial arrangements for membership but encouraged Names to compare the services and charges of agents before deciding which one to use.[14]

Commenting on these matters the chairman revealed, in his November 1986 speech to the general meeting of members, that regulatory progress on the registration of brokers had been substantially delayed because of the time and effort devoted to the submission of evidence to the Neill Inquiry.

The Neill Report is almost as long as Sir Henry Fisher's Report which had been at my elbow throughout my time at Lloyd's. But it differs significantly because it was prepared by a committee of objective outsiders: both the Fisher Report and the Cromer Report that had preceded it were prepared by committees whose majorities were working members of Lloyd's. Like Fisher, Neill received written evidence from hundreds of parties, but a review of a list of those who gave oral evidence shows how the balance had shifted towards outsiders in seven years: apart from a sprinkling of journalists all Sir Henry's witnesses came from within the Lloyd's community; more than half of Sir Patrick's came from outside Lloyd's.

Neill's conclusion that Lloyd's fails the test of matching the requirements of the Financial Services Act is based on three examples, each of which has been discussed above. He noted that Lloyd's failed to honour its undertaking to Parliament in 1981 to publish a register of agents' charges; he observed that the standard underwriting agency agreement failed to recognize and protect the interests of Names as opposed to those of agents and recommended that it be rewritten; and he condemned Lloyd's handling of parallel syndicates, both as to the time taken to deal with the problem and the means of dealing with it: he felt that parallel syndicates should have been banned. While he regards these shortcomings as funda-mental, he also makes a large number of additional recommendations for changes in Lloyd's regulatory arrangements.

Many of these go far further than would have been possible in my time at Lloyd's because they weaken the power of the agents vis-à-vis that of the Names. Such changes could never be proposed while the agent-dominated committee ruled the roost. The principal recommendations included: more detailed guidance to new Names, including the publication of data facilitating the comparison of the relative performance of members' agents; the introduction of a direct contractual relationship between the Name and the managing agent even though the Name may have obtained access to the syndicate indirectly through the intervention of a members' agent; a right on the part of the Name to appeal to the chief executive against the application of the 'pay now, sue later' clause in the underwriting agreement; the appointment of an ombudsman, under the aegis of the nominated members of the council, to deal with Names' complaints against the corporation; the replacement of the Names Advisory Committee, chaired by an external member of council, by a Names Interests Committee, chaired by a nominated council member; the establishment of a Names Compensation Fund; and the introduction of proper professional examinations for those who seek to become underwriters at Lloyd's. These changes, and other more detailed ones upon which I have already commented, will greatly strengthen the protection of Names.

Considering the three tasks[15] which the Council of Lloyd's set itself, and me, at the beginning of 1983, Neill gives Lloyd's full marks for the cleaning-up operation: 'We have identified no serious deficiencies in Lloyd's procedures for investigations and disciplinary proceedings.'[16] As far as the rule book is concerned Lloyd's is commended for the progress so far, but more is needed. But when it comes to the third task, altering the structure of the society, it is clear that, as I had pointed out at the time of my resignation and the Berrill Report had confirmed four months later, it remains fundamentally unchanged. Sir Patrick's analysis of this problem is so fundamental to the argument of this book that it is worth discussing it in detail.[17]

The question is defined in the request for evidence by the Neill Inquiry: 'Whether the present constitution of Lloyd's is, in principle and practice, adequate and effective in overseeing the operation of the Lloyd's market and in protecting the interest of Names'.[18] Lloyd's critics argued the need for external supervision. Neill confirms that Lloyd's is subject to less external supervision than other self-regulatory organizations recognized under the Financial Services Act who are answerable to the Securities and Investment Board, and points out that while the DTI has a duty to protect the interests of policy holders which it discharges through the solvency procedures, it has no duty to protect the interests of Names. The Governor of the Bank of England has a formal role in confirming the appointment of nominated members of the council: informally he may go further when, for example, he took the initiative in persuading Lloyd's to create the new post of Chief Executive. One of the four nominated members, the chief executive is charged by his terms of reference with the responsibility for the quality of the self-regulatory arrangements, both as to the rules and their application.[19] Nevertheless, Neill concludes: 'External influence, particularly in terms of independent oversight of the process of regulation, is much more limited in relation to the Council of Lloyd's than it will be in the context of the monitoring of Self Regulatory Organisatins (SROs) by the Securities and Investments Board (SIB). At the level of principle, therefore, some changes in the current arrangements would be needed before they could be judged comparable with those envisaged by the Act.'

Neill then advances a fundamental prescription in relation to the development of self-regulation in the City of London: 'The Financial Services Act reflects a public policy that practitioner based regulation in the investment field requires some element of independent oversight.' He examines three examples of defective regulation: agents' charges – 'a desire on the part of working members to preserve the traditional secrecy surrounding this aspect of their affairs'; the standard underwriting agency agreement – 'the working members of the Lloyd's community were not able themselves to take a sufficiently objective view of the interests of the Names'; and rules in relation to parallel syndicates – 'the problems are seen from within, not from without': a phrase which aptly sums up Neill's whole judgment about Lloyd's.

Clearly more outside influence was needed. The presence of nominated members of the council, an independent chief executive and committees reporting directly to the council, notably the Accounting and Auditing Standards Committee, the Investigations Committee and the Rules Committee, all contribute to an outside view. Nevertheless, Neill points to the continuing influence of insiders through the Committee of Lloyd's: composed entirely of working members of the council, headed by the elected chairs who are required by statute to be working members and who also chair the council, meeting weekly, in spite of the recommendation of the Berrill Report that they meet fortnightly, and until recently reviewing all council papers before the council meets.

Pointing out that the balance between the council and the committee has been affected by the appointment of the chief executive, Neill notes that no provision was made in the Lloyd's Act for such an appointment. Referring to my resignation he says: 'Moreover, although terms of reference were drawn up for the new post, complementary terms of reference were not prepared for the Chairman and the elected Deputy Chairs. There was as a result some degree of uncertainty of what the relationship should be between the elected Chairs and the Chief Executive, and over their respective roles in the organisation. This uncertainty was clearly visible in the explanation given by Mr Hay Davison of the reasons for his resignation.' Referring to these uncertainties Neill goes on: 'A number of significant submissions to the Inquiry have, however, been critical of the continuing substantial executive activity on the part of the elected Chairs. We have noted in this connection the conclusions of the Berrill Report (para. 2.5) that the work load of the elected Chairs had not, in the period up to beginning of 1986, been changed to the extent that it should have been and that "the roles at present performed by the elected Chairs need to be scrutinised and wherever possible delegated to the Chief Executive and other senior staff". We support the recommended delegation.'

Pointing out that the appointment of an independent chief executive postdates the 1982 Act, Neill describes the appointment as providing comfort both to the Names and to the public interest. 'The success and effectiveness of any supervisory body depends heavily on the quality and independent-mindedness of its staff and their ability to take decisive actions regardless of whether such action accords with the wishes of those who are being regulated or is seen as a threat to their interests.' Despite the appointment of men of calibre to the staff of the corporation there remains the difficulty that the chief executive and his staff 'are answerable to a Council which is dominated numerically by working members of the community, a domination enhanced by the substantial executive roles performed by the Chairman and the elected Deputy Chairs'.

Reviewing the options for change Neill explores two alternatives: the designation of an external body whose authority could be invoked when the insiders were not taking a sufficiently disinterested view of matters, leaving the domestic structure more or less as it is; and modifying the domestic structure so that the Council of Lloyd's itself becomes a supervisory body.

In the former option the SIB is the obvious body to do this job. Here the difficulty is that it is devoted to investor protection, yet whatever body supervises Lloyd's must have the interests of both investors and policy holders in mind. This duality makes Lloyd's a unique regulatory problem, one for which the SIB is not well suited. Here I agree with Neill. Furthermore the whole legal thrust of the Financial Services Act, under which the SIB operates, is directed towards the protection of investors as narrowly defined in the Act. Lloyd's Names do not easily fit within the definition. However, it is difficult to see why a purpose-built supervisory body, or even the DTI itself, could not discharge the role of balancing the interests of Names and policy holders: the Council of Lloyd's is not unique in possessing this capability. However, Neill chooses the second alternative – to modify the Council of Lloyd's.

Recognizing that 'the balance of initiative on regulatory as well as market matters rests with the working members', Neill proposes to redress this so that the working members of the council cease to have a majority. This is to be done by doubling the number of nominated members from four to eight and reducing the number of working members, and the Committee of Lloyd's, from sixteen to twelve. One of the nominated members should always be the chairman for the time being of the SIB or his deputy. Neill sees the nominated members as discharging a role on the council and its committees not markedly different from that which board members of any external supervisory authority could be expected to undertake. He concedes that they lack a separate staff and argues that a small high-powered staff should be established.

Neill rightly dismisses the criticism that additional nominated members might not be available or that the reduction in the number of working members will seriously damage the input of market expertise into the regulatory process. A more serious criticism is that the nominated members will be chosen by the Council of Lloyd's and endorsed by the Governor of the Bank of England. The task of selection is a critical one in which the authorities should play an active part.

The additional nominated members will make it possible for them to hold the reserved chairmanships already referred to, and to play a larger part in the work of the ombudsman, the Names Interests Committee and the registration of agents. In particular, as Neill sees it, the chief executive and his senior colleagues would be answerable to a body where the power of initiative clearly lay with the outsiders. This solution is likely to offer a much more effective guarantee of the independence of the chief executive than the entrenchment of paper terms of reference. A view with which I concur.

The publication of the Neill Report in January 1987 coincided with revelations about dubious practices in the City in connection with the Guinness takeover of Distillers in March 1986. Here the DTI had taken more vigorous steps to pursue alleged malpractices than had been the case at Lloyd's four years earlier. With an election in prospect the Government was sensitive to allegations that it was soft on wrongdoing in the City of London. Over four months, from October 1986 to January 1987, the tone of ministerial speeches had changed, from robust support for the concept of self-regulation to the argument that the new regulatory framework in the City was proving itself capable of handling the alleged skulduggery firmly and briskly. In such a political climate the Council of Lloyd's had no alternative but to accept at once Neill's principal recommendation: that the balance of the council should be altered. Presenting the report to Parliament, the Secretary of State, Paul Channon, promised to legislate within a year if Lloyd's did not act properly and promptly.

Press reaction to Neill accepted that it was not a whitewash but was a thorough independent examination of Lloyd's regulatory problems: the headline in the *Financial Times* was 'A Salutary Kick for Lloyd's'. In its leader on the subject the *Daily Telegraph*, pointing out that it was my 'volcanic departure' that led to the Neill Inquiry, accepted that supervision was the key to the reform of Lloyd's.

The attitude of the Room turned on the question of divorce. Neill's request for evidence indicated that the inquiry would be reopening the discussion of divorce between members and managing agents deferred by Parliament in 1982 after rejection by a ballot of Lloyd's members.[20] Divestment of managing agents from brokers had already caused a massive upheaval in the market: the prospect of further extensive changes in the ownership of agencies filled it with dread. Commenting on the question Neill said: 'We think that there are strong practical arguments against any scheme of mandatory divorce and that Names benefit from being able to choose between different types of agent.'[21] As soon as Neill was published and it became clear that divorce was not to be required the Room relaxed: the active underwriters, agents and brokers were largely indifferent to the political manoeuvrings upstairs where the working members were discussing which of their number would resign.[22]

XX

The Future of Lloyd's

Much of this book has been devoted to the regulatory problems of Lloyd's during a momentous period of its constitutional history. A new legislative structure was introduced against a background of doubt about its suitability for the job to be done. Meanwhile the business of Lloyd's has gone on remarkably unaffected by events on the second floor at Lime Street and down the road in Whitehall. In the four years since I went to Lloyd's the overall capacity of the market increased 2.3 times from £4.3 billion in 1983 to £10 billion in 1987. In the same period the membership increased by 50 per cent from 21,000 to nearly 32,000. Despite its well-publicized difficulties there was no shortage of business coming to the market and of Names willing to join Lloyd's.[1] These facts should encourage reformers not to be deterred by warnings to leave Lloyd's alone lest changes spoil the business and the valuable flow of international earnings. Clearly there are measures which, if taken, could seriously damage the market and drive business and Names away: there is no evidence that the ideas under consideration and the proposals in the Neill Report would come within a mile of doing that.

However, there are real threats – external and internal – to the future of Lloyd's and its ability to continue to compete effectively in world insurance markets.

Externally the biggest and most important market is the USA. Here legislative proposals from time to time threaten new regulatory restrictions on Lloyd's. They are met just as regularly as they are proposed: by the lobbying skills of Le Boeuf Lamb Leiby & MacRae – Lloyd's US counsel – and by the undoubted muscle Lloyd's has in congressional corridors, thanks to the size and importance of its dollar business, and by the flexible response of Lloyd's brokers and underwriters to changing markets, a flexibility due in part to Lloyd's unique organizational structure with its emphasis on highly decentralized decision-making.

The threat to Lloyd's financial strength of a steadily declining pound is more serious. The more the pound falls against the dollar the more Lloyd's capital base is eroded. Premiums are taken in dollars and held in trust in dollars. Claims are settled in dollars. But the reserve margin to cover any adventitious deficit is provided in sterling. Would it not be more sensible to denominate syndicate capacity in the currency in which the syndicate trades, that is in dollars?

A Name who wishes a join a syndicate writing dollar business, or mixed dollar/sterling business, should be required to provide part of his deposit in dollars and show that the dollar value of part of his means was consistently maintained. If the pound falls against the dollar the under-writer would not then have, as he has today, a capacity problem but his Names would have to cover the shortfall: by showing more assets in sterling terms or, more probably, by hedging the exchange risk.[2] This is nothing more than the Names insuring themselves against the risk of currency fluctuations and such insurance would be a tax-deductible expense covered by part of the resulting underwriting profit. An alternative stratagem – to make Lloyd's a dollar business, in view of the fact that 70 per cent of its trade is in dollars – would be more dramatic than the situation requires. But there is nothing very radical in what is proposed. At present Lloyd's accounts for premiums and claims in three currencies – sterling, US dollars and Canadian dollars; the suggestion is that the calculation be extended to the security base as well.

The second threat to the non-marine business in the United States today is that posed by the capricious and often extravagant settlements in US tort cases. Here Lloyd's underwriters are a small voice among many sufferers. The issue is a political one and calls for a political solution. It seems likely that an answer will be found, probably first on the medical front: the disappearance of medical services from certain regions of the United States where medical malpractice claims have been particularly heavy results in angry letters to Congress. Meanwhile Lloyd's underwriters are protecting themselves and their Names by more restrictive policy wordings, despite the complaints of the assureds and their brokers.

The third external factor is the continual difficulty in applying the Treaty of Rome to insurance services in Europe. Lloyd's, by its low rates and extensive covers, demonstrates the advantages of competition in the field of insurance. Assureds in those countries which continue to treat insurance like a public utility suffer from the disadvantages of monopoly supply. Freeing the European market would not only remove these to the customers' advantage it would also help European insurance companies to provide an international service for a worldwide market.[3]

Factors outside Lloyd's are largely outside Lloyd's control but internal factors, which are in principle capable of being resolved internally, look in fact just as intractable. During 1983 the new council established a committee to look into the future – the Policy Review Advisory Committee. In its short life this committee, which was served by the planning department of the corporation, devoted its efforts to obtaining the views of brokers, underwriters and corporation staff about the future of Lloyd's. The concerns from all quarters were the same and fell under four headings: cash flow, claims handling, documentation and training.[4] Failure to resolve the difficulties in these areas would make it increasingly difficult for Lloyd's to compete internationally in the twenty-first century.

The disadvantages of the club-like traditions of Lloyd's are most clearly seen in the arrangements for handling the settlement of premiums and claims. The underwriter's attention is most clearly focused on the risk at the moment when he signs the slip. His box will make a note of the risk but the collection of the premium by the broker will be left until later. The broker has a direct financial interest in delaying the payment of the premium to the underwriter because he enjoys the interest on his customer's money until he hands it over. The more financially astute among the broker's customers will agree late settlement terms with the broker to obtain a share of this interest benefit. Originally the underwriters were the unwitting victims of these arrangements, but in recent years a terms-of-credit scheme has been introduced which tracks the settlement record of each broker and calls to account anyone who delays settlement unduly. At the same time it formally recognizes the lengthy credit terms normally allowed. The underwriter has his opportunity to retaliate by delaying the payment of claims and forcing the broker to use premium funds held pending transfer to the underwriter to settle outstanding claims, a practice which some might argue comes perilously close to breach of trust.

With high real interest rates and low inflation the benefits to the brokers' earnings in closely controlling, not to say manipulating, the cash balances in their hands are tremendous.

In this tug of war between broker and underwriter the losers are too often Lloyd's customers, the assureds. They wonder why, when dealing with Lloyd's, premiums are often invoiced very slowly and cash settlements of agreed claims are so frequently delayed. There can be no doubt that poor cash-handling practices are damaging the reputation of Lloyd's compared with the company market. It is difficult for Lloyd's to discipline this behaviour. Accounting arrangements in the market need tightening up, particularly the introduction of a system of slip registration and inception-date accounting, so that the broker cannot delay filing the completed slip with the LPSO or the date for the due settlement of the premium.[5]

The second internal difficulty is claims service. Lloyd's operates a unique procedure by which the broker is responsible for lodging the claims on behalf of the assured. Thereafter he acts also as the agent of the underwriter in obtaining information and settling the claim. Two court cases in 1969 and 1970 drew attention to the conflicts of interest inherent in these arrangements, and since then Lloyd's has discouraged brokers from acting too much as the agent of the underwriter.[6] But, for the most part, the underwriter has no other field force available to deal directly with the claimant.

In an attempt to improve claims service Lloyd's bought Toplis and Harding Inc. (THI) in 1984. This is an American firm of loss adjusters whose primary role is to advise underwriters on the settlement of claims. THI deals directly with underwriters, both marine and non-marine, and is able to provide a service free of the conflict of interest that the broker has. To the extent that delays in claim settlement are attributable to delays by brokers, THI gives the underwriters a means to cure the problem.

Further delays in claims handling originate from the fact that the underwriter who signs the slip is the person with the authority to settle any claim arising on the consequent policy. Most boxes have a claims clerk who handles claims presented by the broker; some of the larger syndicates have a separate claims box. But the need in principle to get the approval of every underwriter on the slip makes for substantial delays. All the markets have sought ways to solve this problem. The marine market uses Lloyd's Underwriters Claims and Recoveries Office (LUCRO), a part of the corporation. LUCRO receives claims from brokers, sees that underwriters are notified, and then settles claims either on its own authority or with the consent of the leading underwriter on the slip. The more idiosyncratic non-marine market operates LUNCO, Lloyd's Underwriters Non-Marine Claims Office, under the aegis of the Non-Marine Association. This organization has less delegated settlement powers but serves to provide a similar information role. A third agency operates in the aviation market. These organizations have clearly improved the speed of settling claims.

The final weakness in claims service lies, again, in the handling of cash. The underwriters' cheques pass through the hands of the brokers who may delay paying the funds to the claimants. In any case, under current practice, the final payment is out of the hands of the underwriters. Direct payment schemes are in operation in some parts of the market: these give the underwriter more control over the service Lloyd's gives to the assureds.

The critical legal position of an insurance policy is defined in the law: 'A contract of marine insurance is inadmissible in evidence unless it is embodied in a marine policy in accordance with this Act. The policy may be executed and issued either at the time when the contract is concluded, or afterwards.'[7] Similar provisions apply to other classes of insurance. Essentially the policy is needed as evidence of the contract when a claim is made. It is clear that the policy can be issued after the insurance starts and that is commonly the case. The London market is unique in the insurance world in making the broker responsible for preparing and issuing, but not signing, the policy. In respect of risks written at Lloyd's the last task is that of the LPSO on behalf of the underwriters who are bound by the policy. The procedure is this: the broker describes the risk on a slip – a standard form; having completed the slip with the initials of a sufficient number of underwriters the broker advises the client with a cover note and, usually at the same time, issues the invoice; the broker then files the completed slip with the LPSO together with a draft policy. This is checked by the LPSO to see that the policy agrees with the slip – that the underwriters' intentions when signing the slip have been faithfully reproduced in the policy. The LPSO then signs the policy and returns it to the broker to be forwarded to the client. In the course of this checking process the LPSO collects the data needed to effect the accounting settlement between the broker and the underwriters.

This is a cumbersome process and fraught with delay. In many cases policies are not finally prepared until after the insurance has expired. Attempts have been made to streamline the preparation of policies. For example, Lloyd's policies no longer list on the reverse the names of all the members of the syndicates backing the policy. Nevertheless, one of the disadvantages of Lloyd's from the assured's point of view is the long delay before the necessary insurance documents are produced.

The long-term solution to these problems – cash flow, claims processing and documentation – lies in data processing. Lloyd's was among the earliest users of computers in the UK. The LPSO installed one of the new IBM machines in 1960 and since then the corporation has been a major user of computers. In 1983 there were almost four hundred people working in the data-processing department – in Chatham and London – both in production and in systems development work. But the present system of central accounting is out of date. It produces its daily output of advices to underwriting boxes about the risks that have been booked to them in the form of punched cards: 90,000 a day, or 45 boxes of cards.

Punched cards are now an obsolete data-processing medium and the fact that Lloyd's must now be the world's largest user of them is not a source of pride. This fact alone illustrates the efforts that must be made to bring the corporation, and the Lloyd's market, up to date.

An early step in this process was a paper to the Council of Lloyd's in November 1983 which proposed that Lloyd's should be transformed into an electronic market by 1988. There were to be three stages in the transition. In the first stage data would be entered into a common network by brokers who would continue to present a printed slip to underwriters at the box. A second phase would involve the underwriters entering their lines electronically, having seen the slip on a screen at the box. A third parallel phase would cover the computerization of claims handling.

Further study showed that the plans laid in November 1983 were over-ambitious. The problem was that there were four separate classes of computer system in the vast Lloyd's market. Each of the major brokers had its own data-processing network; some of the larger agents had computers for risk analysis and some accounting functions, but many of the smaller ones relied on data-processing bureaux for their accounting figures; the LPSO had its own central processing system to handle the central accounting settlement, and the claims offices had their own arrangements. The aim was to bring these four into some kind of common network in which the role of the corporation would be similar to that of British Telecom – to provide a network of channels through which brokers and underwriters could transmit messages.

But this would need a common language and common data-processing standards. Here the disparate nature of Lloyd's showed itself. It is a market place, not a company. Each agent and broker is running his own business and is very jealous of his independence. The council is prepared to legislate on regulatory matters because it has legal powers over these, but it is not prepared to do so in commercial fields, and it did not feel it appropriate to impose on the market over such a commercial matter as data processing. The business of negotiating a common approach between brokers on the one hand and the market associations of underwriters on the other is long and difficult. Yet if Lloyd's does not do this its success in world markets, when all its major competitors are highly automated and are able to make the fullest use of computers, will be very doubtful.

But even if the data-processing solutions are found and the electronic market becomes a reality rather than a dream, Lloyd's will not succeed without the right people to operate the market. Business, especially the City, now hires graduates in large numbers, but Lloyd's has been slow to take advantage of this trend. The brokers now operate graduate entry schemes, as they must because they compete in worldwide insurance markets and their customers are large corporations who are also staffed by graduates. But the underwriters have no such arrangements. The problem is that most agencies employ no more than twenty people and there are not enough places on the boxes each year for the typical agent to have a graduate entry scheme. So recruits come in dribs and drabs, at a much lower salary and with lower ambitions, from secondary schools, or some, already trained, from brokers. Training is, except for the larger brokers, exiguous to a degree. The traditional method of 'sitting next to Nellie' ensures a lot of experience but does not ensure its relevance. There is little training in theory, or in the legal background to the market. One very senior underwriter told me that in common with most underwriters at Lloyd's he never had any form of business training in the fields of company law, agency law and taxation. His training was limited solely to underwriting. The very narrowness and inadequacy of these training arrangements were in part a cause of the widespread misunderstandings that led to the scandals, as Neill points out.

At the end of 1985 Lloyd's introduced a bye-law requiring each new entrant to the Room to take a simple examination – Lloyd's Introductory Test – soon after he or she starts at Lloyd's.[8] It is the first time that Lloyd's has required any technical qualification. Such qualifications exist in the insurance world: the Chartered Insurance Institute is the examining body and its examinations are required in the company market and to a lesser extent in the broking field. But not at Lloyd's.

Underwriting is not a profession – like law, medicine or accountancy – and the practitioner is not dealing with the public: the protection of a statutory body is not needed to ensure that practitioners are qualified, because their customers – the public – have no easy means of doing so. A bad underwriter will not last long at Lloyd's, his errors will soon become known, although the lesson may cost his Names money. There is no compelling need to require underwriters to be professionally qualified, yet this lack has meant that the calibre of entrants to the market has not been as high as it should have been.

Neill rightly points to these defects, commenting on the absence of any adequate system of examinations. He refers to Lloyd's introductory test but does not consider that this goes far enough. Experience is no doubt an excellent school for a market trader: but Lloyd's underwriters and agents must now be far more than this, as Neill says: 'We for our part are in favour of mandatory examinations. We find the arguments against them unconvincing. Active underwriters at Lloyd's assume considerable responsibilities in conducting insurance business on behalf of Names.

Furthermore, Lloyd's have taken great trouble to introduce a substantial volume of legislation covering many aspects of the market. It is imperative that those who work in the market should be thoroughly familiar with this body of law, and, as we have said elsewhere, a knowledge of the law of agency is essential to the proper conduct of the business.'[9] The weight of this argument is borne out by the finding of the PCW investigators that many members of the Lloyd's community in senior positions were not even vaguely aware of their legal obligations as agents.

These difficulties are reflected, on a much smaller scale, in the corporation's staff. Most of the jobs in the corporation are clerical and are easily and well filled. But the more taxing posts in the regulatory, systems, market support, finance and administrative areas are filled in a variety of ways, too many of them informal. Lloyd's should urgently introduce a programme to recruit graduates to the corporation staff and provide them with proper training, accepting that a proportion will leave the corporation to work in the market after three to four years. The balance who remain would provide enough to service the managerial ranks of the corporation. But such policies can not be achieved in a three- or four-year time span: they are more likely to take twenty-five years.

Progress on these four fronts is essential if Lloyd's is to continue to be an effective commercial force in world insurance markets. Better control of cash flow, tighter claim settlement procedures, and more streamlined documentation can all be achieved with the help of more sophisticated computer systems. This will require a cultural change in the Room, one that is more likely if the calibre of entrants is raised and their training improved. Signs of this are clearly visible in the greater openness and acceptance of change exhibited by the younger generation of brokers and underwriters.

If these changes do come about there is no reason why Lloyd's should not continue to make an excellent contribution to the British balance of payments and to the fortunes of its Names. The recent commercial results show that, far from damaging Lloyd's, the greater openness associated with the reforms of the last four years has brought greater public understanding, and very much greater understanding by Names, of the market in which they participate. But the continued commercial success of Lloyd's can only be assured in a well-regulated market in which investors can have confidence that they will get a fair deal. Sir Patrick Neill points the way towards a better and more robust regime at Lloyd's. Couched in dense and dispassionate prose, his report is a mine of constructive and effective proposals for improving the relative position of Names at Lloyd's vis-à-vis agents. The more I read it the more I find in it: there is no recommendation that is not well considered and capable of urgent implementation.

I must however still ask: is the day of agent domination in the Council of Lloyd's really coming to a close; do the Neill proposals for constitutional change really go far enough to shift the balance of initiative permanently away from the working members; is Neill's solution adequate to right the balance? I doubt it. The policy initiative at Lloyd's still rests as it has for seventy years with the Chairman of Lloyd's and his deputies. It is O Group that is responsible for laying down the policy line to be proposed to the council; and the elected chairs dominate O Group. O Group, which controls the council agenda, must bear responsibility for the specific defects in the regulatory reform programme identified by Neill. But it is important to see those defects in the context in which Neill places them. He does not condemn the Council of Lloyd's for getting three policy questions wrong: instead he judges correctly that the erroneous conclusions reached by Lloyd's in relation to the disclosure of agent's charges, parallel syndicates and the standard form of underwriting agency agreement are symptomatic of an imbalance in the power structure of the corporation by which the interests of working members and agents have too much play.

If such errors are to be avoided in the future it is essential that the office of Chairman of the Council be separated from that of Chairman of the Committee: a division for which the Lloyd's Act makes provision. The Chairman of the Council should be a nominated member: Sir Patrick is quoted as saying that he expects this to come about in five to ten years. Indeed it will be a rum sort of council in which the chairman and the elected deputy chairman can only be selected from a minority of the councillors. It is no more logical to argue that the Chairman of the Council of Lloyd's must be a working member than to argue that a working stockbroker must chair the Securities and Investments Board or a miner the National Coal Board. The voice of the market should be provided by the Chairman of the Committee, the voice of the Chairman of the Council should be the voice of the regulatory body. After all Sir Patrick proposes the Council of Lloyd's as a Lloyd's surrogate for the SIB.

But such a change cannot happen without legislation because the Lloyd's Act 1982 reserves the Chairmanship and Deputy Chairmanships of the Council to working members. An amendment to the Lloyd's Act would be essential, but simple. The Government should not shirk this vital element in its battery of City regulatory reforms. Until this is done the initiative at Lloyd's will still rest with the working members. What confidence can we have that they will turn to and actively assist in dismantling their own power base along the lines proposed by Neill? Certainly judging from my own experience progress on critical issues will be as slow as external pressures – the press, Whitehall and the bank – permit.

I resigned from my position at Lloyd's because the power structure of the corporation was not adequate to maintain and continue the reforms that would be needed before the Names could get a fair deal. As a direct result of my resignation Sir Patrick's Inquiry was appointed. His report confirms the validity of the reservations which prompted my resignation and charts the way for further reforms that would not have been accepted under the regime within which I worked.

Appendix I

1 Reports to the Chairman and to the Council of which he is a member.
2 Attends meetings of the Committee.
3 Forms part of a team with the Chairman and the other two Deputies who together preside over the affairs of the Society.
4 As Deputy Chairman he will be particularly concerned with supporting the Chairman in connection with the external relations of the Society. As the senior member of the Society the Chairman must continue to discharge his ambassadorial role and to lead negotiations at the highest level. The Deputy Chairman and Chief Executive will assist with negotiations with regulatory and tax authorities both here and overseas at official level. He will also be particularly concerned with relations between the Society and the Press.
5 As Chief Executive he will be responsible to the Council for:
   a) Overseeing the establishment of the new self-regulatory regime at Lloyd's. He will recommend proposed byelaws to the Council; he will see to the setting up and monitor the progress of necessary task forces; he will consult with the market and outside regulatory authorities on proposed rules; he will see to the setting up of the necessary machinery to implement new byelaws; he will be responsible to the Council for the quality of the new self-regulatory arrangements, both as to the rules and as to their application; and he will exercise general supervision over the disciplinary arrangements.
   b) The management of and accountability for the resources of the Society.
   c) The direction and, with the exception of the Secretary General, the appointment of the senior staff (after consultation with the Chairman of any policy board where appropriate and subject to the approval of the Council).
   d) Overseeing the implementation of policy decisions of the Council and the Committee.
   e) Maintaining proper channels of communication and responsibility within the Society.

f) Co-ordinating the work of the Society's various sub-committees, advisory boards and other investigatory and advisory bodies.

g) Laying the foundations for the future management of the Society and the development of the Corporation of Lloyd's.

6 The Deputy Chairman and Chief Executive will not make directions to the Market. However, he will be expected to become known to underwriters and brokers in the market place so that he may be able to earn their confidence and exert influence on behalf of the Council.

7 The appointment is seen as a temporary one with a term of three to five years. Whether there is to be a successor and what his duties might be remains to be considered.

Appendix II

11 November 1985

Gentlemen,

As Chief Executive of Lloyd's, I report to the Council of Lloyd's and I am, therefore, addressing this, my notice of resignation, to you.

When I came to Lloyd's in February 1983, it was with these Terms of Reference which I required as a condition of accepting the appointment and which were confirmed by the Council at the time:

As Deputy Chairman to be concerned with external relations, notably with regulatory and tax authorities and the Press.

As Chief Executive to be responsible to the Council for:
- overseeing the establishment of the new self-regulatory regime envisaged by the Lloyd's Act 1982
- exercising general supervision over disciplinary arrangements
- managing the resources of the Society
- appointing and directing staff
- overseeing the implementation of policy decisions
- maintaining proper channels of communication and responsibility
- laying the foundations for the future management of the Society

With the approval of the Chairman and the Council, I set myself three principal objectives: to bring to book those in the Lloyd's community who had misbehaved themselves; to establish a new regulatory framework for Lloyd's, based upon higher standards of disclosure, accounting and auditing; and to improve the staffing, organisation and management of the Corporation. I undertook this assignment for a term of three to five years. I saw, and see, myself principally as an agent of change and had no intention of continuing permanently in post.

Thanks to the readiness of the Council to embrace the major changes called for and the energy of the Chairman in pressing them forward, those principal objectives are now largely achieved. We expect, today, to complete the last of the major disciplinary cases; the new rule book called for by Sir Henry Fisher is mostly in place; and the re-staffing of the Corporation is evident by the substantial influx of new people and the major reorganisation that has occurred since I joined Lloyd's.

My conclusion that now is the time to resign is prompted by the Council's recent initiation of an internal inquiry into the structure of Lloyd's, which has started discussions about changing the Terms of Reference and status of the post of Chief Executive. The preparation of the Corporation's evidence for this inquiry has revealed divergent opinions about the continuing need for the Chief Executive to be independent and responsible directly to the Council.

My own views on the paramount necessity of an independent Chief Executive, with appropriate terms of reference, responsible directly to the Council, have not changed and, therefore, I would find it impossible to continue in office were those terms to be significantly altered. At the same time, the argument is a perfectly proper one for a self-regulatory body and, by resigning at this time, I remove an obstacle to the Council's freedom of discussion and to my freedom to argue for the retention of the position of the Chief Executive with independent powers without any suggestion of self-interest.

My contract requires me to give six months' notice of resignation. This I now do and propose to leave the Corporation's employment on 11 May 1986. In view of the circumstances of my appointment, I am sending copies of this letter to the Secretary of State for Trade and Industry and the Governor of the Bank of England. In order to obviate any speculation about the reasons for my decision, I am also sending a copy to the Press.
Yours faithfully,

Ian Hay Davison

Bibliography

BRUCE-GARDYNE, Jock, *Ministers and Mandarins – Inside the Whitehall Village* (Sidgwick & Jackson 1986).

CLARKE, William M., *Inside the City. A guide to London as a Financial Centre* (George Allen & Unwin. Revised paperback 1983).

COCKERELL, Hugh, *Lloyd's of London – A Portrait* (Woodhead-Faulkner Limited 1984).

GIBB, D. E. W., *Lloyd's of London – A Study in Individualism* (The Corporation of Lloyd's 1957 reprinted 1978).

HODGSON, Godfrey, *Lloyd's of London – A Reputation at Risk* (Penguin Books Revised Paperback Edition 1986).

MACVE, Richard, *A Survey of Lloyd's Syndicate Accounts – Financial Reporting at Lloyd's in 1985* (Prentice-Hall International in association with the Institute of Chartered Accountants in England and Wales 1986).

MANSER, W. A. P., *The Institutional Insurance Market – A View from London.* Special Report No. 193 – The Economist Intelligence Unit (The Economist Publications Ltd. 1985).

PLENDER, John, and WALLACE, Paul, *The Square Mile. A Guide to the New City of London* (LWT/Century Hutchinson: reprinted 1986).

WIDLAKE, Brian, *In the City* (Faber & Faber 1986).

INQUIRY REPORTS

BERRILL, Sir Kenneth, Lloyd's Corporation Structure. Report of the Berrill Working Party (Corporation of Lloyd's March 1986).

BOYD, S. C., and DUBUISSON, P. W. G., Department of Trade and Industry – Minet Holdings plc, WMD Underwriting Agencies Limited – Investigation under Section 165 (1) (B) of the Companies Act 1948 (HMSO 1986).

COLMAN, Anthony, and HAILEY, Stephen, Report of Lloyd's Committee of Enquiry – Syndicates Underwritten by T. R. Brooks and other – Fidentia Marine Insurance Co Ltd., Final Report Part 1 'The Fidentia Report' (Circulated to members of the syndicates by the Corporation of Lloyd's August 1983).

CROMER, Rt Hon The Earl of, Report of Working Party to Study the Future of Lloyd's 1969 (Corporation of Lloyd's, published October 1986).

DAVIS, A. J., Inquiry into the Management of Syndicates by Richard Beckett Underwriting Agencies Ltd. Report of the Davis Committee (Corporation of Lloyd's July 1986).

FISHER, Sir Henry, Self-Regulation at Lloyd's – Report of the Fisher Working Party (Corporation of Lloyd's, May 1980).

GOWER, L. C. B., Review of Investor Protection Report Part 1 (HMSO January 1984 Cmnd 9125).

GOWER, L. C. B., Review of Investor Protection Report Part 2 (HMSO 1985).

NEILL, Sir Patrick, Regulatory Arrangements at Lloyd's – Report of the Committee of Inquiry. Chairman Sir Patrick Neill QC (HMSO 1987 Cm 59).

PAPERS BY THE AUTHOR

DAVISON, Ian Hay, 'Reform at Lloyd's – 1983–1984' reprinted in *The Future of Lloyd's – Papers from a Technical Briefing Conference* 14 February 1985 (Risk Research Group – 1985).

DAVISON, Ian Hay, 'The Auditor's Role at Lloyd's'. Paper delivered to the Conference of the National Association of Accountants, Paris, 19 April 1985.

DAVISON, Ian Hay, Lloyd's – 'The Case for Self-Regulation'. Paper delivered to the London Meeting of the American Bar Association 16 July 1985.

DAVISON, Ian Hay, 'Statutory Divestment at Lloyd's of London and the Financial Services Revolution'. Paper delivered to the Manchester Business School Conference on New Strategies in Financial Services 11 June 1986.

CONSULTATIVE DOCUMENTS

September 1982 Underwriting Agency System at Lloyd's – Working Party's Consultative Paper on Ownership and Control of Underwriting Agencies – *Higgins* Working Party.

March 1983 Underwriting Agency System at Lloyd's – Part I – Working Party's Report on Ownership and Control of Underwriting Agencies – *Higgins* Working Party.

July 1983 Membership of the Society – Consultative Document – Draft Bye-Laws.

August 1983 Disclosure of Interests by Underwriting Agents – Draft Bye-Law and Detailed Proposals – *Plaistowe* Working Party.

September 1983 Underwriting Agency System at Lloyd's – Part II – Working Party's Report on Preferred Underwriting and Parallel Syndicates, Character and Suitability – *Higgins* Working Party.

November 1983 Lloyd's Accounting Manual – Accounting to Underwriting Members of Lloyd's – *Randall* Task Group.

May 1984 Umbrella Arrangements – *Batchelor* Working Party.

July 1984 Lloyd's Syndicate Audit Arrangements – Accounting and Auditing Standards Committee chaired by Brandon Gough.

July 1984 Underwriting Agency Agreement – *Barber* Task Group.

October 1984 Membership Requirements at Lloyd's – The Report of the Long
  Term Review Working Party – *Bird* Working Party.
March 1985 Exposure Draft Rules for Binding Authorities and Approval of
  Correspondents – *Parry* Working Party.
August 1985 Related Party Interests and Transactions Bye-law – Exposure Draft.
November 1985 Extended Warranties and Consumer Guarantees – *Clucas*
  Working Party.

PRINCIPAL BYE-LAWS ISSUED BY LLOYD'S
1871 –   Lloyd's Bye-laws under Lloyd's Acts 1871–1951 published by the
             Corporation of Lloyd's 1973.
1983 – 2   Administrative Suspension
       3   Inquiries and Investigations
       4   Information and Confidentiality
       5   Misconduct, Penalties and Sanctions
       6   Disciplinary Committees
       7   Appeal Tribunal
       8   Council Stage of Disciplinary Proceedings
      17   Deputy Chairman and Chief Executive of the Society
1984 – 2   1983 Annual Reports of Syndicates
       3   Disclosure of Interests
       4   Underwriting Agents
       6   Syndicate Premium Income
       7   The Syndicate Accounting Bye-law 'Explanatory Notes – Reinsurance
             to close – December 1985'
       9   Membership
      10   Syndicate Audit Arrangements
1985 – 1   Agency Agreements
       4   Binding Authorities
       7   Multiple Syndicates
       8   Lloyd's Introductory Test
1986 – 2   Related Parties
       5   The Review Powers Bye-law

PRINCIPAL REPORTS OF LLOYD'S DISCIPLINARY PROCEEDINGS
Case Number:

8401/4	Brooks & Dooley – 'The Fidentia Case'	December 1984
8502/3	Peers, Brooks, Parry & Raven – 'The Fidentia Case'	August 1986
8402/6	Sasse – 'The Sasse Syndicate'	July 1985
8403/4	Denby & Posgate – 'The Wigham Poland Policy'	October 1984
8404/4	Grob, Comery, Posgate & Benbassat – 'Southern International Reinsurance and Banque du Rhone'	December 1984 Appeal May/June 1985

8404/4	Carpenter – 'SIR and B d R'	June 1985
8501/9	Hart – 'The Hart Syndicates'	April 1986
		Appeal July 1986
8401/5	Hardman, Oldworth, Davies, Hill,	January 1985
	Sampson, Dixon – 'The PCW Case'	Appeal by Mr Sampson
		October 1985
8401/W	Wallrock – 'The PCW Case'	November 1985
		Appeal June 1986

STATUTES
Marine Insurance Act 1906
Insurance Brokers (Registration) Act 1977
Insurance Brokers Registration Council (Code of Conduct) Approval order 1978
Lloyd's Act 1982 – Incorporating those sections of the Lloyd's Acts 1871–1951
    currently in force
Insurance Companies Act 1982
Financial Services Act 1986

MISCELLANEOUS
Lloyd's Annual Report and Accounts 1981–1985
Lloyd's of London Global Report and Accounts 1982–1985
A.L.M. – 1982 Lloyd's Syndicate Results (Association of Lloyd's Members September 1985)
Self-Regulatory Policy at Lloyd's – from 'Lloyd's Log' July 1983 (Corporation of Lloyd's 1983)
WILLIS C.J.P. and others – Lloyd's Market 1984 (Risk Research Group Ltd, November 1984)
The Future of Lloyd's – Papers from a Technical Briefing Conference (Risk Research Group Ltd, March 1985)
New York Insurance Exchange Annual Report 1985
Underwriters' Corporation Staff' and Brokers' View of Lloyd's, July 1985
REW, John, and STURGE, Charles – 1982 Lloyd's League Tables (Chatset Ltd 1985)
Lloyd's of London Membership: The Issues – published by the Council of Lloyd's December 1986

Notes

Chapter I   A Necessary Rupture

1 The Committee of Lloyd's was formed in 1771 and took over the regulation of the society from the Master, or proprietor, of the coffee house, of which Edward Lloyd was the first.
2 Eighty-two per cent of the 1987 members do not work at Lloyd's.
3 Neill, *Regulatory Arrangements at Lloyd's – Report of the Committee of Inquiry.*
4 Allegations were current at the end of 1986 that there had been improprieties in supporting the share price of Guinness during its bid for Distillers earlier in the year.
5 See Appendix II.
6 The precise terms of reference were: 'To consider whether the regulatory arrangements which are being established at Lloyd's under the 1982 Lloyd's Act provide protection for the interests of members of Lloyd's comparable to that proposed for investors under the Financial Services Bill.' Neill, op. cit., Appendix I.
7 Ibid., para. 3.22, p. 13.
8 Ibid., para. 1.6, p. 1.
9 Fisher, *Self-Regulation at Lloyd's*, 1980.

Chapter II   Lloyd's in the World Insurance Market

1 Lloyd's Act 1871 – Schedule – Rule 3.
2 By one of those illogical extensions which are so common at Lloyd's, the insurance of goods in transit by land is included. This is small beer to Lloyd's and peanuts in relation to North American trucking business, most of which stays firmly in the USA where, no less logically, it is known as dry marine or inland marine business.
3 Not all will be directly insured at Lloyd's, many such risks will be *reinsured* there.
4 For 1983 the premium income figures were:

Marine	40%
Nonmarine	42%
Aviation	7%
Motor	11%

5 Also loss of profits, specie, householder's, builder's and contractor's, accident and illness, employer's liability, banker's blanket bonds, abandonment of functions, contingency risks, travel and holiday 'all risks', and professional indemnity.

6 Gibb, *Lloyd's of London, a Study in Individualism*, pp. 61–5.

7 Total world non-marine insurance premiums in 1983 were approximately $290 billion; Lloyd's non-marine insurance premiums in 1983 were approximately $2.6 billion.

8 The current revolution in City of London investment markets may be changing this. But although London's share of world investment business may grow, much of this growth will be engendered by American and Japanese investment houses increasing their London operations.

9 This varies by class: ships, goods in transit and property damage are 80–'90 per cent export while only 8 per cent of motor business is export.

10 December 1985.

11

	1985 £bn	Ten Years to 1985 £bn
Lloyd's underwriting and investment earnings	1.2	5.3
Lloyd's brokers' earnings	0.7	3.5
	1.9	8.8
Banking	2.1	8.2

Note that most of the Lloyd's brokers' earnings relate to non-Lloyd's business.

12 In 1985 the US Federal Government Deficit amounted to $198 billion; Lloyd's holdings of US Government paper were $5 billion.

13 'Covers' – the perils that are covered by an insurance policy.

14 Manser, *The Institutional Insurance Market, A View from London*, p. 29.

15 'Lloyd's Global Report' 1985, p. 4.

16 Recently American legislators have made the captive insurance company rules even more stringent by requiring no shareholder to hold more than 10 per cent of the shares. US captives seem set for a decline.

17 Hodgson, *Lloyd's of London – A Reputation at Risk*, p. 149.

18 New York Insurance Exchange Report 1985.

19 1983 – £4.2 billion. 1986 – £8.5 billion.

Chapter III The Structure of the Market

1 Pepys records the practice: 'Called at the coffee house and there hear by great accident that a letter is come that our ship is safe come to Newcastle.

With this news I went like an asse presently to Alderman Blackwell and told him of it. . . . Now what an opportunity had I to have concealed this and seemed to have made an insurance and got £100 with the least trouble and danger in the whole world!' Quoted in Plender & Wallace, *The Square Mile*, p. 165.

2 Plus a further 550 sub-agents.

3 Bowring's, Sedgwick's and Willis Faber.

4 Fisher, *Self-Regulation at Lloyd's*, p. 74; and see Chapter XII below.

5 Commission rates vary between 3 per cent (on a large reinsurance) and 30 per cent on small direct personal lines. Although Lloyd's may allow a higher commission than a company underwriter, brokers frequently complain that the amount of work is no less on risks written by companies because in many cases the slip will be signed by underwriters from both markets.

6 Until quite recently Lloyd's policies continued to bear, on the reverse, a list of the members of the syndicates committed to the policy. This has now ceased. Instead the policy indicates the numbers of the syndicates and reference must be made to the syndicate book at Lloyd's in order to determine who precisely is liable for the risks under a policy.

7 The change in these proportions since the advent of divestment and re-registration, discussed in Chapter XII, is interesting:

	April 1984		Expected in July 1987	
	No.	%	No.	%
Managing Agents	38	12	57	24
Members' Agents	110	36	83	34
Combined Managing/				
Members' Agents	158	52	101	42
	306	100	241	100

8 Sturge, A. C. L., 'Lloyd's – An Outside Member's View', quoted in *Technical Briefing Conference* 1985, p. 122.

9 Ibid., p. 121.

10 In 1969 non-commonwealth male nationals were admitted, in 1970 British women domiciled in the UK, and in 1971 women of any nationality were allowed to join.

11 The requirements for 1987 are:

Minimum –Means	£	100,000
–Deposit	£	50,000
–Premium Income Limit	£	250,000
Maximum –Means	£	520,000
–Deposit	£	260,000
–Premium Income Limit	£1,300,000	

Foreign residents must deposit a higher sum. Names working at Lloyd's may qualify at a lower level of means and make a reduced deposit. Names may make a lower deposit, as little as £25,000 in the case of UK Names, but their premium income limits will be reduced pro rata.

12 Lloyd's Policy Signing Office – LPSO – is the largest employer among the departments of the corporation. It receives the draft insurance policy, prepared by the broker, compares the policy with the slip to see that the conditions laid down by the underwriters have been reflected in the policy and, if all is in order, signs and seals the policy on behalf of the underwriters. Its function is therefore essentially one of providing a check on behalf of underwriters but it also has a regulatory role: irregularities that come to light in the LPSO are reported to the advisory department for investigation and, in extreme cases, disciplinary action can ensue.

13 Lloyd's Act 1982, s. 6.

Chapter IV The Legal and Financial Structure of Lloyd's

1 Cockerell, *Lloyd's of London – A Portrait*, p. 13.
2 This was the Forwood case in which the committee's improbably illegal conduct led to pressure for reform. See Gibb, *Lloyd's of London – A Study in Individualism*, p. 135.
3 This has since changed at the instigation of the Neill Report. See Chapters I and XIX.
4 It was upon this area that the Neill inquiry focused.
5 Smith, *The Wealth of Nations*, Chapter X, Part 1.
6 Insurance Companies Act 1982, s. 83 (2).
7 Lloyd's of London, *Membership: The Issues*, 1986.
8 Before making allowance for sums earmarked to cover the contingent deficits of members in suspense of £82 million. See Lloyd's of London: 'Global Report and Accounts', 31 December 1985, p. 43.
9 See Chapter XVIII.
10 The Burnand scandal of 1903 when an underwriter and three of the four other Names on his syndicate were bankrupted. This led to a programme of reforms. Gibb, op. cit., p. 183.
11 In 1985, Neill *Regulatory Arrangements at Lloyd's* para. 9.51, p. 61.
12 See Chapter V.
13 Neill explores the question of protection of Names' interests at considerable length. See Chapter XVIII.

Chapter V The Advent of Speculation

1 Cromer, *Report of Working Party to Study the Future of Lloyd's*, 1969.
2 Ibid., para. 50, p. 14.
3 Ibid., para. 195, p. 41.
4 Ibid., para. 231, p. 47.
5 Ibid., para. 340, p. 66.
6 Fisher, *Self-Regulation at Lloyd's*, para. 1.12, p. 3.
7 Lloyd's Act 1982, s. 3 (2)(c).
8 The *Higgins* Inquiry into the Underwriting Agency System at Lloyd's found

in September 1982 that 308 out of 431 syndicates would have to suffer a change of ownership as a result of the Act. That represents 71 per cent of the syndicates. The Fisher report, in para. 12.03, said '... the eight largest "Broker-Controlled" Agencies are controlled by the eight largest Lloyd's Brokers who between them account for 58.8 per cent of the premium income of Lloyd's.'

9 Chapter III, p. 24.
10 Cromer, op. cit., paras. 252 and 253, p. 50, quoted in Fisher, op. cit., para. 12.10, p. 75.
11 Fisher, op. cit., para. 12.19, p. 77.
12 This passage is largely drawn from a paper given at the Revenue Law Conference at Cambridge by the author on 5 July 1986.
13 Report of Lloyd's Disciplinary and Appellate Proceedings in the matter of C. L. R. Hart, p. 19.
14 This passage is largely drawn from a paper given at the National Association of Accountants Conference in Paris by the author on 19 April 1985.
15 Cromer, op. cit., para. 181, p. 37.

Chapter VI   The Autumn of 1982
1 See Chapter II.
2 For a discussion of the Howden, PCW and Brookes & Dooley affairs see Hodgson, *Lloyd's of London – A Reputation at Risk*, and the reports of the Lloyd's disciplinary committees into 'The Fidentia Case' 8401/4 and 'The PCW Case' 8401/5. The Howden affair is developed and analysed in 'The Wigham Poland Policy' 8403/4, 'Southern International Reinsurance and the Banque du Rhone' 8404/4, and 'The Hart Syndicates' 8501/9.
3 Hodgson, op. cit., p. 79.
4 Boyd and Dubuisson, 'Minet Holdings et al. Investigation under s. 165 of the Companies Act 1948', paras 5.16, 5.17 and 5.21, pp. 59–62.
5 Ibid., para. 7.33, p. 80.
6 Ibid., para. 7.35, p. 81.
7 See Chapter V, p. 45.
8 For a lengthy description of this task see Davis, 'Inquiry into the Management of Syndicates by Richard Beckett Underwriting Agencies Ltd.'
9 The Neill Report attempts an estimate in paras 3.18–3.20 p. 13 as follows:

	£m
Brooks & Dooley	£ 6.2
Howden's $30 million at 1.5 $/£	£20.0
PCW	£29.0
	£55.2

10 Report of Lloyd's Disciplinary Proceedings 'The PCW Case' 8401/5.
11 Ibid., para. B 9(6), p. 21.
12 Ibid., para. B 11, p. 24.

13 The relative roles of the DTI and the Bank are interesting at this stage. The Governor of the Bank of England, Gordon Richardson, was a popular figure at the height of his powers. Clearly he saw the Lloyd's difficulties as a City problem for the resolution of which he had better take responsibility if the Bank were to retain its traditional influence in City markets. The Treasury and Whitehall were known to be flexing their muscles about City regulation. The DTI, under Lord Cockfield, acquiesced, and although he clearly signalled his approval by telephone to my appointment, I never had a face-to-face interview with him about Lloyd's at that time. See Bruce-Gardyne, *Ministers and Mandarins*, Chapter 6.

Chapter VII The New Council of Lloyd's

1 Gough until December 1986, Walker-Arnott until December 1987 and Berrill until December 1988. Sir Kenneth Berrill later became Chairman of the Securities and Investment Board.
2 The Neill Report drew attention to this matter and proposed that the Council of Lloyd's should keep the question of remuneration under review. Para. 12.36, p. 84.
3 Since I left Lloyd's at the end of February 1986 the corporation has moved across Lime Street into the new building. The committee room is now on the eleventh floor and the executive offices on the twelfth. What used to be known as 'the second floor' has therefore become the 'the twelfth floor'. Following the recommendations of the Berrill Committee one of the weekly committee meetings has been replaced by the monthly council meeting.
4 Neill's proposal to remove the working members' majority will have the effect, as he points out at para. 12.38 p. 84, that the special resolution procedure, designed to give a blocking veto to the nominated and external members, will instead give it to the working members. To that extent his proposal is defective and the Act should be amended to correct this.
5 See Appendix I. The Bank of England played an influential part in drafting this document.

Chapter VIII Cleaning up the Market

1 Much of this passage is drawn from a paper given at a Risk Research Group Conference on 'The Future of Lloyd's' by the author on 14 February 1984.
2 *Financial Times*, 10 December 1982.
3 Regrettably since the summer of 1985 the old carping tone has returned.
4 Section 20 of the Lloyd's Act 1871 reads, in part: 'If any member of the Society 1. Violates any of the fundamental rules of the Society; or 2. Is guilty of any act or default discreditable to him as an underwriter or otherwise in connection with the business of insurance he shall be liable to be excluded from membership of the Society.' To enforce this section Lloyd's and the defendant had each to appoint an arbitrator who would jointly report as to the member's guilt. If found guilty the member could

then be expelled by an 80 per cent majority at a general meeting, provided that at least one hundred members voted.

5 Lloyd's Act 1982, s. 7.

6 Bye-Law No. 2 of 1983 – Administrative Suspension.
Bye-Law No. 3 of 1983 – Inquiries and Investigations.
Bye-Law No. 4 of 1983 – Information and Confidentiality.
Bye-Law No. 5 of 1983 – Misconduct, Penalties and Sanctions.
Bye-Law No. 6 of 1983 – Disciplinary Committees.
Bye-Law No. 7 of 1983 – Appeal Tribunal.
Bye-Law No. 8 of 1983 – Council Stage of Disciplinary Proceedings.

7 Neill commends this course of action in his report and goes further to propose that a nominated member of council should always chair the Investigations Committee and that working members of that committee should be in a minority.

8 Bye-Law No. 2 of 1983 – Administrative Suspension.

9 Called the Advisory Department because it advises underwriters of miscreants who are known to be about in the insurance world.

10 By 18 January 1987 eight investigations had been carried out by outsiders and seventeen by Lloyd's staff, assisted in one case by two working members of the council.

11 Colman & Hailey, 'The Fidentia Report, Part I'.

12 Bye-Law No. 9 of 1984 – Membership.

13 There are those who would argue that Lloyd's disciplinary proceedings are a lawyer's paradise. During 1984 I was a guest at the Annual Dinner of the Senate and the Inns of Court, and was made most welcome. Inquiring why I had been singled out for such excellent hospitality I was told: 'You do realize, don't you, that cases surrounding Lloyd's provided 20 per cent of the fee income of the entire London bar last year?' I do not know whether or not this was true, but men of Lloyd's are litigious, especially when livelihoods and large sums are at stake.

14 Report of Lloyd's Disciplinary Proceedings. Appeal by Ian Richard Posgate 8404/4, para 7(a), p. 4.

15 This had not always been the case. Instances had occurred in the past when Lloyd's settled matters, and expelled the miscreants, without calling in the police.

16 The contrast with the promptness with which the authorities have pursued those accused of insider dealing in securities at the end of 1986 is striking.

17 Neill confirms this at para. 11.45 p. 76: 'We sympathise with those who have expressed exasperation that alleged frauds remain untried in the criminal courts. The sooner the lengthy investigations have been concluded the better. It is certainly beyond doubt that no blame can be attached to Lloyd's for the fact that public prosecutions have not been instituted.'

18 See Chapter V, p. 49 et seq. This passage, like the earlier one, is largely drawn from a paper given at the Revenue Law Conference at Cambridge by the author on 5 July 1986.

19 This view was confirmed by the Neill Report which recommends at para. 9.25, p. 57 the introduction of rigorous professional examinations for underwriters so that those who work in the market are thoroughly familiar with the law of agency.

Chapter IX   The Rule Book

1 Lloyd's Bye-Laws under Lloyd's Acts 1870 to 1951.
2 Bye-laws were required to be passed by a general meeting. See Chapter IV, p. 31.
3 For example, members were required to sign a general undertaking on election, and conditions and requirements were imposed by means of undertakings before admission to the register of Lloyd's brokers permitted 'to show a brokerage account in the Room'.
4 See Chapter V p. 50.
5 An example is the 'War & Civil War Risk Exclusion Agreement' which excludes the insurance of property on land against war risks, and delegates the control of underwriting marine and aviation war risks to the relevant sub-agreements. The philosophy behind the agreement is that the accumulation of value on land could exceed an insurer's capital base, so not only would insurers be destroyed, but the assured would not be indemnified. Ships and their cargoes are less of an accumulation risk, as they can move away from potential danger, in absolute terms the values involved are far less, and the insurances offered contain exclusions and cancellation clauses which would not be acceptable to owners of land-based property.
6 The discussion that follows was published in *Lloyd's Log* in July 1983 under the title 'Self-Regulatory Policy at Lloyd's'.
7 See Chapter VI p. 61.
8 'Self-Regulatory Policy at Lloyd's'.
9 Fisher, op. cit., para. 1.20, p. 6.
10 This passage draws upon the arguments in a paper given to the American Bar Association in London by the author on 16 July 1985.
11 On reflection I am forced to conclude that codes of conduct are most appropriate for identifying existing best practice in order to encourage a minority of backsliders to mend their ways: they are not so suitable where existing practices are inadequate and in need of reform. Neill confirms this view at para. 8.49 and adds the further powerful argument: 'Whether or not failure to comply with the provision of a code would give grounds enabling a Name to mount an action for breach of contract, it is beyond doubt that a clear and specific bye-law dealing with the same matter would enhance his prospects of success.'
12 For an explanation of baby syndicates see Chapter VI, p. 62.
13 Such green papers had to conform to certain basic desiderata: the reason for the report had to be clearly stated; the document should be self-sufficient, containing within itself all that the reader would need in order to consider the policy discussed; the issues were to be explained as far as possible in

layman's language, remembering that underwriters and brokers are not lawyers; the arguments for and against the proposed course of action should be rehearsed and the conclusion clearly stated; and finally, readers should be directed to the issues on which comments were specifically required. Consultative documents were issued with a deadline for response after which action would be taken.

14 It is noteworthy that legislation about baby syndicates, related party reinsurance, disclosure of agents' charges to their Names and the production of information for new Names all got a fresh impetus as a result of Press pressures following the disclosure of the large PCW losses in Summer 1985 and the subsequent appointment of the Neill Inquiry.

Chapter X Syndicate Accounts

1 Fisher, *Self-Regulation at Lloyd's*, Recommendation No. 71, p. 9 and para. 23.22, p. 139.
2 The Companies Act refers to the Companies Act 1985, a consolidating statute which incorporates all Companies Acts since the last consolidating statute of 1948.
3 See Chapter I, p. 5.
4 Plaistowe, 'Disclosure of Interests by Underwriting Agents Draft – Bye-Law and Detailed Proposals', *Plaistowe* Working Party.
5 Randall, 'Lloyd's Accounting Manual'.
6 See Chapter VI, p. 62.
7 *Higgins*, 'Underwriting Agency System at Lloyd's – Part II'.
8 Bye-Law No. 3 of 1984 – Disclosure of Interests, s. 3.
9 The other three being the disciplinary rules, the rules for members and those for the registration of agents.
10 Despite fears that the publication of syndicate accounts would attract hordes of curious gossips the opening of the files passed quietly. The number of inquiries has been:

   1984 – 51
   1985 – 69
   1986 – 45

11 MacVe, *A Survey of Lloyd's Syndicate Accounts*.
12 Bye-Law No. 7 of 1984 – Syndicate Accounting. Explanatory Notes – Reinsurance to Close, 9 December 1985.
13 Neill supports this view at para. 5.9, p. 23.
14 Ernst & Whinney, the Corporation of Lloyd's auditors, now give a report that the LPSO figures are correctly prepared. But they are not able to give an assurance that the premium income booked in the year relates to insurance covers which start in that year.
15 MacVe, op. cit., p. 111; see also Neill, para. 5.13, p. 24, who agrees.
16 IBNR – Claims incurred but not reported.
17 Neill supports this view, see para. 5.8, p. 23.
18 It recommended that net premium income should be analysed by major

business category, geographical area, and source – reinsurance treaty, binding authority, etc. The review of the closing year would compare premium income with capacity, identify significant claims affecting the year and report on the performance of the reinsurance to close of the previous years. Similar details would be disclosed, as far as possible, about the open years.

19 MacVe, op. cit., p. 191, a view supported by Neill, p. 25.

20 Ibid., pp. 228–9.

Chapter XI The Audit Panel

1 Chapter IV, p. 38.

2 'Lloyd's Syndicate Audit Arrangements'.

3 Ibid., para. 3.6, p. 3.

4 Insurance Companies Act 1982, s. 83(4).

5 See Chapter I, p. 5.

6 Although some argued that the 15 per cent rule should be interpreted so that no panel auditor could depend upon work in the Lloyd's market for more than 15 per cent of his total fees, this was felt to be too restrictive and the test was applied only at the managing agency level: no auditor could earn more than 15 per cent of his total fee income from any one managing agent's group of syndicates.

7 'Lloyd's Syndicate Audit Arrangements', para. 7.4.1, p. 7.

8 Ibid., para. 7.4.4., p. 8.

9 Ibid., para. 8.5, p. 10.

10 Ibid., para. 8.6.1, p. 10.

11 Neill, *Regulatory Arrangements at Lloyd's*, para. 5.22, p. 26.

12 Some accountants are associates, a class of person outside the membership entitled to enter the Room and use Lloyd's facilities.

13 Bye-Law No. 10 of 1984 – Syndicate Audit Arrangements – Schedule 2.

14 'Lloyd's Syndicate Audit Arrangements', para. 5.3, p. 4.

15 Neill, *Regulatory Arrangements at Lloyd's*, para. 10.21, p. 65.

16 At 31 December 1986 the distribution of syndicate audit assignments was as follows:

	%
Ernst & Whinney	24
Neville Russell	22
Littlejohn Frazer	18
Arthur Young	15
	79
Others (7 firms)	21
	100

Eight panel firms had no audits at all.

17 Neill, op. cit., para. 9.51, p. 61; and Fisher, *Self-Regulation at Lloyd's*, para. 23.22, p. 141.

Chapter XII   Divestment and the Re-registration of Agents

1 Divestment, at Lloyd's, means the legal separation of Lloyd's brokers from managing agencies who have the management of the underwriting syndicates, so that the conflict between the duty of the broker to his customer, the insured, and the duty of the managing agent to the Names on the underwriting syndicates he manages is eliminated.
2 Fisher, *Self-Regulation at Lloyd's*, para. 12.19, p. 77.
3 Daniels, 'Underwriting Agencies After Divestment,' Papers from a Technical Briefing Conference published by the Risk Research Group Ltd, March 1985.
4 Ibid., p. 18.
5 Fisher, op. cit., paras 10.06–10.09, p. 60.
6 *Higgins*, 'Underwriting Agency System at Lloyd's – Part 1'.
7 Ibid., para. 2.02, p. 13. This passage throws an interesting light on the attitude of the working party to self-regulation at Lloyd's. The implication is that outsiders might not be trusted to abide by the rules. But Lloyd's problem was that it was the insiders who had broken the rules, and some, admittedly guilty of milder transgressions, sat on the governing Council of Lloyd's.
8 The Stock Exchange frowns upon such a capital structure in the case of a quoted company.
9 See Chapter III, p. 24.
10 This was the very position in which Minet Holdings PLC were to find themselves vis-à-vis their agency subsidiary PCW.
11 *Higgins*, op. cit., para. 3.17, p. 18. Stamp capacity refers to the total premium income the syndicate is permitted to accept: its capacity to accept premium income. Years ago, when syndicates consisted of only a handful of Names and there was no LPSO or central accounting, underwriters had rubber stamps made which showed their syndicate's membership and the individual Names' shares. This was stamped on policies when they were signed at the box.
12 Bye-Law No. 4 of 1984 – Underwriting Agents, s. 8, p. 11.
13 Ibid., s. 15(a), p. 17.
14 *Higgins*, 'Underwriting Agency System at Lloyd's – Working Party's Consultative Paper on Ownership and Control of Underwriting Agencies', September 1982.
Appendix 2 – Analysis of Agencies as at September 1982.
Total Number of Underwriting Agents in the Market:

(i) Number of pure Managing Agents	35 (11%)
(ii) Number of pure Members' Agents	105 (35%)
(iii) Number of Managing/Members' Agents	163 (54%)

Total Number of Managing Agents Identified as having a Divestment Problem:

(i) Number of pure Managing Agents   19 (17%)

(ii) Number of Managing/Members' Agents   95 (83%)

                                                      114

Syndicates:

Total number of syndicates in the Lloyd's Market = 431

Number of Syndicates managed by the 114 Agents = 308 (71%)

15 Much of the commentary on the effects of divestment that follows is drawn from a paper on 'Statutory Divestment at Lloyd's of London and the Financial Services Revolution'. Given at the Manchester Business School Conference on New Strategies in Financial Services by the author on 11 June 1986.

16 Neill comments on this and suggests a relaxation of the strict rule that outsiders may not exercise voting control over Lloyd's agencies, para. 9.9, p. 53.

17 *Bird*, 'Membership Requirements at Lloyd's'. This proposal was vigorously endorsed by Neill, para. 5.36, p. 28.

Chapter XIII Relations between Members and Lloyd's

1 The other three were: the audit and publication of syndicate accounts; the re-registration of agents; and the disciplinary rules.

2 *Bird*, 'Membership Requirements at Lloyd's'.

3 'Membership of the Society' consultative document.

4 In 1985 11,000 application forms for membership were issued and 4,330 completed forms returned; 3,178 applicants attended a Rota interview and 3,085 new members were finally elected.

5 Bye-Law No. 9 of 1984 – Membership.

6 See Chapter VIII, p. 84.

7 Several liability is required by Bye-Law No. 9 of 1984 s. 18(a) replacing Lloyd's Act 1871 s. 40: Underwriting is confined to Lloyd's by Bye-Law No. 9 of 1984 s. 17(b) replacing Lloyd's Act 1871 Schedule – Rule 3.

8 Cromer, *Report of Working Party to Study the Future of Lloyd's* (1969).

9 Fisher, *Self-Regulation at Lloyd's*.

10 *Barber*, 'Underwriting Agency Agreement'.

11 Fisher, op. cit., para. 9.31, p. 58.

12 *Barber*, op. cit., para. 6, p. 3.

13 Ibid., para. 6, p. 3.

14 Cromer, op. cit., para 222 et seq., pp. 46–8.

15 Fisher, op. cit., para. 9.30, p. 58.

16 Lloyd's gave an undertaking to the House of Commons Committee on the Lloyd's Bill in July 1981 that the recommendation in paras 9.15 and 23.22 of the Fisher Report would be implemented within two years of the Bill receiving Royal Assent, i.e. July 1984. Paragraph 9.15 of the Fisher Report called for a bye-law specifying the information to be disclosed to prospective

Names including the maintenance by the corporation of a register of the terms and conditions of business offered by all agents and the disclosure by agents of their other business interests. Paragraph 23.22 called for rules about syndicate accounts. Paragraph 9.15 was not implemented in accordance with the Parliamentary undertaking. See Neill, *Regulatory Arrangements at Lloyd's*, Appendix 8, p. 102.

17 Higgins, 'Underwriting Agency System at Lloyd's Part I,' para. 9.03, p. 26.
18 Barber, op. cit., para. 9, p. 4.
19 MacVe, *A Survey of Lloyd's Syndicate Accounts*, Chapter 9, p. 84.
20 The position was improved when, under the pressure of the Neill Inquiry, the council agreed to maintain a detailed register of all managing and members' agents' charges to be available publicly. See Lloyd's Press Release, 9 December 1986.
21 Neill, op. cit., Chapter 6, p. 29.
22 Bird, op. cit. The working party included two external members, a number of agents, and two members of the corporation staff.
23 This has now been corrected and arrangements are in hand to bring all members into line by 1 January 1988.
24 Bird, op. cit., para. 2.11, p. 15. This is also to be implemented by 1 January 1988.
25 The political implications, for the management of the society, of the decision about maximum premium income are immense. Without such a limit the market's capacity could well be provided by far fewer wealthier members. But such a structure would reduce the power of the agents because their Names would be fewer in number and more influential. By deciding to retain a maximum premium income limit Lloyd's has ensured that it will have a numerous membership as it grows. But this has produced a society in which the Names think of themselves as investors and not as members of a club. The pressures this change has brought about are the theme of this book.

Chapter XIV Rules for Underwriters

1 Chapter V, p. 46.
2 Lloyd's Report of Disciplinary Proceedings against F. H. Sasse, Exhibit No. 1, p. 3, and Statement of Case, paras 2.3 and 2.7, pp. 2 and 5.
3 Such overwriting could not escape the eyes of a reasonably vigilant auditor. Delayed signings risk discovery in a market where there are many syndicates on one slip.
4 See Chapter X, p. 106.
5 Fisher, *Self-Regulation at Lloyd's*, para. 21.19, p. 128.
6 Ibid., para. 21.26, p. 130.
7 Bye-Law No. 6 of 1984 – Syndicate Premium Income.
8 Ibid., para. 2(a), p. 5.
9 Fisher, op. cit., para. 22.02, p. 131.
10 Bye-Law No. 4 of 1985, Schedule 1.

11 Quoted in Fisher, op. cit., para. 22.10, p. 133.

12 Bye-Law No. 4 of 1985.

13 Fisher, op. cit., para. 22.13, p. 133.

14 Code of Practice on operation of Binding Authorities. Issued on 5 August 1985 by the Council of Lloyd's with Bye-Law No. 4 of 1985.

15 See Chapter IX, p. 91.

16 The result of the unfortunate experience of the market when it insured the Liberal Party's deposits in 1950.

17 Hodgson, *Lloyd's of London – A Reputation at Risk*, p. 255.

18 Fisher, op. cit., para. 27.03, p. 150.

19 Report of Lloyd's Disciplinary and Appellate proceedings in the Case of C. L. R. Hart. Decision of the Disciplinary Committee, para. 51, p. 32.

20 *Higgins*, 'Part I', op. cit., para. 9.12, p. 27.

21 Colman and Hailey, 'The Fidentia Report Part I', para. 18.22.

22 Related Party Interests and Transactions Bye-Law – Exposure Draft – August 1985.

23 Related Parties Bye-Law No. 2 of 1986.

24 Neill says: 'It seems to us that the prohibitions contained in Bye-law No. 2 of 1986 combined with the continuing requirement (imposed by Bye-law No. 3 of 1984) on managing agents to disclose any transactions in which they, their executives, or related companies have material interests, go a very long way towards ensuring that past abuses are not repeated.' Para. 8.26, p. 47.

25 *Higgins*, 'Part II', para. 11.1, p. 4.

26 Association of Lloyd's Members, '1982 Lloyd's Syndicate Results'.

27 Bye-Law No. 7 of 1984 – the Syndicate Accounting Bye-Law – Schedule 7, para. (j) p. 48.

28 The Neill Report charts the collapse of baby syndicates. The percentage of syndicates having 99 or fewer members changed as follows:

1978	43	1981	32	1984	18
1979	37	1982	29	1985	11
1980	34	1983	24	1986	8

The rapid decline after 1983 is noteworthy. See Neill, op. cit., Appendix 12.

29 *Higgins* Part II was published in September 1983, the Multiple Syndicates Code and Bye-Law was passed in December 1985.

30 Neill reports the percentage of parallel syndicates, where one underwriter manages more than one syndicate, as follows:

1978	31	1981	27	1984	21
1979	33	1982	27	1985	20
1980	30	1983	24	1986	16

The decline after 1983 was noticeably rapid. Unlike the earlier table showing the numbers of small syndicates these figures are not affected by the growth in the membership. Source, Neill, op. cit., Appendix II.

31 Neill, op. cit., para. 8.49, p. 51.

32 Code attached to Multiple Syndicate Bye-Law No. 7 of 1985.

33 These matters, originally part of the legislation, were once again deferred at the committee's request and will no doubt be swept up in the programme of reforms that will follow the Neill Report.

34 Bye-Law No. 7 of 1985 – Multiple Syndicate Bye-Law, para. 2, p. 5.

35 Neill reports that only three syndicates were affected by this bye-law. Neill, op. cit., para. 8.39, p. 49. It was in effect a hollow gesture, helpful in creating an impression of determined action but of little real effect.

Chapter XV   Lloyd's Corporation Structure

1 Chapter VII, p. 70.

2 Quoted in full in Appendix I.

3 Throughout this and the next chapter, unless the context calls for a fuller title, the deputy chairman and chief executive is referred to as the chief executive.

4 Cockerell, *Lloyd's of London – A Portrait*, p. 18.

5 A position first established by John Bennett in 1804.

6 Gibb, *Lloyd's of London – A Study in Individualism*, p. 147.

7 In 1967 the number of deputy chairmen had been increased from one to two to cope with the increasing work of the society's administration.

8 Chapter XIV, p. 137.

9 The largest department of the corporation, the Lloyd's Policy Signing Office was set up in 1916 and only taken over by the corporation in 1924 when all underwriters were, for the first time, required to use the LPSO.

10 The sole exception was the marine intelligence department. Once the biggest department of the corporation, it had been hived off in 1973 when Lloyd's of London Press was established at Colchester to publish *Lloyd's List* daily, the regular weekly and monthly shipping publications, and a list of maritime and legal works.

11 See Chapter IX.

12 Berrill, *Lloyd's Corporation Structure*, para. 2.3, p. 7. See also Chapter XVI, p. 158.

13 Ibid., para. 3.15, p. 14.

14 Ibid., para. 2.5(i), p. 8.

15 Ibid., para. 7.6, p. 38.

16 In 1985 the Corporation of Lloyd's showed an operating surplus of £24 million and a total revenue of £103 million. Of this revenue rather more than half came from members' subscriptions and entrance fees and the balance from charges for services provided to the market. There had been little variation in this pattern during preceding years.

17 See Chapter IX, p. 98.

Chapter XVI   The Position of the Chief Executive

1 Unless the context requires otherwise this chapter uses the phrase 'chief executive' to mean the deputy chairman and chief executive.

2 Lloyd's Act 1982, s. 4.

3 See Terms of Reference, Appendix I.

4 Lloyd's Act 1982, s. 6(8) and Appendix I.

5 Neill, *Regulatory Arrangements at Lloyd's*, para. 12.16, p. 80.

6 See Chapter XV, p. 148. Assignments continued until well into 1987.

7 See Chapter XV, p. 148. This committee was unique among committees of the council in that although the chairman was a member it was chaired by an external or nominated member of the council to emphasize the fact that staff matters belonged to the chief executive and he reported about them to the council directly and not through the chairman, who had ceased to have executive responsibility for staff matters.

8 This phrase echoed Sir Henry Fisher's comment that the Secretary General of Lloyd's should play a role akin to that of a permanent secretary in a ministry. See Fisher, *Self-Regulation at Lloyd's*, para. 26.04, p. 148.

9 Fisher, *Self-Regulation at Lloyd's*, para. 26.06, p. 149.

10 Just before the press conference in September at which the chairman traditionally announces Lloyd's results an error was found in the Global returns for 1984 (see Chapter VIII, p. 78). The error had arisen because of a misunderstanding by a panel auditor about one of the syndicate returns. It had been discovered because of a new system of accounting checks introduced for the first time that year. Because the annual deadline for filing syndicate returns had been repeatedly put back to accommodate the difficulties of the PCW Names, insufficient time had been left to resolve errors revealed by the new checks.

11 Berrill, *Lloyd's Corporation Structure*, para. 2.3, p. 7.

12 Ibid., para. 2.4, p. 8.

13 Ibid., para. 2.5(i), p. 8.

14 My letter of resignation is included at Appendix II.

15 Berrill, op. cit., para. 4.9, p. 21.

16 Locke, *Of Civil Government*, Book II, Chapter 12, para. 143.

Chapter XVII   Unfinished Rule-making

1 Lloyd's Act 1982, s. 8(3).

2 Fisher, *Self-Regulation at Lloyd's*, para. 13.04, p. 8.

3 For a further description see Chapter II, p. 17.

4 Fisher, op. cit., para. 13.19, p. 89.

5 Lloyd's Act 1982, s. 8(3).

6 This brief bye-law gives legal effect to the Direct Motor Regulations. Motor business may be accepted fron non-Lloyd's brokers provided that it complies with the regulation.

7 The Insurance Brokers Registration Council (Code of Conduct) Approval Order 1979, s. 3.

8 See Chapter IV, p. 32.
9 The Lambert Coles Committee.
10 Fisher, op. cit., para. 14.02, p. 95 and Appendix 7, pp. 181–4.
11 Anglo-African Merchants Ltd v. Bayley, 1970, 1 QB 311; North, and South Trust Co. v. Berkeley, 1971, 1 WLR 470, both discussed in Fisher, op. cit., para. 13.27, p. 90.
12 Neill points out that sixteen years after the above cases the legal conundrum that they propound has still not been resolved. Neill, op. cit., para. 9.45, p. 60.
13 Insurance broking accounts.
14 Fisher, op. cit., para. 13.39, p. 93.
15 See chairman's speech to the general meeting of members, 25 June 1986.
16 See Chapter XIV, p. 137.
17 Clucas, *Extended Warranty and Consumer Guarantee*, para. 6.2.3, p. 10 and para. 8.12, p. 16.
18 *Batchelor*, 'Umbrella Arrangements'.
19 See House of Lords Debate on the Criminal Justice Bill, 10 February 1986. Hansard, Columns 49–54.
20 At which members of the Investigations Committee are absent.
21 Fisher, op. cit., para. 9.08, p. 51.
22 Neill, op. cit., Appendix 8, p. 102.
23 Fisher, op. cit., para. 9.15, p. 53 et seq. This was one of the two paragraphs specified in the Parliamentary Undertaking. The other was para. 23.22 concerning syndicate accounts – see Chapter X, p. 104. The discussion in the Fisher Report carries interesting echoes of an earlier age: the non-Lloyd's members of the working party favouring disclosure of syndicate accounts, the Lloyd's members believing that the publication of syndicate results for the purposes of comparison might be positively misleading. The conclusion was that the non-Lloyd's members were prepared not to press for more radical proposals (for the general publication of syndicate results), but to rest content with the more limited proposals which all members of the working party were willing to support.
24 Neill, op. cit., paras. 4.14 to 4.22, pp. 17–18.
25 'Lloyd's of London – Membership: The Issues', December 1986.
26 See Chapter XIII.
27 Such a proposal would be as fair as and more workable than the suggestion for auctioning places on syndicates considered and rejected by Neill at para. 5.32, p. 27.
28 See Chapter III, p. 39.
29 Bye-Law No. 5 of 1986, s. 1.

Chapter XVIII   PCW and the Names
1 The story is introduced at Chapter VI.
2 Bye-Law No. 7 of 1984.

3 President of the Institute of Bankers and Vice-Chairman of Lloyd's Bank PLC.
4 The name of the agency was changed from P.C.W. Underwriting Agencies Limited to Richard Beckett Underwriting Agencies Limited in September 1983.
5 Davis, 'Inquiry into the Management of Syndicates by Richard Beckett Underwriting Agencies Limited'.
6 Ibid., para. 3.91, p. 53.
7 'Lloyd's Global Report and Accounts', 1985, p. 4.
8 Davis, op. cit., para. 3.114, p. 59.
9 Ibid., para. 7.2, p. 128.
10 Names should be better placed in future by the adoption of Neill's Recommendation 20 which calls for a direct contractual nexus between Name and managing agent.
11 Davis, op. cit., para. 9.106, p. 199.
12 Bye-Law No. 7 of 1984 – The Syndicate Accounting Bye-Law, Explanatory Notes on Reinsurance to Close, 4 December 1985.
13 A total of 517 members failed to file solvency certificates by 31 July 1985. As a result £66 million of the Central Fund, which then stood at about £200 million, was 'earmarked'. By October, 199 Names had failed to provide proof of their solvency and were suspended: £56 million was still earmarked. A year later no less than £238 million was earmarked out of a Central Fund which then stood at £265 million. (Neill, op. cit., para. 7.32, p. 41.) The increase in earmarking is due to dramatic worsening of the PCW losses during 1986. The number of Names then facing losses of over one hundred thousand pounds was probably between three hundred and five hundred.
14 Sir Ian Morrow is a former President of the Institute of Chartered Accountants of Scotland. He is not a member of Lloyd's.
15 Lloyd's agreed to foot the bill through a policy of insurance. Gibb's history of Lloyd's reports at p. 273: 'A premium of 2/6d per cent was paid by the Corporation to the underwriters for writing a risk that was known to be a loss before it was written. A slip was initialled and a policy signed. The original policy is still in existence – a document of no little significance which, even if it is never exhibited, should be kept permanently in the Corporation's archives. It has indeed a twofold interest. It is the first outward and visible sign of the sense of Corporate responsibility which marks the modern Lloyd's. And it is probably the only policy in the history of underwriting in which has appeared the signature of every Lloyd's syndicate and every person underwriting for himself alone. In that respect it is unique.'
16 Gibb, *Lloyd's of London*, p. 283. This concerns the Wilcox Syndicate.
17 Insurance Companies Act 1982, ss. 83(4) and (5).
18 'Explanatory Notes on Reinsurance to Close', op. cit.

19 In order to avoid commercial harassment Lloyd's is careful to keep the private addresses of Names confidential. Mail addressed to a Name at Lloyd's is forwarded to his agent who should then pass it on. Unhappily it can happen that if the contents of the letter are critical to the interests of the agent, it may not be forwarded.

20 Neill, op. cit., paras 7.9–7.28, pp. 36–40.

21 Bye-Law No. 4 of 1984 – The Central Fund Bye-Law.

22 The matter of a compensation fund put the Neill Inquiry into something of a quandary. Such funds are an essential part of investor protection under the Financial Services Act. Lloyd's has none and it is not easy to see how one could be established. Neill, op. cit., paras 7.31–7.39, pp. 40–42.

23 'Lloyd's Global Report and Accounts', 1985, p. 42.

24 Confirmation that I am not the only one to hold this view is provided by the Neill Report. 'We should record the scepticism expressed by a number of the witnesses about whether unlimited liability continues to provide a practical basis on which to run the market. They have argued that a Name's liability should be limited to his shown means.' Neill, op. cit., para. 4.27, p. 19.

Chapter XIX   Lloyd's and the Legislators

1 Notably Jonathan Aitken MP on the Savonita affair. See Chapter V, p. 45.

2 For a detailed description of the events surrounding the passage of the Lloyd's Act 1982 see Hodgson, *Lloyd's – A Reputation at Risk*, Chapter II, p. 306. For the Parliamentary Undertaking see Neill, *Regulatory Arrangements at Lloyd's*, Appendix 8.

3 Messrs Grob, Wallrock and Posgate were later disciplined by Lloyd's disciplinary committees.

4 Gower, *Review of Investor Protection – Part I.*

5 Ibid., para. 4.12, p. 31.

6 Financial Services Act 1986 – Schedule 1.

7 Insurance Companies Act 1982 – s. 83(2).

8 Financial Services Act 1986 – s. 42.

9 It is very doubtful that such resources would have been made available had the Civil Service been given the job.

10 Neill, *Regulatory Arrangements at Lloyd's*, para. 1.4, p. 1.

11 Ibid., para. 1.6, p. 1.

12 Ibid., para. 1.10, p. 2.

13 Bye-Law No. 5 of 1986 – Review Powers.

14 'Lloyd's of London – Membership: The Issues', December 1986.

15 See Chapter I, p. 7.

16 Neill, op. cit., para. 11.47, p. 77.

17 Ibid., Chapter 12, p. 78; unless otherwise indicated the quotations on the following pages are drawn from this chapter.

18 Ibid., Appendix I, para. 8(9).

19 Appendix I, para. 5(a).

20 See Chapter V.
21 Neill, op. cit., para. 1.18, p. 3.
22 See Chapter I.

Chapter XX   The Future of Lloyd's

1 However Names are clearly much more careful of their interests. Almost half now have stop loss policies and the number of resignations rose in 1986 to 1.3 per cent of the membership after averaging 0.5 per cent for ten years.
2 See Chapter XIV, p. 134.
3 Matters were considerably advanced on this front by the settlement in December 1986 of four cases brought by the EEC Commission against the governments of West Germany, France, Ireland and Belgium. It was successfully argued that EEC-based insurers should enjoy greater freedom to operate elsewhere in Europe.
4 'Underwriters' Corporation Staff and Brokers' View of Lloyd's', July 1985.
5 A view which Neill endorses, admittedly for different reasons. See Chapter X, p. 106 and Neill, *Regulatory Arrangements at Lloyd's*, para. 5.9, p. 23.
6 But the issue remains unresolved as Neill explains in para. 9.45, p. 60. See Chapter XVII, p. 168.
7 Marine Insurance Act 1906, s. 22.
8 Bye-Law No. 8 of 1985 – Lloyd's Introductory Test.
9 Neill, op. cit., para. 9.25, p. 57.

Index

Index

Index

Dixey Working Party – underwriting
    agents manual 117
Dixon, Peter 57, 58, 61, 175
DPP and criminal prosecutions of Lloyd's
    offenders 85, 219

Englefield, Rear-Admiral Sir Gilbert
    Bart – Secretary to the Committee
    of Lloyd's 1906–22 146
Exchange controls 51
External members of Council – election
    of 64

Farrar, Mark 60
Fidentia Report 83, 139
Financial Services Bill/Act 1986 2, 159,
    186
Fisher, Sir Henry:
    Report 5, 47, 59, 94, 123, 126, 131,
        135, 185
    recommendations divorce 48
    recommendations divestment 47, 116
    re-registration of agents 117
    re agents charges 128
    re binding authorities 136, 137
    re tonner policies 138
    on Lloyd's brokers 165, 168
Funding policies 49–52

Gang of Four 56, 140
General Undertaking 131
Goschen, G. J. – Chairman of Lloyd's
    1869–86 and 1893–1901 146
Gough, Brandon 64, 102
Governor of Bank of England 6, 190
Gower, Prof – Review of Investor
    Protection 186
Graduate recruitment 200, 202
Green, Sir Peter 5, 57, 58, 67–68, 88,
    98, 154
    relationship between Name and agent
    88
Green papers 98, 220
Grob, K. V. 56, 57, 59, 139

Hailey, FCA, Stephen 83

Hardie, Jeremy 60
Harrison case 179
Hart, Report of disciplinary proceedings
    51, 139
Heath, Cuthbert 5, 12, 22, 38, 109
Higgins Working Party 69, 103, 117,
    120, 123, 129, 139, 216
    on Baby Syndicates 141
Holland, Nigel 59
Howden 2, 3, 59–61, 139, 181
    DTI Inquiry into 57
    acquisition by Alexander & Alexander
    56
Hozier, Sir Henry – Secretary to the
    Committee of Lloyd's 1874–1906
Hurricane Betsey 43, 49

Imperial 58
Inception Date Accounting 106, 135,
    198
Information to prospective Names 171,
    189
Inland Revenue:
    relations with 86–88
    settlement 1985 87
Insurance Brokers (Registration) Act
    1977 32, 167
Insurance Brokers Registration Council
    32, 167
Insurance Companies Act 1982 30, 179,
    230
Insurance Cycle, the 16
Investigations Committee 80

Japan 14

Lambert Coles Committee – on brokers
    168, 229
Law of Agency 31, 61, 87, 93
Lawrence, Murray 119
Le Boeuf Lamb Leiby & MacRae–Lloyd's
    US Counsel 195
Leeds Castle – first meeting of new
    Council of Lloyd's 64, 67
Lineslip – definition of 137
Lloyd, Edward 20, 213

235